Executable UML

HOW TO
BUILD CLASS MODELS

LEON STARR

Prentice Hall PTR

Upper Saddle River, NJ 07458

www.phptr.com

Library of Congress Cataloging-in-Publication Data is available.

Editorial/Production Supervision: *Donna Cullen-Dolce*
Acquisitions Editor: *Paul Petralia*
Manufacturing Buyer: *Alexis Heydt-Long*
Cover Design: *Nina Scuderi*
Author Photograph: *Judith Jauhal*
Cover Design Director: *Jerry Votta*
Marketing Manager: *Debby vanDijk*

Printed in the United States of America
ISBN 0-13-067479-6

Pearson Education LTD.
Pearson Education Australia PTY, Limited
Pearson Education Singapore, Pte. Ltd.
Pearson Education North Asia Ltd.
Pearson Education Canada, Ltd.
Pearson Educación de Mexico, S.A. de C.V.
Pearson Education—Japan
Pearson Education Malaysia, Pte. Ltd.

Executable UML

ISBN 0-13-067479-6

90000

For mom and dad

Foreword

This book is about that step between the requirements gathering and the construction of an executable model, the step that no one talks about: abstraction.

We are all familiar with the concept of requirements gathering, whether by use cases, requirements documents, conversations with users or something less formal still. We are also familiar with the concept of modeling, first to sketch out roughly what we want and then to capture the semantics of a subject matter in executable form. But how do we go from a requirements statement to a complete, detailed executable model?

The answer (which no one wants to hear) is that *we have to think*. This thinking takes the form of figuring out some way to approach the problem and writing it down precisely.

The trouble is, it's all too easy to slap down a bunch of classes with attributes and associations and declare the problem solved, barring perhaps the odd paragraph of Object Constraint Language (OCL) to distinguish the behavior of the various instances. This sloppy approach speeds the process of getting a code fix, but the approach often fails to address the real issue of working out what the problem really is, in detail.

To achieve this feat, we need a precise modeling language to help us think clearly about our selected abstractions. This language is Executable UML, a profile of UML that can be compiled into the appropriate software platform. An Executable UML model comprises a class diagram, a set of state charts, and a set of procedures comprising actions. The language places great emphasis on precise expression. If you assert that an Aircraft has an attribute numberOf-

Seats, then each individual aircraft can have a different value for the numberOfSeats. You can't *pretend* that you meant, because this aircraft is a Boeing 747-400, then it must have 270 seats. Each distinct fact must be captured separately.

What this means is that Executable UML has rules, and these rules confer meaning. In the hands of a skilled practitioner, and Leon Starr is one very skilled practitioner, these rules enhance expressiveness and precision, which allows you to examine an abstraction and determine if it's appropriate. The fact is that the abstraction, written down with expressiveness and precision that can also be compiled to code, is a bonus.

Leon's book is aimed at transferring his skill to you. Happily for you, reading Leon's work — if not always easy — is always fun. Leon brings more years of experience than he (or I) are willing to own up to, and this shows in his wealth of example material. Real examples from real projects. If you can abstract your way out of a paper bag, you can apply these examples as patterns to your own problems.

So read, absorb, and enjoy. I know you'll find the effort you put in to acquiring abstraction skills will pay off.

Stephen J. Mellor
Worcester,
Worcestershire
(where the sauce comes from)
United Kingdom

Author's preface

This book is a collection of models, modeling tips and analysis techniques that have worked for me (and my colleagues) on real projects. It conveys the experience that I have gained in 15 years of building executable object-oriented models. I have written this book for especially for those of you who have already had an introduction to an executable, translation driven modeling method such as Executable UML or the Shlaer-Mellor method. I presume that you are either about to start applying Executable UML on your project or that you have been building executable models for a year or two. This text is geared toward those of you who do the hard work of boiling down application requirements, formalizing these requirements into fully detailed models and getting those models translated into working software.

This book is not a complete statement or grammar of the Executable UML language. For that please see Steve Mellor's text listed in the "Where to learn more" section at the back of the book. Instead, I show you some of the ways that I use important features of the object modeling language. I also provide some guidance in how to deal with a few thorny issues.

Experience on multiple projects has taught me many things. One of the most important lessons is that you can't skimp on the class models and get away with it. You must ensure that your application requirements are thoroughly captured, in great detail, in your class models. This takes time and hard work. Whenever my colleagues and I have cut corners we have run afoul of the following consequences: (1) the state charts become ridiculously complex; (2) one or two critical requirements lie hidden until late in the modeling process, leading to time-consuming rework; and (3) new requirements that should have been anticipated arise late in the modeling process and wreak havoc. On the other hand, a good class model leads to stable state models and simple threads of control. This book focuses on the key to success: building quality class models.

Like most of us, coming originally from a function-oriented programming background, learning to build class models has been challenging to say the least. I've noticed that engineers new to object-oriented analysis grapple with many of the same questions that I did: What model structures are legal? (Can I do *that* with a generalization relationship?) How much detail should go into the class model? How do I build a model that won't fall apart when the requirements change? What's the difference between a good class model and a bad class model? Why do I need to write model descriptions? What's the best way to express an association involving a specific number of instances (not 0, 1 or *). What's the best way to model a hierarchy of things? This book contains answers to these questions and many others.

Another big key to success is to use your time effectively. A common mistake is to spend too much time modeling and not enough time doing analysis. Few software engineers appreciate the value of distinguishing the activities of analysis and modeling. I don't know how many times I've seen a novice analyst spend hours building the perfect model to suit a set of *perceived* requirements. Later on the requirements change, or they turn out to be the wrong requirements, or they turn out to be based on some aspect of the system that is so volatile that no attempt to nail down the requirements can be successful. As a consequence the whole model unravels. I wrote Part 2 of this book to show how this kind of disaster can be avoided.

To become a good programmer, not only do you need to write a lot of code, but you also need to look at code written by other people. The same is true when it comes to analysis and modeling. The models in this book will give you something helpful to look at from time to time as you build lots of models. Have fun.

Leon Starr
San Francisco, California

Acknowledgments

This page is for all of the colleagues and friends that helped me to create this book and get it out the door.

Here is a list of my beta testers (technical reviewers). They were invaluable in the task of rooting out flaws in the text, tables, figures and models: Tonya Bargash, Yeelan Johnson, Michael M. Lee, Steve Mellor, Walt Murphy, Linda Ruark, Jonathon Sandoe, Sally Shlaer and Phil Zakhour.

Highly entertaining conversations with Michael Lee about project management, politics, training and technical issues provided considerable guidance and inspiration, which fueled my enthusiasm throughout this project.

Thousands of hours of intensely focused project work with most of my reviewers, as well as Ruth Knipe, provided me with the analysis and modeling experience that made this book possible. Tracy Yim deserves credit for convincing me to start this project and for providing support and encouragement all along the way.

I am thoroughly indebted to Walt Murphy for his highly technical and meticulous evaluation of every chapter and for helping with the index.

I would like to thank Judith Jauhal for the author's photograph.

Finally, but most importantly, I want to thank Steve Mellor and Sally Shlaer for all the training, support and especially their contributions to the theory of analysis and model translation.

Last minute stuff

Here are a few helpful notes hastily added before I upload this book to the publisher:

Models vs. diagrams

Throughout this book you may notice that I sometimes use the term "class model" and other times I refer to a "class diagram." This is neither sloppy use of terms or disrespect of the UML standard terminology. A *class diagram* is a drawing consisting of standard symbols such as classes, attributes and relationships. It is just one way of viewing a *class model*. A class model can be rendered in other ways, such as text in a scripting or markup language. This distinction between diagram and model is equally relevant to the other Executable UML model types. The same state model, for example can be represented as a UML state chart or as a state table. The same procedure model can be represented as a data flow diagram or as action language script. Furthermore, a class model includes documentation. When you review a class model, you should expect to see class, attribute and relationship descriptions in addition to the class diagram.

Attribute data types

One of the nice things about UML is that the display of many diagram elements are optional. This allows you peer through the potential clutter of a complex diagram and focus on the information you care about at the moment. You may also notice that I omit the UML data type and value initialization components in most of my class symbols. That's because in most examples, this data would clutter the example and, in some cases, force me to reduce the font size so that you would need a scanning electron microscope to read the class diagram. On real projects, when I bring up my favorite model editing tool, the first thing I do is turn off all of the display options I don't need so that any errors I am looking for are immediately apparent. I've noticed that most people don't do this and I think that explains why a lot of errors slide by unnoticed.

Naming conventions

I use the following naming style. Class names: Initials capitalized as in **Flot Shape**. Attribute names: First initial capitalized, underscore spacing (in descriptions only) as in **Desired_quantity**. Data type names: first word lower case, following words initial caps, squashed together as in **barCodeNumber**. When class and attribute names are concatenated, underscores replace spaces in the class name as in: **Flot_Shape.Desired_quantity**. Why do it this way? Class names and attribute names appear frequently in notes and model descriptions. Underscores are a compromise in keeping a long name cohesive with spacing for readability. Data types appear less frequently in notes so squashing is an acceptable way to keep them distinct.

Your mileage may vary

Most, but not all features described in this book may be supported by your particular set of model editing, execution and translation tools. The Executable UML standard and the supporting tools continue to evolve. Even though plain vanilla UML is a notation standard, few if any tools are 100% compliant with it. Welcome to the leading edge of software technology.

In fact, I think you're development technology must be fairly mature so that the theory, methodology and tooling have sufficient cooling-off time to congeal into something coherent. Perhaps this is the case if you are still writing COBOL, I don't know.

Not to worry, us software types are notorious for our ability to find inventive ways to adapt (sidestep, abuse) existing tooling to meet our needs. None of the model development tools in the late 80s provided sufficient features to build the precise, translatable class models covered in this book, but we never let that stop us. In the early days we resorted to CAD drawing tools enhanced by macros, awk scripts and other homebrew utilities to get the job done. The advanced model editors, software architectures, model simulators and compilers available today are a huge step forward. But there's always room to tweak. I'm sure you'll be able to get the job done.

Contents

INTRODUCTION

What is Executable UML?

BASIC MODEL STRUCTURES

Chapter 1 Classes

Chapter 2 Attributes

Chapter 3   Relationships

Chapter 4   Binary associations

Chapter 5   Association classes

Chapter 6 Naming Associations

Chapter 7 Loops and constraints

Chapter 8   Generalization: the basics

Chapter 9   Advanced generalization relationships

HOW TO BUILD USEFUL MODELS

Chapter 10   How to avoid model hacking

Chapter 11   Why write model descriptions?

Chapter 12 How to write class descriptions

Chapter 13 How to write attribute descriptions

Chapter 14   How to write relationship descriptions

MODEL PATTERNS

Chapter 15   Is zero-one-many specific enough?

Chapter 16   Reflexive patterns

Chapter 17   Network patterns

Chapter 18   Linear patterns

Chapter 19   Tree patterns

Where to learn more 389

Bibliography 395

Index 399

Introduction

What is Executable UML?

Executable UML is a graphical specification language. It combines a subset of the UML (Unified Modeling Language) graphical notation with executable semantics and timing rules. You can use this language to build a fully executable system specification consisting of class, state and action models that runs just like a program. Unlike traditional specifications, an executable specification can be run, tested, debugged and measured for performance. The tested specification (models) can then be translated into target code.

Code for real-time systems

The target code may run on a single processor or a network of processors. Unlike traditional fuzzy specifications, executable models resolve detailed application timing and synchronization behavior, mutually exclusive modes and resource contention issues. The source models may be colored[1] with performance and deployment decisions which direct the translation to produce suitably fast, efficient code targeted to multiple tasks and processors. Many model compilers support open translation, which allows experienced programmers to tune and significantly adjust the translation process. This means that the development team is not at the mercy of a vendor's proprietary compilation process. Open translation is necessary to ensure that the generated code runs effectively in customized hardware and software environments. Consequently, Executable UML is suitable (and is used extensively) to specify complex real-time distributed and embedded systems.

Specification and implementation are always separate

The process of translation leaves the source specification intact and unaltered after the target code is generated. This contrasts sharply with the process of elaboration where the source specification is "filled in" and otherwise distorted to yield an implementation. With

---

[1] More about coloring on page 19.

translation, the source specification is always kept separate from and untouched by the implementation. Consequently, development and testing of the specification models may proceed unabated while the implementation technology (new languages, new protocols, hardware in development) evolves.

Why use Executable UML?

Any experienced developer knows that the biggest difficulty in designing software isn't writing the code. That's the easy part.

The hard part — the thing that kills projects, the thing that makes the schedule go from 6 months to 6 years, the thing that gets projects cancelled and managers prematurely turned out to pasture, is this:

Defining the problem.

Specification is key This is especially true of large, complex systems. If a specification for a toolshed is misinterpreted, it is relatively easy to modify or replace the faulty toolshed. If you incorrectly specify your dream house, a skyscraper, or a hypersonic aircraft, the cost of getting it wrong can be astronomical.

In the world of physical construction, specification tools have evolved for hundreds and thousands of years. Today we have blueprints, CAD systems and math models and wouldn't dream of committing physical resources without them. Most modern marvels of engineering would be impossible without specification technology.

Take away blueprints and math models and we are quickly back to living in mud huts and driving mules across rope bridges.

Modern physical structures are possible only with advanced specification technology.

Mud huts and rope bridges are not far from the software reality we live in now. (When was the last time your desktop operating system[2] crashed?) Unfortunately, software specification technology is not as evolved as its physical world counterpart, and we suffer from the consequences every day. Futuristic software skyscrapers won't be possible without advanced specification technology.

But all is not lost. Dramatic leaps in software specification technology have been made in the last few years. Executable, translatable specifications are the latest result. Let's take a quick look at how specifications have evolved to put these developments in context.

---

[2]This statement was not intended for Linux/Unix users. Substitute other desktop software you hate.

The evolution of specifications

Text specifications

In the beginning, specifications were all text. Recall the last time you received (or delivered) an impressively bound numbered copy of a 300-page functional specification? You know, with all those neatly indented bullet items and multi-indented paragraph headings with more numbers and periods than your IP address. The only thing more fun than reading the weighty spec, was reviewing it — for 3 days in 10-hour meetings (that seem like 18) attended by everyone in the company except the receptionist[3].

The limitations of text quickly surface at these horrible meetings. Issues that are complicated or controversial are frequently deferred under the "we'll sort that out in the design phase" mantra.[4] Of course, some of these are truly design issues, but most can't be solved now, because, well — they require *thinking*.

When you write code, by contrast, thinking has to happen because what you write either works or it doesn't. The details have to be sorted out and you just can't argue your way out of a complicated problem — you have to solve it. When you write a text spec, on the other hand, you can choose the level of detail as it suits you. It is all too convenient to gloss over critical subtleties. In fact, the level of attentiveness is always inversely proportional to the current page number.

---

[3] Oh, let's invite the receptionist too, we want to make everyone part of the process.

[4] American Heritage Dictionary, 3rd edition: mantra, n. — A sacred verbal formula repeated in prayer, meditation, or incantation, such as an invocation of a god, a magic spell, or a syllable or portion of scripture containing mystical potentialities.

The real trouble with the text spec materializes after all the reviews are done and it's time to actually build something. When you start solving the real problems it becomes apparent that many terms used in the specification aren't well defined. The same term is used to mean different things and different terms are used to mean the same thing. The deeper you get into the problem solving, the more contradictions you discover. The critically important feature on page 40 negates the critically important feature on page 128.

All of this fuzziness erodes the integrity of the original document to the point where it is derided and largely ignored by the developers. The users and the application experts are consulted, but they are kidding themselves to think that they actually *specified* what was eventually constructed. The terms "suggested" and "guided" would be more realistic.

In fact, it seems strange that you could even hope to specify a complex software system with its myriad layers, protocols and processor interactions using such an inherently one-dimensional medium as narrative text. Can you imagine specifying your dream house in a text document, handing that to contractors and then getting what you want? No way! You would want to have a good look at those blueprints before letting the contractors loose.

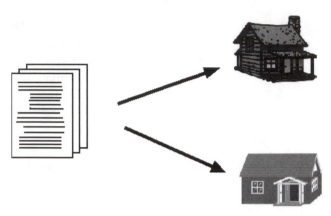

No one would trust a system even as simple as a house to a text specification.

Graphical specifications

The shortcomings of the text specification inspired the introduction of graphical specification methods in the late 70s and early 80s. Blueprints for software, right? Well, sort of.

First there were data flow diagrams (I'm skipping flowcharts since they were never seriously touted as the software equivalent of blueprints). Then state models and entity-relationship diagrams came into use. Competing methods proposed different ways of developing and integrating these diagrams to specify requirements. And many CAD-like tools, analogously named "CASE" tools, sprang up to provide environments for drawing and managing these diagrams.

Graphical specifications wrenched us loose from the confines of a one-dimensional narrative. Dependencies are easier to see as a network of symbols than as a sequence of paragraphs. This is a critical feature since software specifications are replete with interdependencies.

Multiple diagram types make it possible to organize a system's requirements into a compatible set of projections. For complex systems this is easier than intertwining all requirements into a single model. Structural, electrical, HVAC and plumbing schematics are kept separate. This makes it possible to break a complex system down into a series of problems which can be solved separately and in a specific sequence. You don't want to lay out the wiring BEFORE you design the structure. Separation and sequencing are *critical* engineering concepts.

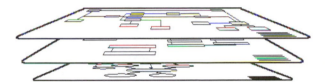

Fundamental aspects of computing (data, control and processing) can be modeled in separate projections.

The projections relevant to software specification separate the three fundamental aspects of computing: data (variables, data structures), control (if-then, jump, while) and processing (crunching on data). In the 80s these corresponded to entity-relationship diagrams for the data projection, state diagrams for the control projection and data flow diagrams for the process projection. The methods were mostly differentiated on the proposed sequencing (or total lack thereof) of the construction of these projections.

But did these graphical methods really do for software what blueprints have done for skyscrapers and hypersonic aircraft? Absolutely not — as *anyone* who has ever tried to apply any of the methods of the 80s on a real software project will tell you. What went wrong?

Standard semantics were missing

Unlike their blueprint and schematic counterparts, software symbols were not usually well defined. The same symbol would often have different interpretations depending on who you asked. A process might be considered interruptible by one engineer and atomic by another engineer on the same project. You couldn't lay out a circuit board, much less a skyscraper, with this kind of confusion. Hardware engineers don't debate the meaning of a capacitor symbol. Real engineering blueprints require more than a standardized symbology — they require standardized semantics. And that was one key element missing from the so called "software blueprints".

Physical engineers don't debate the meaning or intention of their symbols. A capacitor is a capacitor!

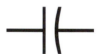

What is the structure of the accessed data? Can the process be interrupted? At what granularity? These are points of debate on a typical software symbol.

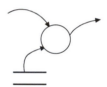

Projections couldn't be tightly integrated

But that's not all. Techniques for integrating the projections were more art than science. Most methods provided no clear rules for connecting the processes on a data flow diagram, the states on a state chart and the elements on an entity-relationship diagram. The rules for sequencing construction of the diagrams were fuzzy as well.

The right level of detail was undefined

As it was with text specifications, the required level of detail was more a matter of political convenience and personal preference. If the problem got too complicated, it was once again deferred to the magical design phase. This happened because there was no clear point defined where the specifications ended and the design began.

The phrase "analysis paralysis" came into vogue in the 80s. This described the situation where a project would enter the specification/analysis box of a PERT chart, like a spacecraft sucked into a black hole, never to emerge again. Since the level of detail necessary to complete the models could never be agreed on — the models could never be completed to meet any objective criteria. Any diagram considered "completed" one week could always be elaborated the next for lack of a limiting condition. And that's assuming fixed requirements!

Testing was impossible

There was an even worse incongruence in the analogy between physical blueprints and graphical software specifications. You could quantitatively measure a blueprint, you could put a CAD drawing through simulation, but the best you could do with a software model was get a bunch of people together and, ugh, *review* it. Now you could argue that it is simply the nature of physical systems that they can be measured. Does this concept really apply to software requirements? Of course it does — we just measure different things than our physical engineering counterparts.

We care about whether the logic is internally consistent, whether or not the data is fully represented and whether or not it is possible to start with certain key pieces of data and access specific pieces of related data. We care about whether or not there is sufficient data to perform critical computations. We want to ensure that instances have certain mutually exclusive states. These all sound like the kinds of things that could be tested objectively rather than debated philosophically.

Summary of graphical contributions

So where does that leave us at this point in the evolution of specification technology? The use of graphics gave us the ability to specify impressive networks of data, control and processing dependencies. That's good. We could split these networks into separate projections to reduce complexity. Also good. But we couldn't rigorously fit them together. That's bad. And the graphical symbols have fuzzy meanings. Very bad. Graphics did nothing to limit and define the required level of detail. Also bad. Finally, whatever you produced could not be simulated or otherwise tested objectively. Very, very bad.

The physical construction analogy would be like sketching a bunch of your own invented symbols and telling the contractors, "Here you go — you get the basic idea." Wherever the contractor loses confidence in the plan during construction, he or she would be free to interpret and elaborate the plans. Once again, you are going to get a system that is partly what you specified and partly what the contractor invented along the way. You might be willing to live with that for your dream house, but you probably don't want Jimmy the welder filling in the gaps in your hypersonic aircraft schematics.

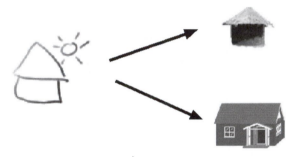

A fuzzy graphical specification isn't much better than a fuzzy text specification.

Executable specifications

Traditional graphic specifications are imprecise, replete with ambiguity and contradiction, expressed at an inconsistent level of detail and impossible to test objectively. Executable specifications fix all that.

That's because an executable specification is built, executed and tested much like a program. The graphical building blocks used to construct an executable specification are not shallow symbols. Each symbol has a concrete, executable definition — just like a statement in a programming language. These building blocks operate in a framework of carefully defined timing rules. These timing rules make it possible to definitively answer questions like "What happens when two events occur simultaneously?", "Are these two events guaranteed to arrive in order?" and "Can this action be interrupted?"

The UML notation serves as the graphical shell — it supplies the expressive symbology. By itself, the UML is not executable, it is just a grab bag of notations. Executable semantics and timing rules are applied to the notation to yield Executable UML. All of the class models in this book are expressed in Executable UML.

Consider some benefits to this style of specification:

No fuzziness   There is no fuzziness. The models work only one way. You may or may not *like* the way the elevator system works, but that's okay. The sign of a good specification is that you can tell that it is or isn't what you want — before the code is written. **A flaky spec can be defended by argument — an executable spec is defended by demonstration.**

Testable models   The models can be tested objectively. You can actually run the specification just like a program. You can set up a scenario, run it, pause it, inspect the activity and then resume it.

Implementation independence   If we specify enough detail to create an executable specification, isn't this really just a high level implementation? Absolutely not! The whole point of a specification is that it does not lock you into a single implementation. Consider, for example, an executable elevator control system specification. The ideal implementation technology for such a system (programming languages, network protocols, hardware, data access methods and protocols, operating systems, etc.) will change every six months. But the fundamental rules, policies and dynamic behavior of an elevator system are pretty much the same now as they were twenty years ago.

The following aspects of elevator behavior are implementation independent: Elevator doors should not open between floors. Pressing the up button calls a cabin in the associated bank. Unnecessary cabin travel should be minimized. Only one cabin should respond to a floor call for service. Floor requests within an elevator are serviced in ascending or descending order. The open door delay following the detection of an obstacle may be shorter than the open door delay upon arrival at a floor.

These are all details that have absolutely nothing to do with the implementation. A choice of an array vs. a linked list implementation should not affect the criteria for selecting a destination floor. A choice of Windows instead of Linux does not change the fact that the doors must never open between floors. (The implementation of this policy may be more tricky on Windows, but that is an implementation problem — it does not negate the correctness of the specification.) Finally, the choice to use embedded processors on each cabin in conjunction with a centralized host may or may not be a good implementation decision — but, again, it has nothing to do with the correctness of the application model.

The same model can be targeted to an infinite variety of implementations.

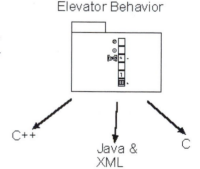

Fundamental model of Elevator Behavior

C++

Java & XML

C

The debut of a new protocol, operating system or language has no effect on the essential behavior of elevators.

**Deployment
independence**

In fact, once you get the elevator application model correct it shouldn't matter whether the model is running on a single CPU in a single task, several tasks on a single CPU, or several tasks on several CPUs with potentially different operating systems. It's still the *same* model of essential elevator behavior. This means that once you get the model built, debugged and tested, you never have to change it to accommodate a new implementation strategy. You change the model only when the application requirements change. If marketing asks for the ability to lock out certain floors for maintenance purposes, then you must change the model. So the model of the application changes only when the application requirements change.

The same model can be deployed many ways.

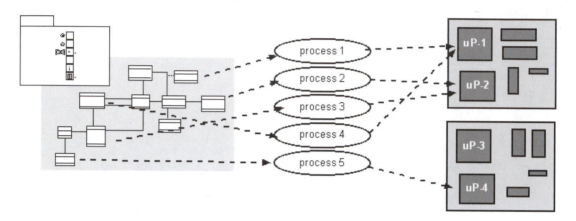

A change in deployment to improve performance has no impact on the essential behavior of elevators.

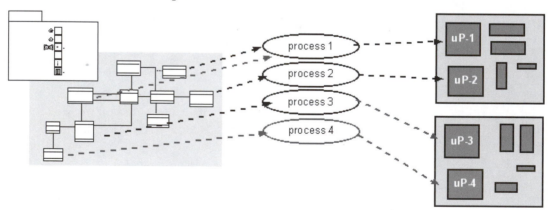

How is the specification implemented?

Okay, so now you have one of these wonderful executable specifications. What do you *do* with it?

It may seem like a difficult task to turn an executable specification into code — until you consider the ugly alternatives. What if you started with no specification at all? Nothing is more difficult than creating a system out of thin air. The right system, anyway. Alright, so let's say that you start with a loose text specification. You still have lots of problems to solve. How do you ensure that once the cabin is on its way to a floor that it can be interrupted by a late request? Which late requests should be allowed to interrupt the elevator? What happens to a request that can't be serviced immediately? How do you ensure that only one cabin responds to an up button request at a floor? The text specification is not going to solve all these problems for you.

Now imagine that you have an executable specification. All you have to do is code it! What could possibly be easier? You don't have to interview the users. You don't have to attend any stupid meetings with marketing or management. You just have to write the !@#$! code. Now THAT's extreme programming!

Don't muck up the specification

The model is a statement of the essential requirements. Interviews with customers and product managers, subtle application policies, critical analysis decisions are all crystallized in that specification. Since the model already works by itself, the last thing you want to do is monkey around with it.

At the same time, you have to express that model in the implementation language — or languages — on your target platform. And if you have a complex embedded, distributed (either or both) environment, then you will have to split up and repackage the model elements to meet your performance requirements.

Translate the models

Translation is the process of mapping model elements to implementation units. For example, you might map a UML class in your specification to a chunk of code defining a C++ class and a linked list to manage the collection of instances. But for performance reasons, you might choose to implement that same UML class as an array of instances of a C++ class. Or maybe you want to collapse two UML classes connected by a 1:1 association into a single C struct. The possibilities are endless and depend entirely on your target language, system software, deployment decisions, performance requirements and programmer ingenuity. The goal is to map EVERY model element to a suitable implementation structure. There is NOTHING for the designer to add with regard to the requirements side of the problem. The designer focuses on choosing the most effective implementation structures to make the models work efficiently.

The process of translation can be manual, automated or some combination of both. Partial automation is common in practice, but full automation has been successfully applied, even on embedded, real-time projects. There is no magic to this process. Once a programmer manually maps a set of model elements to an implementation structure, his or her natural instinct[5] is to devise a tool which automates this process.

Use a model compiler

Full automation is possible if you have a model compiler. But, how does a model compiler work?

---

[5] To quote a colleague of ours: "The best programmers are inherently lazy." — Larry Levin

All of the elements are illustrated in the following diagram.

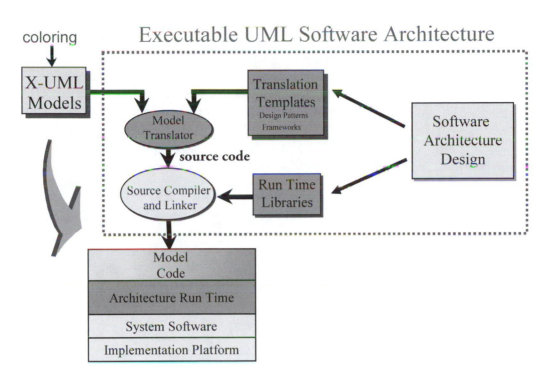

As you can see, the executable models are only a portion of the input to the compilation process. There are several elements of translation technology required to produce efficient code for complex platforms.

Elements of translation technology

Coloring The analyst may tag or "color" portions of his or her models to direct the translation process. Perhaps a group of model elements should generate code for a specific CPU or task. Or maybe certain classes should persist in a database. Certain state transitions may have to complete within a hard time window. Color guides a model translator in much the same way that command line directives guide a code compiler.

Why is it called "coloring"? Let's say you want to specify deployment of the elevator models. You want to split the output code so that some of it runs on a host processor and some of it runs on a processor embedded in each elevator cabin. Picture taking two color magic markers. You highlight part of the models in one color and the rest in another color. These colors tell the model translator where to deploy specific model elements.

Few user interfaces support the magic marker paradigm as of this writing. These days analysts perform coloring by filling in special tables and files that the model translator scans. "Tagging" may be a more accurate term.

The nice thing about coloring is that it is layered on top of the models like an acetate sheet. The models themselves are never modified. If a particular coloring scheme yields suboptimal results, you can easily recolor. If the underlying platform technology changes (in the same project or in a future spin-off project) you can try a new color scheme. In fact, the platform technology may improve to the point that you don't need any coloring at all.

Translation templates

To understand how the translator works, imagine writing the code by hand. You could follow a simple strategy where you translate every class in your UML model to a corresponding C++ class in your code. You've got a lot of classes to code, so you might as well be systematic about it. Consider an arbitrary class named "A" with the attributes a1, a2, and a3. You can write the code for this class easily enough. Now that you've created this coding template, it is easy enough to apply it to another arbitrary class named "B" with attributes b1 and b2. It's kind of like filling out a form. You take your template, scan the input UML model and for each modeled class you fill out your template and generate a corresponding C++ class. Sounds tedious doesn't it? That's why we use a model translator.

Now I just described a *simple* strategy to illustrate the principle of template based translation. In reality, the model translator has a variety of templates at its disposal. Templates are chosen based on the type of scanned model element (class, state chart, association, etc.), the coloring, if any, and any rules built into the model translator.

The cool thing about this is that you can edit the templates used by the model translator. So if the output code offends your programmer sensibilities, you can supply your own templates and design patterns.

Run time libraries   Some of the code in the target is produced through translation — but not all of it. Universal mechanisms required throughout all models, regardless of modeled content, are provided by run-time libraries in the software architecture. These libraries are purchased with the model compiler, or developed by systems programmers inhouse if you are designing your own model compiler.

The state machine engine is a perfect example of a universal service. You wouldn't want to translate each UML state chart into its own autonomous state machine code. That's because the mechanics (state transitions, event generation, event receipt, action execution, etc.) is the same for all state charts. More importantly, you want to force it to be the same!

So instead of translating each state chart into code, you translate each state chart into data. This data is entered into structures defined by the state machine executor. The run-time state machine executor processes all of the state charts as table structures and event queues. So the modeled state charts must be entered into a tabular structure. A state table may consist of rows and columns which are populated with states and events. Transitions and actions are entered into the cells of the table. Actually, a certain amount of code will be generated for each state chart. This code will call functions in the state machine executor library. For example, an action that generates an event will invoke the event generation code fragment which makes the appropriate library call.

The state machine executor is just one example of a universal model run-time service. Other services access data in the classes, navigate associations, set timers, perform intertask and interprocessor communication, and so forth.

Source compiler and linker

The code output by the model translator must be compiled and linked into the run-time libraries. It produces model-based code running on top of model service code which runs on the system software on the implementation platform.

Why translate?

Because elaboration is stupid

To appreciate the benefits of a translative approach to design, consider the ugly alternative, elaboration. To elaborate, you start with the specification and add implementation detail to it. New associations, attributes, states, data type definitions and so forth are sprinkled into the model. Some elements are removed or merged. Other model elements are combined or split apart to yield an efficient implementation. Eventually you end up with an implementation.

Elaboration destroys the original specification. In fact, the process of mucking up the specification with implementation details usually starts long before the specification itself is complete. So the boundary between specification and implementation is always fuzzy with this approach.

Translation on the other hand leaves the specification intact in the same way that a C++ compiler leaves your original source code intact. There are numerous benefits to this approach:

Stability

The specification can be independently maintained. Let's say that a new feature is added to the elevator control system — automatic return to the first floor, for example. This necessitates a change in the elevator application model. There is no change required in the design. The models will simply be updated and re-translated. Only the elevator subject matter experts are involved in this update.

But let's say a new performance feature is added — the search algorithm needs to execute faster. And for this example, let's assume that the search algorithm is optimal as it stands. Then this requirement calls for programmer expertise — not elevator application expertise. The model compiler team must find a different set of implementation structures to express the search algorithm. An array implementation instead of the doubly linked list scheme might save the day. Only the programmers are involved in this update. (Unless, of course, it really does turn out to be a boneheaded search algorithm!)

The specification hovers above the churning sea of evolving implementation technology. Let's say that halfway through the project the team decides to put the elevator application on an intranet and code half of it in Java. The model compilation process certainly changes — but the elevator specification is untouched. The fact that you are running an intranet doesn't change the fact that doors shouldn't open between floors!

I don't know about you, but I've yet to see a project running longer than six months where some key aspect of the implementation technology didn't change midway through the project. It's really nice to be able to forge ahead with the application analysis unperturbed by these hiccups in the design.

Reduced risk

Translation is less risky. Imagine a worst case scenario where your programmers are total idiots[6]. They devise a translation scheme that yields piggish code that would bring a Pentium 8 to its knees. Okay, so you have to throw out the whole design and start over. But the models are safe. Since they weren't elaborated, they didn't melt down with the rest of the design.

Leverage one design in multiple products

The design also benefits by staying separate from the specification. Let's say that a spin-off product is proposed. A horizontal/vertical transit system will be built to move people around an airport. Obviously changes will be necessary in the application — there are many

---

[6]Speaking hypothetically, of course.

new requirements. Perhaps the core of the models will be retained, but change is inevitable in the elevator application. The performance requirements are probably the same, however. And there is a good chance that the same programming languages and system software will also be used. So it may be possible to deliver this new system by doing a new analysis, creating a new specification and then using the same design developed for the original elevator system.

Separation by domain In a real system there is always a huge gap between the application and the implementation. Intermediate layers referred to as "domains" are defined to bridge this gap. The application is just the domain in the very top layer. The design (also called the software architecture) is the domain at the bottom and service domains pick up the slack between.

Domains are beyond the scope of this book, but are defined and explained in Executable UML: The Models are the Code, cited in the "Where to learn more" section at the back of this book.

Summary

Advanced specification technology is necessary to build the sophisticated software systems of the future. Text and graphical notation methods are notoriously flaky. Executable models allow us to test the specification and solve the hard problems up front.

If a specification is executable, it is translatable. Translation generates code from a specification without altering the specification itself. This ensures that the specification is always kept separate from the implementation. To perform an efficient translation, it is usually necessary to color the specification with performance and deployment qualifiers. The model compiler can use these qualifiers to chose the appropriate code fragments as it translates the model elements. Open translation permits developers to alter this process to get appropriately efficient code.

In complex systems there can be a large gap between the application and the implementation. This gap is bridged by organizing the system into domain layers extending from the application down to the implementation.

Basic model structures

1

Classes

Class isn't something you buy. Look at you. You have a $500 suit on and you're still a lowlife.

— Jack Cates (Nick Nolte), 48 Hours

What is a class? Consider a set of things, all of which share the same characteristics, behave the same way, and conform to the same rules and policies. Let's go get a bunch of things — cameras for example, and put them together into just such a set:

A bunch of cameras

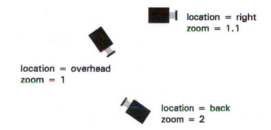

location = right
zoom = 1.1

location = overhead
zoom = 1

location = back
zoom = 2

Figure 1.1

Each camera is a distinct real-world entity. Each camera has its own location and zoom setting.

It's hard not to stare at Figure 1.1 without abstracting a prototypical camera. This abstraction is what Executable UML calls a *class*. A class is the abstraction of a set of real-world things such that all things in the set:

- have the same characteristics

- exhibit the same behavior

- and are constrained by the same rules.

The class symbol   Here's the notation for our prototypical camera:

```
┌─────────────────┐
│     Camera      │
├─────────────────┤
│ Location        │
│ Zoom            │
│                 │
└─────────────────┘
```

This symbol states that there is a thing called a Camera. It also says that every Camera has a Location value and a Zoom value. Just as importantly, it asserts that all Cameras behave the same way and conform to the same rules and policies.

The difference between classes and instances

It is important not to confuse the prototypical camera — the Camera class — with a specific camera — an *instance* of Camera.

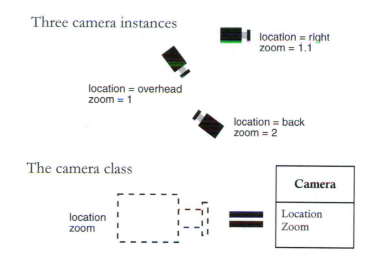

Three camera instances

location = right
zoom = 1.1

location = overhead
zoom = 1

location = back
zoom = 2

The camera class

location
zoom

Camera
Location
Zoom

Figure 1.2

Note: An instance of a class is also known as an *object*.[1]

Anatomy of a class table

Tables make it easy to organize data about class instances.

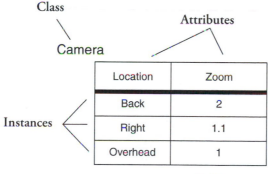

Class

Attributes

Camera

Instances

Location	Zoom
Back	2
Right	1.1
Overhead	1

Table 1.1

[1]So we are really doing class oriented analysis — but it's too late to change the names!

Each row in a class's table contains data about one instance of the class. Each column of the table contains values for each instance corresponding to a single attribute.

Class table rules

The rules described in this section are borrowed from the relational model of data.[2] These rules keep the formalism uniform and minimal. Uniformity means that we keep one real-world fact in one place. So when we update a piece of information, we won't have to worry about cleaning up any loose ends. We also don't have to worry about accidentally losing critical data. Relational theory wipes out an entire class of bugs long before we draw the first state chart. Minimalism means that we build models using a handful of simple, rigorously defined constructs. With a little skill, these constructs can be assembled like building blocks to describe extremely complex applications. Finally, if we faithfully follow our table rules, we ensure that our models can be translated into implementation structures — like program language statements — in a straightforward manner. Let's move on to the first rule.

All attribute values are atomic

The data found at a row-column intersection has no structure (or at least no structure that has meaning in the domain[3] in which it is

---

[2]C.J. Date, *An Introduction to Database Systems*, Addison-Wesley, ISBN: 0201385902. Forget the database part — this book lays out the mathematics of data that must be understood so a developer can properly organize data in ANY language. If you want to engineer rather than hack your data structures, you must read this book.

[3]That's subject matter domain (not attribute domain). A single fact in a client domain may be parsed into multiple facts that make sense in a service domain.

modeled). Here's an example class taken from a household inventory application:

Inventory Item

ID	Location	Condition
OW8	Cellar	Excellent
CD19S	Lroom	Good
SCUS	Closet	Okay

Table 1.2

If you retrieve a value like CD19S from the ID column, all you know is that you have found the item CD19S. You can print the value, transmit it, store it, retrieve it, and use it as an index into some other table. In all these cases you are dealing with one unit of information.

This atomic data rule, like the other rules borrowed from relational theory, helps us maintain the integrity of data in our models, and it also simplifies the mechanics of data access. This rule also forces us to model our application precisely.

So what do you do if your domain requires knowledge of the internal format of a piece of data? Simple — you model it. Let's say that instead of a household inventory system you are designing a system to organize your audio library.

In that case, you would have to break down Inventory_Item.ID using a table like this:

Album

ID	Medium	Compilation Type
A19	CD	Single
A34	Record	Multi
A55	Record	Single

Table 1.3

The information encoded as CD19S in Table 1.2 has been expanded in Table 1.3 to extract the relevant attributes. These attributes now describe a single class named Album.

Sometimes an encoded format breaks down into attributes corresponding to multiple classes and associations. A part number in a catalog, for example, might contain attributes pertaining to a Manufacturer, Supplier, and Part.

Instance order is ignored

Since a class table represents the contents of an unordered set like this...

A set of instances

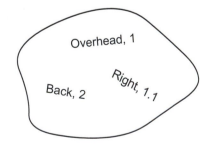

Figure 1.3

...it makes sense that the following tables are equivalent.

Location	Zoom Setting
Back	2
Right	1.1
Overhead	1

=

Location	Zoom Setting
Overhead	1
Back	2
Right	1.1

Table 1.4

Attribute order is ignored

The same reasoning applies to attributes. A class table header constitutes an unordered set of attributes.

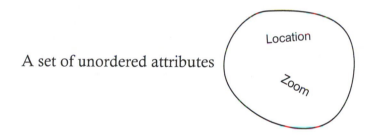

A set of unordered attributes

So these two table headings are equivalent:

Location	Zoom

=

Location	Zoom

Each instance is unique   An entity can be represented only once in a table. There can be no duplicate elements in a set.

Location	Zoom
Back	2
Back	2
Overhead	1

No duplicate instances allowed

Table 1.5

There may be nothing wrong with having two Cameras that each happen to share the same Zoom setting and general Location. But you cannot represent the *same* instance twice in a table. How can we tell whether or not we have an illegal duplicate instance by looking at the data in Table 1.5? We can't. To prevent duplicate instances, we define and use identifiers. Identifiers are discussed in Chapter 2.

Class categories

Novice analysts aren't always playing with a full deck.

What I mean is that, in the context of class modeling, beginners often ignore types of classes that would make complex requirements easy to capture. I know I did when I started out! To become a good analyst, you need to learn when to use — and when not to use — several categories of classes.

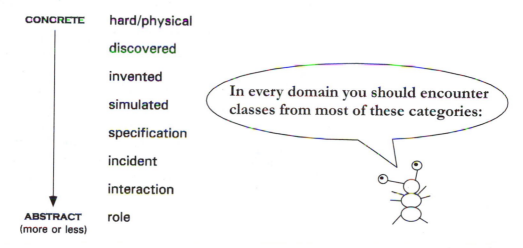

CONCRETE   hard/physical

discovered

invented

simulated

specification

incident

interaction

ABSTRACT   role
(more or less)

In every domain you should encounter classes from most of these categories:

Figure 1.4

The categories I am about to describe are not rigorously defined. They are empirically derived from the models my colleagues and I have produced and reviewed over many years. As a novice, I depended too much on the more concrete categories. With increased experience I found that the abstract categories were necessary to support the intricate policies and control layering essential to building sophisticated systems.

You may find classes that fit more than one category or are difficult to categorize. Don't worry about it. I don't want you to memorize this list or walk around with it taped to your head. It is important, however, to avoid the novice trap of seeing only the physical classes in a system.

Hard or physical classes

A *hard or physical class* is one that you can kick. Physical classes tend to come in closely related clusters: Elevator, Floor, Shaft, for example. Here's another cluster: Mirror, Laser, Motor. Not surprisingly, physical classes appear in any domain that controls or tracks physical things. An elevator control application would consist of physical classes like Elevator, Floor, Building and Shaft. But physical classes are not restricted to high-level application domains. A low-level robot control service domain might consist of classes like Robot, Arm, and Gripper. This service might be used by an application like Factory Material Transport, which also has physical classes like Part, Subassembly and Process Station. On the other hand, it might be used by an artificial intelligence application with more abstract classes like Goal, Condition and Path.

Hard/physical classes are useful for monitoring the current values of real-world entities: the actual speed of a motor, for example. They are also necessary when you need to synchronize your software with the changing states of a real-world entity: commanding a door to close after the landing gear has retracted, for example.

Soft classes

A *soft class* is one that you can't kick. Sometimes they are already defined and sometimes you need to invent them. All the following class categories are soft (nonphysical).

Discovered classes

Discovered classes are defined by application experts long before the analysts arrive on the scene. An operating system domain needs classes like Process, Semaphore and Queue. An accounting application needs classes like Account, Asset, Liability and Corporation. You can't kick any of these things, but in every other sense they are just like physical classes.

Discovered classes generally appear in domains that don't directly track or control the physical world. Some example domains are board games, accounting systems, flight simulators and other types of simulators.

Invented classes

Sometimes you invent classes to make a system of rules work. In an animation record and playback service domain, my team invented classes like Parameter, Event, Timeline and Animatable Entity. The behavior and attributes of these classes were defined according to rules that we invented to fulfill the requirements of this domain. In fact, the application that used the animation service was also full of *invented classes*. This application generated special-effects images for professional video, so we abstracted classes like Camera, Light, Screen and Stage, which behaved according to our invented rules.

Invented classes often appear in service[4] domains. The analysts are free to invent whatever classes are necessary to support the requirements imposed on the service domain.

Simulated classes   Say that you are building a flight simulator. You model the class Airplane. Is that a hard class or a soft class? Since you are building a simulator, you would model the Airplane that you were interested in supporting. While it would be inspired by your knowledge of real-world airplanes, you will probably model your own special version. Your airplane might be a simplified version of the real thing or it might do things that a real-world airplane doesn't (like fly under water). It is soft in the sense that it is not intended to be a real-world airplane (as would be the case if you were building an onboard navi-

---

[4]A service domain is a generic utility directly or indirectly subservient to your application domain. In an elevator control application, for example you might have classes like Cabin, Elevator System Specification, Door, Floor, Shaft and Bank: all elevator specific concepts. A subservient motor transport domain might use classes like Motor, Load, Axis, and Acceleration Profile: all physical transport concepts. This service domain contains no model elements that have *anything* directly to do with elevators. To support the elevator application it is necessary to configure the service domain with application specific data. Cabin 34 in the application, for example might be configured as Load L17 in the motor transport service. This "coupling through configuration data only" principle allows us to reuse the motor transport domain in an entirely different application, wafer transport in a semiconductor process station, without having to change any model content in the service domain! More importantly, it allows us to make changes in the application without having to touch any model elements in the service domain and vice versa. Only configuration data changes.

gation system for real planes). It is discovered in the sense that you didn't invent the airplane concept. It is invented in the sense that you have poetic license with the concept. So we have a new soft category called "simulated".

Specification classes   A *specification class* is a design, plan, blueprint, scheme or definition of one or more less abstract classes. Here is a specification of an aircraft:

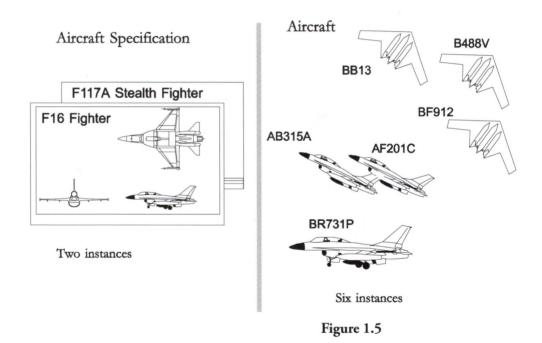

Figure 1.5

The class diagram looks like this:

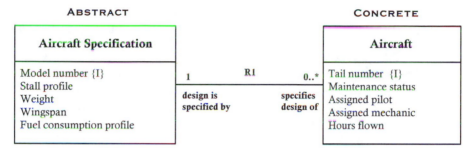

Model 1.1

Being a hard class, an instance of Aircraft is something that you can kick. An Aircraft Specification, on the other hand, is nonkickable. An Aircraft Specification is simply a set of blueprints and design parameters.

Note the introduction of the {I} constraint. It represents a unique identifier (known as a primary key in the database world). In the world of Executable UML, an identifier is a type of constraint. In Model 1.1, the Model_number attribute is constrained so that no two instances of Aircraft Specification may have identical values for this attribute. It would also be an error to have two (or more) instances of Aircraft with matching Tail_numbers. Identifiers are discussed in Chapter 2.

The specification class and association are a generic pattern with the following form:

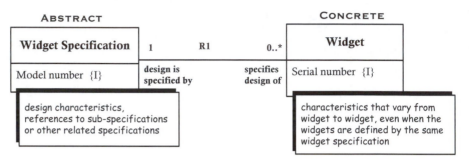

Model 1.2

The specification class takes on the name of the tangible class suffixed by something like:

Model, Type, Class, Design, Template, Specification

The association between Aircraft Specification and Aircraft is a standard form called a *specification association*. The specification association is almost always 1:0..*. In other words, the tangible thing is defined by exactly one specification, whereas the specification defines zero, one or many things. A blueprint can exist long before it is realized.

On a real project this simple two-class pattern is a nice start, but specifications usually become more interesting. Like physical classes, specification classes tend to clump together.

Say that you are building a flight simulator that gives you tools to design your own plane. You will need a class model that constrains the kinds of planes that can be built. Rather than having a single class called Aircraft Specification, you would need a system of classes and associations defining how a plane can legally be constructed. You would have a number of specification classes like Wing Type, Fuselage Type, and Aerodynamic Profile that interrelate to form an Aircraft Specification.

On a typical class model you find a cluster of specification classes that define and restrict a legal assembly of several physical, invented, discovered or simulated classes.

Specification and Physical Classes

Data in a specification, Gas Tank Volume for example, is true for all instances of a given Aircraft Specification, Boeing 777-300 for example.

Data in tangible classes, Current Fuel Level, is true only for a specific real-world instance, UA210 for example.

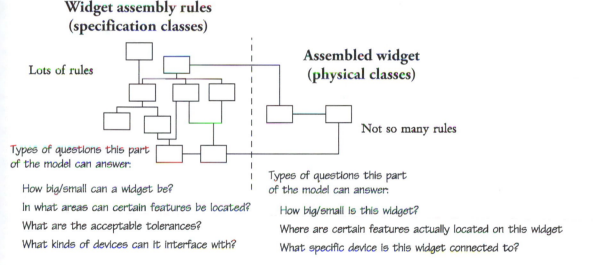

Widget assembly rules (specification classes)

Lots of rules

Assembled widget (physical classes)

Not so many rules

Types of questions this part of the model can answer:

How big/small can a widget be?

In what areas can certain features be located?

What are the acceptable tolerances?

What kinds of devices can it interface with?

Types of questions this part of the model can answer:

How big/small is this widget?

Where are certain features actually located on this widget

What specific device is this widget connected to?

Figure 1.6

Specification classes don't usually exhibit much behavior. Instances of specification classes tend to be written rarely and read frequently. To the degree that editing of specifications is allowed, the editing operations are reflected in the state and procedure models of the specification classes. It is often the case that data in specification classes are written only by the system developers prior to run-time.[5] When this is the case, there is probably no need to build the specification class state models. If reading is the only run-time operation on a specification class, then you can put the read actions in the state models of the referencing nonspecification classes.

Important: Novice analysts often ignore specification classes. It's all too easy to construct a class like the following:

 Bad analysis:

Specification and nonspecification information is intermixed

Aircraft
Tail number {I} Model number Wingspan Stall profile Maintenance status Assigned pilot Assigned mechanic Hours flown

And here's the state model!

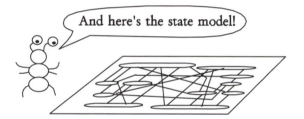

Figure 1.7

The identification of specification class clusters is critical. If you embed specification information and associations in your tangible classes, you will end up with complex and weird associations. The state and procedure models will be unnecessarily awkward and error prone. Specification classes should appear in every domain. Beginners usually miss them completely. Do you have any in your model?

Incident classes
An incident is something that happens. Should a dynamic thing like an incident appear in a class model? If an incident is truly transitory, it is best modeled as an event in a state model. We model an event as

---

[5] You can shorten your schedule by omitting edit functions (and hence the supporting state models) to users in early system releases. In this case, the developers populate read-only data by hand or through the use of quick and dirty initialization utilities prior to compilation.

a class only when the event carries attributes and participates in relationships that must persist in our application.

Here are some examples:

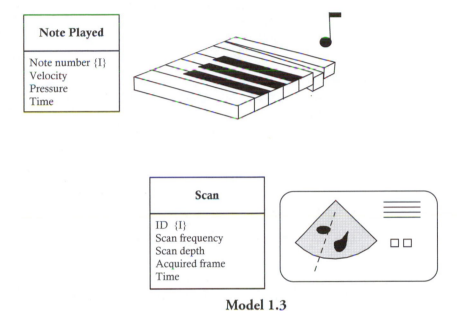

Note Played
Note number {I} Velocity Pressure Time

Scan
ID {I} Scan frequency Scan depth Acquired frame Time

Model 1.3

If you find that many of the classes in a domain have time as an attribute, then you probably need an archival service domain. The archival service will record Events concerning activities in a client domain. As a result, you don't have to model time in the client.

Interaction classes

An *interaction class* is a consequence of an association. Consider this example:

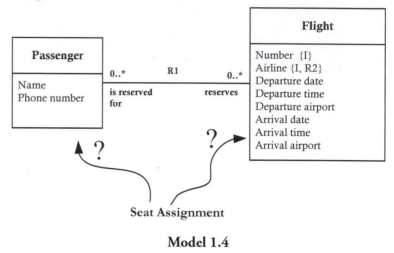

Model 1.4

Where do we put an attribute like Seat_assignment? We can't associate it with Passenger, because a passenger may make more than one reservation. We can't associate it with Flight, because there are many seat assignment possibilities on a flight. We have the same problem with an attribute like Cost and Payment_status. In fact, these attributes are not attributes of either class; rather they are attributes of the reservation association itself.

Also note the introduction of the {R} constraint on the Flight.Airline attribute. More about this in Chapter 2, but for now, it means that the Airline is a reference to an attribute in another class. {R2} means that the attribute is referenced in a class on the other side of association R2 (not shown in Model 1.4). The only reason that the Airline attribute appears in the Flight class is to designate the identification constraint on Flight instances. The combined attribute values found in Flight.Number + Flight.Airline are guaranteed to be unique across the entire set of Flight instances. That's why both attributes are included in the {I} constraint.

How do we assign attributes to an association? We create a class to represent the interaction:

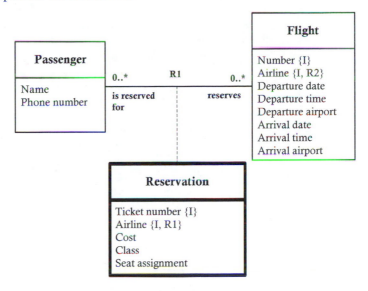

Model 1.5

Here are some more examples:

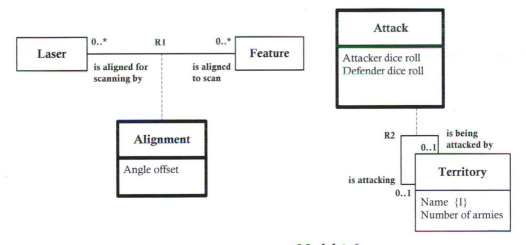

Model 1.6

Interactions are always modeled using association classes. They occur to a small degree in most domains.

Role classes

Sometimes a class has more than one personality. It is difficult to model such a schizophrenic class as a single entity because the unifying behavior varies so much, depending on the time or other circumstances.

Scenario 1: Changing relevance — A class takes on associations or descriptive attributes during one period of time, and during another period of time these same associations or attributes are irrelevant.

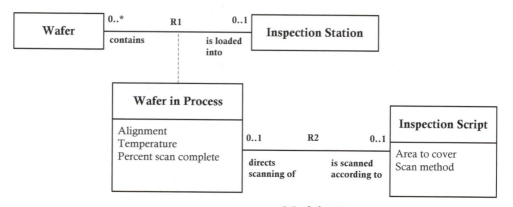

Model 1.7

When the Wafer is loaded, it has an association with an Inspection Station, so an instance of Wafer in Process is created. The attributes Alignment, Temperature and Percent Scan Complete are assigned values and kept up to date. When the Wafer is removed from the Inspection Station, relationship R2 and the Wafer in Process attributes are no longer relevant. But that's okay because we delete the instance of Wafer in Process, leaving behind only the Wafer instance. It's better to vaporize irrelevant attributes in this manner than to leave them lying around with useless values that the state and process models have to remember to ignore! That's what would happen if we tried to make do without the Wafer in Process class.

Scenario 2: Different personality — Common behavior can be defined for all instances of a class, but there is also special behavior that applies to subsets of instances. The defining behavior of an instance never varies over time.

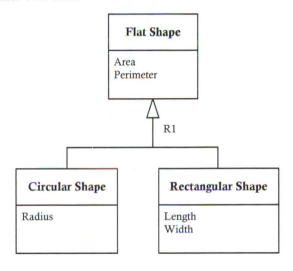

Model 1.8

In this case the instances have *nonmigrating* roles. Once an instance of Circular Shape is created, it never changes into any other type of Flat Shape.

Scenario 3: Relative roles — An instance of one class is composed of or otherwise relates to strict numeric arrangements of some other class.

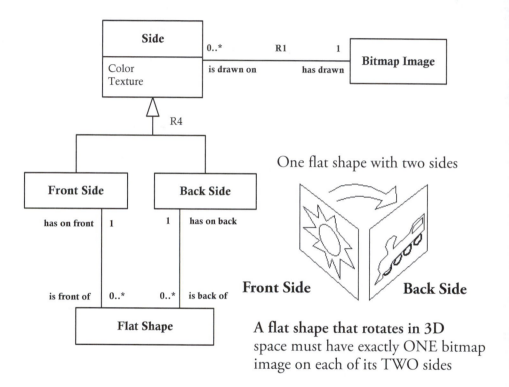

Model 1.9

In this example, all Sides behave the same way. But it is important that every Front Side be paired with a Back Side on a Screen. To see why class roles are a precise way to model this situation, see Chapter 15 on page 303.

Roles are usually modeled using generalization relationships but are sometimes modeled using an association class.

Failure to recognize role classes often results in imprecise class models and excessively complex state models.

Frequently asked questions about classes

Is it okay to have a class with only one attribute?

Yes. There are actually two questions to consider. First, is it legal to construct a single-attribute class? Second, assuming that it is legal, is it useful? Let's consider the following class from a board game like Monopoly.[6]

A single attribute class is legal because it doesn't break any of our table rules. We can construct a table with a single column.

Board ID
8
2
3

The table is legal. What about the class? A class is a bunch of things with the same behavior and the same characteristics. We can argue that a Game Board fits this criterion.

The more relevant question is whether a single-attribute class has any utility. In the game example, we are concerned with things that happen on the game board. We have classes like Space, Player, Token, Hotel, House and Property. The Board doesn't seem relevant because we are concerned only with the contents of the board. We

---

[6]Monopoly™ is a registered trademark of Parker Brothers.

care about how all the elements of a board and the game interact. We need to know the Space where a Token is located or the Player that owns a House. We move a Token, we track allocation of Property, but what do we do with a Board?

Furthermore, while we have multiple instances of the other classes, we notice that there is only ever one instance of Board. This is because we are thinking only of one game being played at a time which suits the immediate requirements.

So it seems that we can do without the Board class. But what happens when our requirements extend so that we must accommodate multiple games in progress? On a network perhaps? Then we need the Board class to distinguish the status of the same instance of Token in two active games.

Another possibility is that Board has some attributes that aren't apparent at first. Money placed in the center of the board might be available to players under certain conditions, like when someone stops at Free Parking. In this case an amount of cash would be an attribute of Board. Even if there are no descriptive attributes in Board, you may want to construct associations to it. If you wanted to model a rule that at all times there is exactly one player that can move or conduct transactions, you could do it with an association like this...

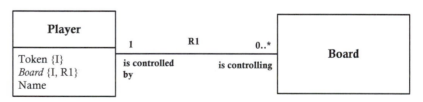

Model 1.10

Note that the Board.ID attribute has been eliminated in Model 1.10. It has been replaced with an implicit identifier as described on page 58. The Player.Board attribute is shown in italics to indicate that it references an implicit identifier. The {I} constraints in the

Player class indicate that no two instances of Player have the same Token on a given Board.

If you were to hand code Model 1.10 in C++, you would probably only define the Player class and write suitable code to guarantee the identification constraints. This is exactly what a good model compiler will do. The model compiler should have a strategy for dealing with implicit identifiers and attribute-less classes. So as an analyst, you can focus on expressing the rules of the application without making sacrifices to optimize the code.

When you model an application, the classes at the focus of your concern tend to have lots of obvious attributes and associations. There are always a few on the horizon that don't seem to add much value at first. They should be included in your model because more than likely they will prove useful homes for attributes and associations that, while not central to the area of study, are nonetheless critical. Of course, if it turns out that a single-attribute class like Board never serves any purpose, then you can always discard it when you complete the model.

Can a class have only one instance?

Yes. Again, there is no problem as far as the formalism goes. An empty table or a table that always contains only one instance is perfectly fine.   If there is always one instance, you have to ask why. Many times it is because the functions at the focus of your interest only apply to one instance. But, as you extend your scope, it becomes apparent that more than one instance is possible.

If we are building a control system for an inspection station, we may know there is only ever one station. But the minute we extend this system to networked control of many stations, more instances are entered into the table.

It is also possible that you have a useless class that really shouldn't be a class. The following class is a bad idea:

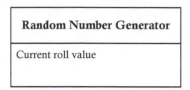

Instead we really have an attribute of something else:

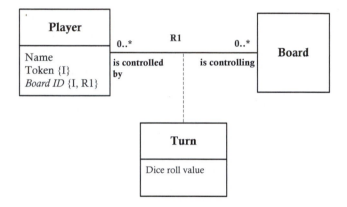

Chapter 2

Attributes

What is an attribute? Let's start with a dictionary[1] definition:

> **at·trib·ute** n. 1. A quality or characteristic inherent in or ascribed to someone or something.

For our purposes, we substitute "someone or something" with the phrase "all of the instances of a single class". It is easier to define with a picture:

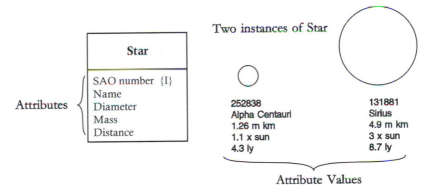

Model 2.1

It is important to distinguish between an attribute and a value assigned to an attribute. An *attribute* is a prototypical characteristic relevant to all possible instances of a class. An *attribute value* is a characteristic of a specific instance in the set.

Attributes have the following properties:

- purpose

- identification role

- dependency on other attributes

- value assignment

---

[1] The American Heritage Dictionary of the English Language, Fourth Edition, 2000.

- universal meaning

- origin

Let's explore them.

Purpose

An attribute either names or describes class instances.

Descriptive attributes

An attribute may tell us about the nature of a class, like its physical appearance, operational status, geometric characteristics, and temporal situation. Here are some examples:

> Size, Wait Time, X Coordinate, Color, Angle Offset, Street Address, Stall Speed

We call these *descriptive attributes*.

Naming attributes

An attribute may attempt to distinguish one instance of a class from another. Here are some examples:

> Company Name, File Name, Driver's License Number, Serial Number, Product Code, Device ID

These attributes exist not so much to describe, but to label, instances. We call these *naming attributes*. A naming attribute may or may not be sufficient to uniquely identify instances of a class. For example, the attribute Employee Name is a naming attribute, but it is possible to have two employees with the same name.

Naming attributes are usually suffixed with a word like ID, name, code or number.

Some naming attributes exist prior to analysis:

> Company Name, Floor Number, Driver's License Number, Aircraft ID

These are *discovered names* because they are discovered by the analyst.

Other naming attributes are invented by the analyst to ensure that each class has at least one identifier. Some examples are:

Camera ID, Event ID, Transaction ID, Segment ID

These are *invented names*. By convention, I stick with the suffix *ID* for all invented names (rather than number, code, etc.) just to keep my models consistent.

Naming or descriptive?

The purpose of an attribute is not always clear. At first glance, the following attribute appears to be a naming attribute:

Runway Number

Consider three runways at an airport, 27, 90 and 19. Each of these numbers seems to be an arbitrary name. But airport runways are numbered by compass direction. Runway 27 is oriented to the west at 270 degrees.

If I cared enough about it, I would argue that Runway Number is really a descriptive attribute since it describes a geometric characteristic of a runway. Whether it's a naming or descriptive attribute doesn't really matter. What's important is that the attribute in this example does more than just provide a name.

Identification role

Every instance of a class is unique. If we have three instances of the Camera class, we know that each instance represents a distinct physical Camera. This concept of distinctness is an important aspect of the real-world that we would like to capture in our models. An identifier establishes a constraint that prevents the illegal entry of duplicate instances in a class.

An *identifier* is a set of one or more attributes in a class that guarantees the selection of a unique instance of that class when values are supplied for those attributes.

Using table examples, we will explore *implicit identifiers, single-attribute identifiers* and *compound (multiple-attribute) identifiers*.

Implicit identifiers

An implicit identifier does not appear on the class model, it is implicit. For example, the Camera class introduced in Chapter 1 has an implicit uniqueness. We know that each instance of Camera must be unique. This could be specified explicitly by adding an invented identifier attribute to the Camera class as shown below.

Camera
ID {I} Location Zoom

ID	Location	Zoom
CAM8	Back	2
CAM3	Right	1.1
CAM19	Overhead	1

Model 2.2

Any value selected for Camera.ID, CAM8 let's say, leads us to a single instance of Camera. Consequently, you can never have more than one CAM8 value in the Camera.ID column.

Zoom is not an identifier because it is possible to have two cameras with the same Zoom value. The same goes for Location.

The Camera.ID attribute serves only one purpose in this example. It makes the statement that, yes, all instances of Camera must be unique. But Executable UML places this requirement on all classes. An unnecessary burden is placed on the analyst if an identifier must be invented for each class: Camera.ID, Lens.ID, Tripod.ID, etc.

We can shed this potential burden by assuming that there is a hidden unique identifier on every class. This means that the software architecture[2] must guarantee uniqueness among instances using keys, pointers, indices, handles, memory co-location or some other mechanism.

By removing the invented ID from the Camera example, we return to the original model from Chapter 1, as shown:

Camera		Location	Zoom
		Back	2
Location		Right	1.1
Zoom		Overhead	1

Model 2.3

Since we can assume that each class has an implicit identifier, why would we ever need explicit identifiers? The answer depends on the world you are modeling. If you invent a class, as is typically the case in a service domain or when it's a policy class in an application domain, you will just use the implicit identification scheme. But if you need to model an existing real-world identification scheme, like a driver's license for example, use an explicit identifier. An explicit identifier may consist of a single attribute or multiple attributes.

---

[2]The software architecture is the domain that supports Executable UML using resources available on the target platform. The software architecture executes the state models, maps the class model elements to data structures and provides for intertask and interprocessor communication of events and data among other things. A software architecture embedded in a medical pacemaker is implemented completely differently than one distributed on a fault tolerant network. While the implementation varies, the exact same services (executing the models and supporting all Executable UML assumptions) must be available.

Single attribute identifiers

Model 2.1 is an example where we must model the real-world identifier explicitly. Unlike implicit identifiers, an explicit identifier is not implementation dependent. We may let the model compiler choose an implementation data type (string, integer, etc.) to represent Star.SAO_number. But the model compiler most certainly will not assign the SAO_numbers! SAO_numbers are assigned by a catalog maintained by the astronomy community. The authority that manages the SAO catalog ensures that no two Stars are given the same name.

The class model can easily specify this constraint. No two instances of Star may share the same value in the SAO_number attribute. The {I} constraint next to the SAO_number attribute marks it as an explicit identifier.

Compound identifiers

A compound identifier is an explicit identifier that consists of two or more attributes. A value must be supplied for each of these components to guarantee the selection of a unique instance.

In the United States, the license plate on a vehicle establishes uniqueness. But it is possible to have a license plate in the state of California with the number 12345 that matches a license plate in the state of Colorado with the same number. You can't, however, have two license plates in the same state with duplicate numbers.

Licensed Vehicle
State {I}
License number {I}
Color
Year
Make
Model

State	License number	Color	Year	Make	Model
CA	12345	Blue	1997	BMW	540i
CA	XUML	Blue	2000	Jeep	Wrangler
CO	12345	Black	1998	Jaguar	XJ8

Model 2.4

In Model 2.4 we see that both State and License_number are marked as the identifier of the Licensed Vehicle class. Two {I} constraints are used to mark a *single* identifier (State + License_number).

To create a compound identifier, you sometimes need to refer to an identifier of a related class. Consider the incorrect model below:

Runway
Direction {I}
Side {I}
Length
Grade

Direction	Side	Length	Grade
13	Single	5000 ft.	Gravel
27	Left	7000 ft.	Paved
27	Right	7000 ft.	Paved

Model 2.5

What's wrong with this picture? Judging from the table in Model 2.5 there doesn't appear to be a problem. But does (Direction + Side) truly guarantee uniqueness among Runway instances? As long as we restrict ourselves to one airport, probably. But we may have a runway labeled 27R at two different airports. The model is not complete — let's try again.

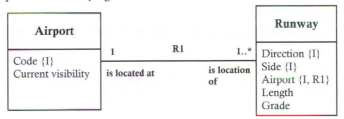

Model 2.6

Referential attributes

The identifier for Runway now consists of three components (Direction + Side + Airport). The Airport attribute is a reference to the Airport.Code attribute. In Executable UML, we call this a *referential attribute*. The {I, R1} constraint in the Runway class tells us that the Runway.Airport attribute refers to an identifier on the other side of the R1 association. It is perfectly legal to rename the attribute in the referencing class.

RULE 1: When you create a referential attribute, make sure that the opposite side of the association is 1 or 0..1. Otherwise, you will break the table rule which says that you can't have multi-valued data for an instance's attribute value. If your association has an * on each side, you may have to create an association class to house the referential attributes. In Model 2.6, a value in the Runway.Airport attribute can only refer to one instance of Airport since the opposite side of R1 has a multiplicity expression of 1, so Runway.Airport is a legal referential attribute.

RULE 2: If the referenced identifier is compound, you must include each of the attribute components in the reference. Otherwise, you wouldn't be referring to a specific instance. A reference to a location, for example would require both the Latitude and Longitude attributes.

Multiple identifiers   A class can have more than one identifier, as shown below:

	Type	Color	Start file	Start rank	Current file	Current rank
	identifier 1		**identifier 2**		**identifier 3**	
king's rook	black	h	8	h	8
queen	black	d	8	g	2
queen's rook	black	a	8	a	4
queen's rook	white	a	1	b	1

Chess Piece

Type {I}
Color {I}
Start file {I2}
Start rank {I2}
Current file {I3}
Current rank {I3}

Model 2.7

In this table of chess pieces you can select a unique piece by specifying the piece type and color, or the start file and rank (no two pieces can start on the same rank and file) or the current file and rank piece position.

The primary identifier (Type + Color) is still marked with {I} constraints. The other identifiers are numbered.

All identifiers, primary and otherwise, must be modeled. There are two reasons for marking all identifiers. First, the identity constraints aren't ignored in the real-world. You can't put two chess pieces at the same file-rank intersection at one point in time. To avoid creating a buggy chess program, you should model all identity constraints. Second, we must be cognizant of all identifiers to ensure proper normalization. (Normalization is a relational theory concept that sorts out dependencies between attributes to improve data integrity). If you don't know all your identifiers, you can't root out troublesome attribute dependencies. Attribute dependency is discussed on page 64.

Overlapping identifiers   Within a class, an attribute may participate in zero, one or many identifiers. In the "many" case, we get an overlap as demonstrated below.

Licensed Vehicle
State {I, I2} License number {I} Title number {I2} Manufacturer {I3} Chassis number {I3} Year of manufacture

Model 2.8

The Licensed Vehicle class above has three identifiers:

1.   State + License Number

2.   State + Title Number

3.   Manufacturer + Chassis Number

The State attribute overlaps identifiers 1 and 2.

Dependence on other attributes

The following normalization rules, borrowed from relational theory, ensure that tables are not filled with redundant, inconsistent or missing data. These rules are applied on each class as it is abstracted.

Dependence on the identifier

Rule: All nonidentifying attributes depend on the identifier (and nothing but the identifier).

Light
Color temperature Intensity x y z

Color temperature	Intensity	x	y	z
1400	3	13	25	1
800	7	55	3	1.7

Figure 2.1

All the nonidentifying attributes in the Light class (Color Temperature, Intensity, x, y, and z) are dependent on the value selected for Light.ID and nothing else. The value of Intensity is not affected by the X coordinate, for example. Picture the dependencies like this:

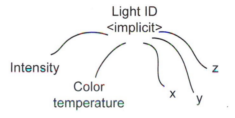

Figure 2.2

Note that there are no interdependencies among the nonidentifying attributes. Also note that Light ID is not a real attribute, it is an implicit identifier. As far as attribute dependency goes, implicit identifiers are treated just like explicit identifiers.

The following class does not fit this rule:

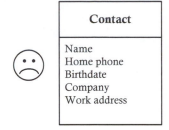

Name	Home phone	Birthdate	Company	Work address
Bob Irving	216-2212	3/18/63	LaST Computers	345 Silicon Sludge Lane
Judith Jauhal	216-9902	12/23/65	DivideByZero Software	10323 Faultline Road
Mike Libby	302-8890	2/16/51	LaST Computers	345 Silicon Sludge Lane

Model 2.9

In this case there is an illegal dependency between Company and Work Address.

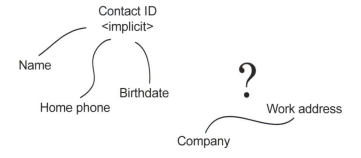

This is bad for a couple of reasons. First, the work address data are redundantly specified whenever you add multiple contacts that work at the same company. If LaST Computers moves to a new location, multiple address values must be updated. Second, if you delete the last person that works at DivideByZero Software from your system, you unnecessarily lose the address information for that company.

When attributes cling together within a class, you should abstract a new class as shown:

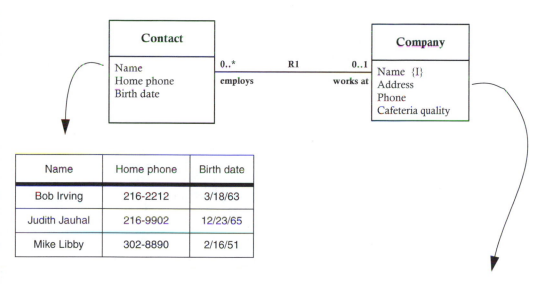

Name	Home phone	Birth date
Bob Irving	216-2212	3/18/63
Judith Jauhal	216-9902	12/23/65
Mike Libby	302-8890	2/16/51

Name	Address	Phone	Cafeteria quality
LaST Computers	345 Silicon Sludge Lane	202-9999	Yechh!
DivideByZero Software	10323 Faultline Road	430-8818	Okay

Model 2.10

Now there are no redundant data. Model 2.10 also sets us up to discover useful attributes which describe a Company that are much farther removed from the Contact (Cafeteria Quality, for example). As illustrated below, the nonidentifying attributes depend only on the identifier in each table.

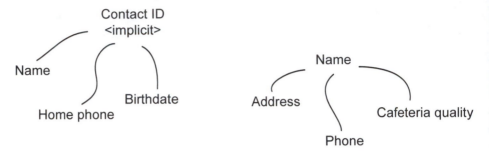

Figure 2.3

Dependence on the whole identifier

Rule: Each nonidentifying attribute must depend on the whole ID. This rule is violated in the class below.

Automated Vehicle on Route
Vehicle ID {I}
Route ID {I}
Accumulated delay
Estimated completion time
Battery charge

Vehicle ID	Route ID	Accumulated delay	Estimated completion time	Battery charge
V15	R503	1:23	27:02	75%
V52	R34	0:17	13:34	90%

Model 2.11

Battery_charge is the offending attribute. Accumulated_delay (time delayed on the route — used by the scheduling algorithm) and Estimated_completion_time are relevant only when a Vehicle is assigned to a Route. These attributes are dependent on both the

Vehicle ID and the Route ID. Battery Charge has nothing to do with a Route.

Partial dependence

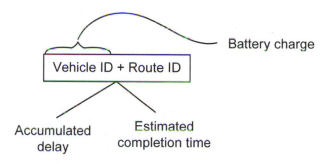

Figure 2.4

The Battery_charge attribute really belongs in the Vehicle class. Otherwise, we would unnecessarily lose the Battery_charge information when a Vehicle is taken off a Route and the corresponding instance of Automated Vehicle on Route is deleted. The Accumulated_delay and Estimated_completion_time, on the other hand, should be thrown away when a Vehicle completes a Route.

Here are the correct classes:

Automated Vehicle on Route
Vehicle ID {I} Route ID {I} Accumulated delay Estimated completion time

Vehicle ID	Route ID	Accumulated delay	Estimated completion time
V15	R503	1:23	27:02
V52	R34	0:17	13:34

Vehicle
ID {I} Weight Battery charge Time since last service

ID	Weight	Battery charge	Time since last service
V15	174 lb.	80%	97:35
V52	245 lb.	12%	3:12

Model 2.12

Value assignment

What are the consequences when you assign a value to an attribute? It depends on whether that attribute is part of an identifier. Let's take a look at each case.

Changing a nonidentifier value

Consider changing the value of the nonidentifier attribute Visibility in the Airport class. Let's change SFO's visibility from 5 miles to 1 mile. (We get a lot of fog here!)

Airport
Code {I} Latitude {I2} Longitude {I2} Visibility

Code	Latitude	Longitude	Visibility
SFO	37.6190019	-122.3748433	̶5̶ →1 mi
LAX	33.9425361	-118.4080744	25 mi
DEN	39.8584081	-104.6670019	12 mi

Model 2.13

No big deal. You should be able to change the value of a nonidentifier attribute without affecting any other attribute values in the same class. (Exceptions are made to this rule when it comes to computational dependency.)

Changing an identifier value

But it is a big deal when you change the value of an identifier attribute. Let's change SFO's Longitude. (We get a lot of earthquakes here!) Before we change the Longitude we have to check to verify that no other Airport has an identical pair of Latitude-Longitude values. Okay, our earthquakes aren't that bad, but the point is that when an identifier attribute value changes, the procedure models must verify that an illegal duplicate instance is not created.

Mess with the identifier and you mess with the whole instance.

Computational dependence

Applications need to perform computations. Attributes in one part of the model may be input to a particular computation while attributes in another part of the class model may reflect the results of that computation. The computations themselves are spelled out in the procedure models. But the class model should highlight those attributes whose values are computationally derived.

Consider an application that computes the rotational speed of a motor shaft using an optical shaft encoder. The encoder is a disk with regularly spaced marks. As the encoder spins, the marks block light detected by an optical sensor. To get the speed of the motor shaft, you multiply the optical pulse rate by the mark spacing. Here's the class model:

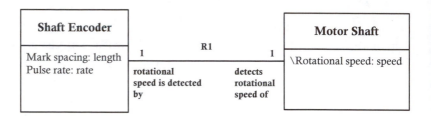

Model 2.14

The value of the Rotational_speed attribute is computed by a procedure associated with the Motor Shaft class:

```
self.Rotational_speed =
my_Shaft_Encoder.Mark_spacing *
my_Shaft_Encoder.Pulse_rate
```

The "\" in front of the Rotational_speed attribute in Model 2.14 indicates that this attribute is computationally dependent on other attributes in the class model.

Universal meaning

Does every attribute of a class instance require a meaningful value at all times? I would like to just say "yes", but the real answer to that question is "Yes, uhm... pretty much..." The principle of universally meaningful attributes varies in severity as we explore different kinds.

Always applicable An attribute that is always applicable will always hold a meaningful value no matter how the class is behaving or what associations the class holds. Here is an example:

Landing Gear.Mode (Extending, Retracting, Up, Down)

Landing Gear.Movement_status (Jammed, Not Jammed)

If we presume that the class refers to landing gear in a fully assembled and operational aircraft, as opposed to being a part sitting on a conveyor belt, we can always assign a meaningful value to each attribute. A class made up of attributes that are always applicable is probably well defined.

While we would like for all attributes to have this property, sometimes trade-offs have to be made. In these cases you need to consider less ideal attribute possibilities.

Never applicable (for some instances)

Sometimes you abstract a class where the instances all behave the same way and have all the same characteristics — except for one attribute that doesn't apply in certain cases.

Consider this class taken from a submarine game:

Torpedo
Guide wire remaining Fuel remaining

As we write the class description, we find that one of the attributes is meaningless for some instances:

APPLICATION NOTE

A torpedo is designed to operate in one of two ways. One type of torpedo is unguided. It uses its own sensors to find a target. The other type is guided by a wire that is reeled out the rear of the torpedo as it swims. At some point the wire runs out, is cut, and then the torpedo follows a preprogrammed search pattern until it runs out of fuel or hits a target.

The Guide_wire_remaining attribute does not apply to the first type of torpedo (self-guided).

To fix the problem you could assign the value N/A (not applicable) to the Guide_wire_remaining attribute for all self-guided torpedoes.

Or perhaps you could permanently assign 0 to such instances. Neither approach is advisable, however.

Whenever you discover an attribute that requires the assignment of N/A or a constant with special meaning (-1, 0, 1, 999999, etc.) you have an insufficiently abstracted class. The troublesome attribute points out that not all instances in this class behave the same way.

We can eliminate the troublesome attribute by abstracting classes that reflect the divergent torpedo behavior (as well as the shared behavior).

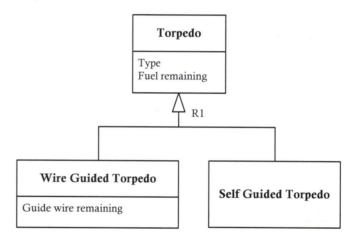

Model 2.15

In this case the problem is solved using generalization. The Guideance_wire_remaining attribute will always have a meaningful value since it is never allocated in the not applicable case. Sometimes you can use an association class to eliminate not applicable values (see Model 5.3 on page 128).

You might be concerned that the Self Guided Torpedo subclass has no specialized attributes. It's really not a problem as far as the analyst is concerned. Model 2.15 simply states that Guide_wire_remaining is relevant only to Wire Guided Torpedoes. The model compiler has many choices when it comes to generating the code to implement this real-world fact. One choice is to generate three classes. Another choice is to generate a single class or maybe two classes. A model compiler targeting C++ might use inheritance. Who knows? The analyst has done his or her job by stating that the Guide_wire_remaining attribute is not always relevant. This fact gives the model compiler real-world information that it can use to optimize memory usage.

Not applicable — at the moment

An attribute may be applicable for all instances, but not at all times. This is generally due to a change in state. There are certain states where the attribute has no meaning at all.

Let's extend the definition of the Landing Gear class to include states where the landing gear is not installed in an aircraft.

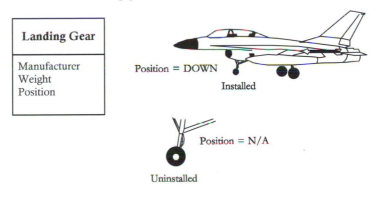

Landing Gear
Manufacturer
Weight
Position

Position = DOWN

Installed

Position = N/A

Uninstalled

Model 2.16

The attribute Position refers to the in-use status of the landing gear (up, down, retracting, extending). This attribute does not apply, however, when we talk about landing gear that has been removed from an aircraft for inspection. Since the gear is detached from the device that moves it into position, the position has no meaning.

We can resolve the problem by assigning an arbitrary value to Position and ignoring it when the landing gear is detached. Or we could create a special position called "uninstalled". But all of these fixes are just pathetic hacks.

Our best bet is to specialize Landing Gear appropriately:

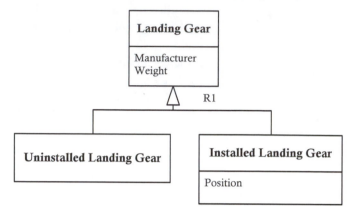

Model 2.17

Delayed assignment   Sometimes an attribute has meaning, but there is an initial period of time, beyond the creation process, when a value is not yet assigned.

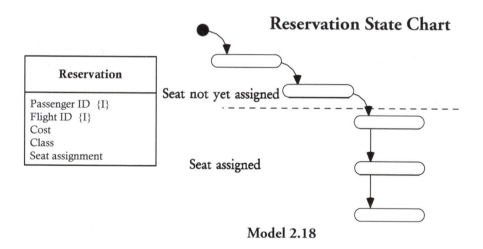

Model 2.18

When a flight reservation is made, a seat may or may not be assigned. We could define the attribute domain of Seat Assignment to be: Any aircraft seat name such as 1A, 12C, and so on, or Unassigned.

We can make the attribute more uniform, as in the landing gear example, through specialization. In this case we could create new classes like Reservation With Seats and Reservation Without Seats. But is the goal of making a single attribute uniform worth the cost of two more classes and a specialization-generalization relationship?

In this case, probably not. But I can never say for sure until I see more of the subsystem and get a feel for what kind of state and process behavior we are going to be modeling. You want the combination of your class model AND state and procedure models to be simple, yet extensible. If you stick with the Seat_assignment attribute, then you can count on adding a special condition, and maybe even a state or two, to your Reservation state model. But this may be less effort than specializing by seat assignment.

More than one meaning   Sometimes you have an attribute that changes its meaning depending on what value is assigned.

APPLICATION NOTE

At a part inspection station we mark parts that fail inspection. There are two ways to mark a part. You can scratch the part or you can spray ink on the part. If you spray ink, you have a choice of colors. For a given type of part and production process, a script specifies a series of inspection and evaluation steps and a marking scheme.

Here's the initial model:

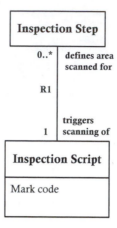

Model 2.19

The Inspection Script.Mark_code attribute specifies how a part is to be marked if it fails a script. The attribute domain is 0, 1, 2, 3, 4, 5, where 1 to 3 specifies ink colors, 4 means scratch and 0 means don't mark at all.

Mark_code has a different meaning depending on the kind of marking to be applied. So what's wrong with that?

- Model 2.19 doesn't expose all marking possibilities. Can a part be marked more than once? Can a part be both scratched and inked? By burying a scheme in the attribute domain, you hide the rule that a part can be either inked or scratched, but not both.

- The model doesn't extend well. What happens when you get a requirement to mark more than once? Mark and scratch?

- Since marking rules are in the attribute domain, new marking requirements will complicate the attribute domain. This will lead to added complexity in the state model that controls marking.

To make the meaning uniform we could do this:

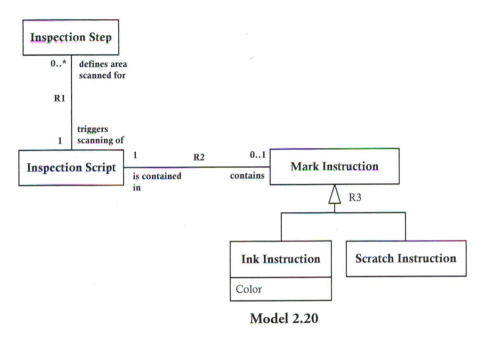

Model 2.20

This model takes the application rules that were previously embedded in the Mark_code attribute domain, and exposes them in the classes and associations.

- 0 — handled by conditional on R2

- 1, 2, 3 — handled by creating instance of Ink Instruction and setting Ink Instruction.Color (Note that more colors can easily be added.)

- 4 — handled by creating instance of Scratch Instruction (If you had degrees of scratching, heavy/light for example, you could easily add the Scratch Instruction.Degree attribute.)

This model easily extends to accommodate new requirements. If we get a requirement to mark more than once, for example, we could change R2 to 1:0..*.

Now, I am not saying that the specialization example is necessarily the best approach. But it is important to recognize an attribute with multiple meanings and to be able to expose these meanings using classes and associations. When I go to this trouble, nine times out of ten I end up discovering hidden application rules. If, by the time you get to the state models, the added classes and associations don't seem to be adding any value, it's easy to drop them. It's not going to kill you to have one or two multiple-meaning attributes with complex attribute domains lurking in the depths of your class model. But it will kill you if you have lots of this type of attribute. Your class model won't expose subtle, yet important, application rules like it should, and it will be difficult to extend as the subsystem assimilates more and more requirements. If you do have a few multiple meaning attributes, keep an eye on them as the requirements develop. Be ready to convert them into more uniform attributes when the model gets weird.

Attribute origin

The attributes in a class originate in one of two places. If an attribute is both defined and contained in a class, then it is a *native attribute*. If an attribute is defined in some class other than the one in which it is contained, then it is a *referential attribute*.

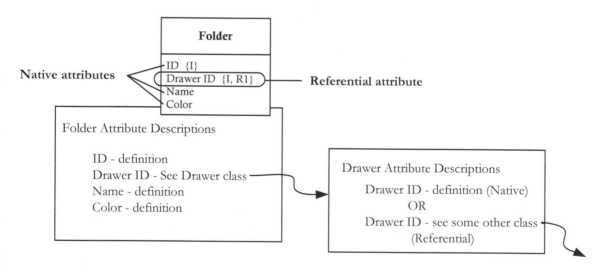

Figure 2.5

Native attributes   A native attribute should have an attribute and domain description. A native attribute can be naming or descriptive. It *may* constitute part or all of an identifier.

Referential attributes   A referential attribute (attribute A) has an attribute description that points to an attribute (attribute B) in the class that the attribute references. Note that attribute B may be either native or referential. If attribute B is referential, then it must point to an attribute (attribute C) in some class. This chain of references can extend through any number of referential attributes, but must eventually resolve to a native attribute somewhere.

A referential attribute can be naming or descriptive. If it plays an identification role, it may constitute part or all of one or more identifiers.

Origin and identifiers   An invented identifier like Point.ID is a native, naming, nonreferential attribute. But other combinations of attribute origin and purpose can yield perfectly good identifiers:

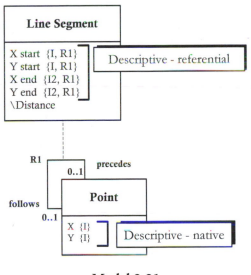

Model 2.21

In this example, the identifier of the Point class is made up of descriptive native attributes. The identifier of the Line Segment class is made up of descriptive referential attributes. Model 2.21 uses referential attributes to formalize R1 according to the referential attribute placement rules described in Model 5.2. This example shows that referential attributes are treated just like any other attribute when it comes to identifier composition. In Executable UML we usually don't need to show referential attributes explicitly[3]. So we could have drawn the model like this instead:

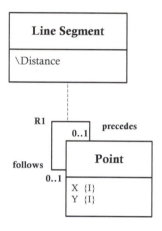

The "\" in front of the Line_Segment.Distance attribute indicates that the value of this attribute is derived mathematically. Every derived attribute is defined by a mathematical expression containing attributes as parameters found elsewhere in the class model.

Summary of attribute properties

Take all the attributes in a single class. All of them are eligible as partial or whole identifiers, assuming that they can collectively or individually do what an identifier is supposed to do. Some of these

---

[3] In fact, they are only necessary in compound identifiers. See page 60.

attributes are referenced and some are native. Some are descriptive and some are naming.

You should be able to fill out this form for every attribute in any class:

- Attribute name
- Class it belongs to
- Referential: Y/N
- Part or all of at least one ID for this class: Y/N
- Type: Naming/Descriptive
- Description (depends on type); for more details, see Chapter 11

An attribute can have only one of the following identification roles:

- Single-attribute identifier
- Part of one compound identifier
- Part of more than one compound identifier
- Not part of any identifier

An attribute cannot be both a single-attribute identifier AND part of a compound identifier. If an attribute is a single-attribute identifier all by itself, it by definition needs no other components.

Frequently asked questions about attributes

How many attributes can a class have?

As many as necessary. In my experience this is between 1 and 15, with an average of 5. If I saw a class with 100 attributes, I would expect to find interdependencies among them that would violate the "dependence on identifier and nothing but identifier" rule explained earlier in this chapter.

You have to make sure that the class definition holds together. In practice, it loses its integrity when you have too many attributes.

How do I know I have all the attributes?

When there aren't any more to find. Sorry, no easy answer. This is where you depend on your skill as an analyst — not a modeler. A novice analyst frequently misses important details. An experienced analyst takes good notes, asks good questions, interrogates experts, reads manuals, looks closely at the hardware, and holds productive walkthroughs. For more about this topic, see Chapter 10 on page 231. All of these activities are required to attain completion. If you just sit there and guess randomly at the attributes, scribble them down in a class rectangle, and move on — then you will probably miss a few.

Can you always guarantee uniqueness in a class?

Yes. Here is an example from a system that inspects defects in propellor blades. In this example a defect is a crack or dent.

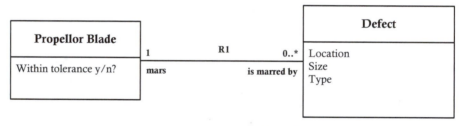

Model 2.22

Here we log and store data about each defect, so we need to distinguish one from the other. We might even need to add an explicit identifier to the Defect class to represent real-world markers that might be annotated on an x-ray image.

But now imagine a system where defects are simply counted. We just want to answer the question, "How badly beaten up is this Propellor Blade?"

In this case, don't abstract the Defect class. Just add the Number_of_defects attribute to the Propellor Blade class.

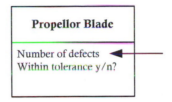

So if you can uniquely identify real-world entities, you can abstract these entities as a class. If you can't tell one apart from the other, you should abstract an attribute representing a quantity.

Another good example is the factory application where you need to know how many bolts are left, but you don't want to create a bunch of bolt instances each time a bin full of bolts arrives. More to the point, there is no bar code or serial number on each bolt, so you can't tell one bolt from the other anyway. The solution is to abstract the Bin class with the Bin.Bolt_quantity attribute that is incremented as bolts arrive and decremented as they are consumed.

Chapter 3   Relationships

Every relationship that does not raise us up pulls us down...

— Friedrich Nietzsche

In UML, a *relationship* is defined as "A connection among model elements."[1] There are four standard types of UML relationships: association, dependency, generalization and flow. Only association and generalization are relevant[2] in Executable UML class models, so from now on, I will use the term "relationship" to refer to these two.

The association relationship type is further broken down into binary nonreflexive, binary reflexive and association class. Add generalization to these and that gives us four basic types of Executable UML relationship types. I realize that this last item, association class, sounds like a type of class rather than a type of association. It's a lot like the wave/particle duality in physics. An association class is both a type of association and a type of class. You'll see how this works soon enough. This chapter takes a quick survey of the Executable UML relationship types. Subsequent chapters delve into more depth on each type.

---

[1] OMG UML Specification, v1.4, February 2001, www.omg.org

[2] In Executable UML data, control and processing are cleanly separated into different models: class, state and procedure, respectively. Association and generalization relationships are relevant to the essential structure of data, whereas the dependency and flow relationships pertain to the dynamic manipulation of the data. Since these last two relationship types are relevant during the state and procedure model phases, they do not appear in the Executable UML class model.

Let's start with a definition of the basic association concept.

What is an association, really?

It is difficult to define the term association. Even the dictionary definition is somewhat circular:

> **as·so·ci·a·tion** *n*. 1. The act of associating or the state of being associated.

The Executable UML definition is more specific:

> An *association* is the abstraction of a correspondence that holds systematically among instances of classes.

This definition is best understood using an application example:

APPLICATION NOTE

A movie player is a system resource that can activate and run a movie. Movies take time to load and, once loaded, take up a lot of memory. But we need the ability to preload up to three movies so that any one of them can be cued (activated) from the control room at a moment's notice. Only one movie can be run by a movie player at a time.

Here is a sketch of some example application entities that "associate" with one another:

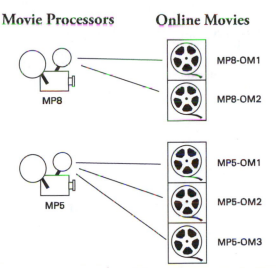

Figure 3.1

This picture suggests a few abstractions. Two movie processors have been drawn, which leads us to abstract the prototypical Movie Processor as a class. Five movies also are shown, which might lead us to abstract the Movie class — but that's not useful enough. The application note leads us to define the concept of an Online Movie — a movie that has been loaded into memory and is ready to be played. That gives us the On-line Movie class. (For the purposes of this exercise we don't have to worry about offline movies, which are saved but aren't ready to play).

Abstracting an association

Figure 3.1 suggests another important abstraction. There are five links, depicted as straight connecting lines, between the Movie Processors and the Online Movies. From the perspective of an Online Movie, each of these lines indicates that the Online Movie is accessible for immediate playback on the connected Movie Processor. From the perspective of a Movie Processor, each line indicates that the Movie Processor can immediately play the connected Online

Movie. With five of these lines drawn, we can abstract the prototypical link as an association.

The association symbol   The class and association abstractions are illustrated below:

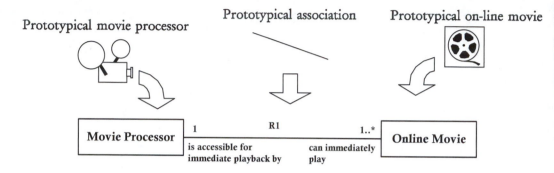

Figure 3.2

Associations and rules   An association formalizes real-world rules. Here are the rules formalized by the CAN IMMEDIATELY PLAY association in Figure 3.2:

- Every Online Movie can immediately be played by a Movie Processor.

- An Online Movie cannot be immediately played by more than one Movie Processor.

- A Movie Processor must have at least one Online Movie available for immediate execution at all times.

- A Movie Processor may have more than one Online Movie available for execution.

If you are new to UML symbology, don't worry about how all this works right now. Subsequent chapters will explain how relationships are drawn and formalized in nauseating detail.

Here's what's important: An association is an abstraction of a real-world correspondence in the same sense that a class is an abstraction of a real-world entity. The process of class abstraction formalizes the characteristics and behavior of real-world entities. The process of association abstraction formalizes the way these same entities relate to one another.

Once you understand the Executable UML definition of associations, the other relationship types are just variations on the same theme. So let's skip past the definitions and see how we can put all the relationship types together to solve a modeling problem.

Relationships define application policies

In a typical object-oriented system, people focus so heavily on the classes that they tend to miss what's happening in the relationships. This is too bad, because the capabilities of a system are largely defined by the number and types of relationships that must be maintained.

I can demonstrate this point by building two different models for part of the same application. Each model will consist of the same basic set of classes. But the relationships in each model will differ, yielding radically different system behavior.

APPLICATION NOTE

Presentation graphics application: Predefined shapes can be dragged from a library and positioned on a sheet. Once a shape is placed on the sheet it may be rotated, resized, or moved around.

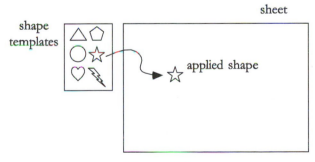

Figure 3.3

Example 1: Master shapes

In this first example shapes are created from a master shape template. A shape is an ordered set of connected points. The point locations are defined in a local shape coordinate system. Here is how a shape is placed on a sheet:

1. A shape template is selected.

2. An (x,y) location on the sheet is specified for the shape's center.

3. Translate, scale and rotation operations are applied to produce a shape on the sheet.

It might look like this:

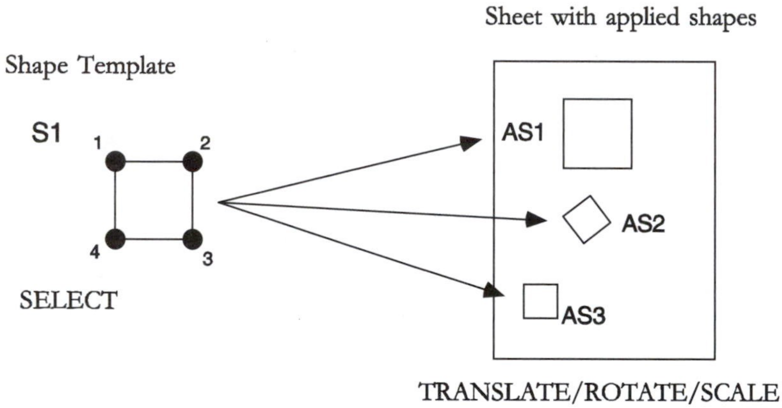

Sheet with applied shapes

Shape Template

S1

SELECT

TRANSLATE/ROTATE/SCALE

Figure 3.4

Now let's take a look at the class diagram:

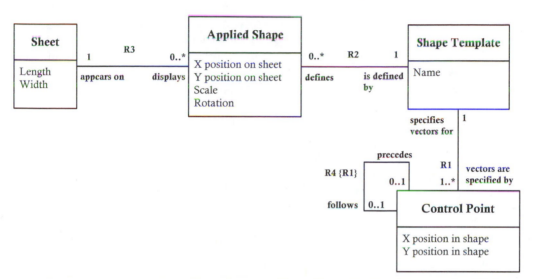

Model 3.1

Each Applied Shape can be translated, rotated and scaled independently. But a *single* set of control points defines the vertices of multiple applied shapes. Consequently, you can't edit the vertices of any individual applied shape. An edit to the control points in Shape Template S1 will simultaneously affect applied shapes AS1, AS2 and AS3.

Note: The constraint notation on association R4 restricts a linkage from one Control Point to another on R4 to be in the same Shape Template. Relationship constraints are discussed in Chapter 7.

Example 2: Copied shapes

Now let's take the same set of classes and change the relationships around.

In this example an applied shape is created by making a complete copy of a shape template. Here is how a shape is placed on a sheet:

1. A shape template is selected.

2. An (x,y) location on the sheet is specified for the shape's center.

3. A new set of control points is copied from the selected shape template.

4. An instance of applied shape is created and associated with the new set of control points.

5. Translation, scale and rotation operations are applied.

Here is the class diagram for this second example:

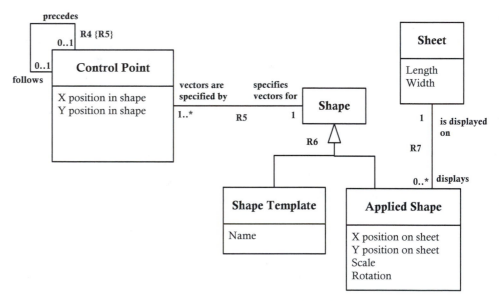

Model 3.2

Here are some example instances:

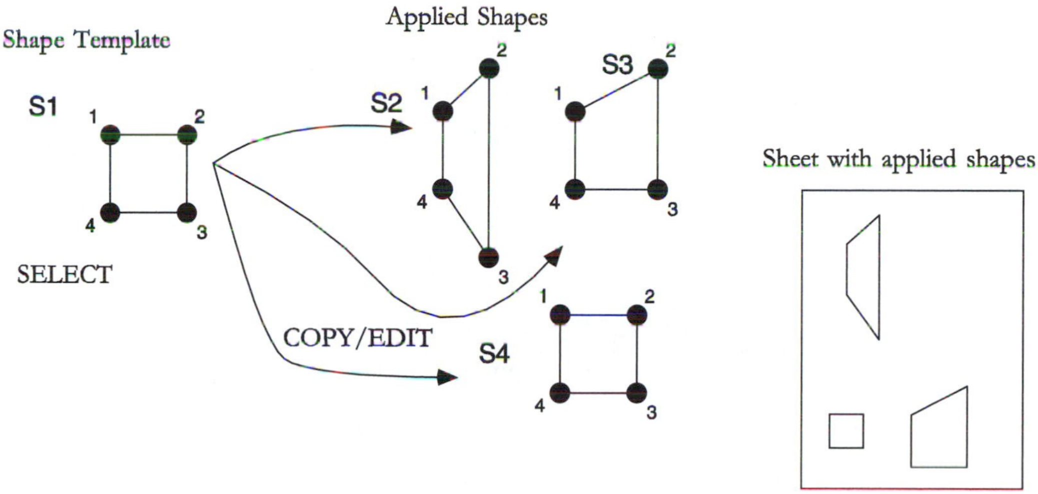

Figure 3.5

As before, each Applied Shape can be translated, rotated and scaled independently. In addition, Applied Shapes can be independently reshaped. Furthermore, you can edit the Control Points in the originating Shape Template (S1) without affecting the generated shapes (S2, S3 and S4).

Relationships are important

It should be clear from these examples that the class model does more than just organize your data. Relationships make powerful statements about system policy and behavior. So do classes and attributes, of course, but novice analysts tend to focus on finding and defining classes at the expense of getting the relationships right. Often a client will show me a model that is difficult to complete. Usually the classes are well named and defined, but the associations aren't even named, let alone defined. Many relationships are missing or are not precise enough. Since relationships define so many of the critical and subtle system policies and behaviors, it is no surprise that skimping on the relationships makes it impossible to arrive at a satisfactory model.

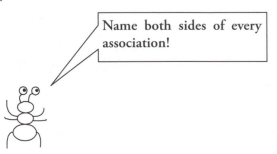

The extra time you spend getting the relationships correct (assuming that you are doing all the other analysis tasks — see Chapter 10 on page 231) will always pay off.

Also see Chapter 6 for more details on creating good association names.

Relationship types

As I said at the beginning of this chapter, the Executable UML class modeling language features four relationship types: non-reflexive binary associations, reflexive binary associations, association classes and generalization. But are these four relationship types adequate to model the magnitude and complexity of information in modern software systems?

Assuming for a moment that the answer is yes, consider some benefits to keeping a language symbolically sparse:

- You don't have to memorize much to be able to read a model.

- The rules for translating a model into design elements are simple.

- The model is more transparent — the application rules are highly visible while the internal modeling rules keep a low profile.

- For a given set of requirements, there tends to be only one optimal modeling solution (so you don't get a different model depending on the analyst's mood that day).

Executable UML relationship types are so expressive because they are based on the relational data model. The relational data model is built up from set theory, which accommodates any kind of information complexity. That's about all I understand from an academic perspective. Speaking from experience, I've modeled complex requirements in numerous high tech, real-time, networked, embedded, multiprocessing (add your own impressive, yet meaningless adjectives here) systems. In all these systems, I've never found myself thinking, "Gee, if I just had more association types I'd be able to capture these really complex requirements." So the answer to the question I started off with is, "Yes, the four Executable UML association types are adequate."

Visualizing association types

One way to appreciate this fact is to visualize the class instances and links between these instances in each type of association. I have drawn one or more snapshots of how some example instances might be intertwined, for each association type. This style of illustration is often useful when you are trying to understand exactly how a specific association type affects the participating class instances. I call it a "snapshot" because it illustrates the objects and links that might exist at a given point in time. A quick scan of all the snapshots in the next few pages should give you the sense that these association types can harness quite a bit of complexity.

In the coming chapters, each relationship type will be described in detail and its snapshot will be revisited. So, if you aren't already conversant with a particular relationship type, I don't expect you to glance at its snapshot and instantly understand everything. By the time you have finished reading all the relationship chapters in this book, however, you should be able to extract any relationship from one of your own class models and do the visual exercise of drawing an appropriate snapshot.

Potato diagrams

Before I move on to the snapshots, let me explain the graphical notation I am using. Take a quick look at Figure 3.1 and you will see icons representing class instances (objects) and straight lines representing relationship instances (links). In the following snapshots I am using generic classes and relationships, so the objects appear as black dots and the links appear as arcs between the dots. A set of objects that belongs to the same class is enclosed in an oblong shape. We call them potato[3] diagrams.

Nonreflexive binary associations

Use a *nonreflexive binary association* when you need to model a correspondence between instances of two different classes.

Nonreflexive binary association: Correspondence between instances of two different classes

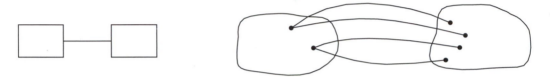

Three unconditional associations
1:1, 1:1..*, 1..*:1..*

Seven conditional associations
1:0..1, 1:0..*,
0..1:0..1, 0..1:0..*,
1..*:0..1, 1..*:0..*,
0..*:0..*

Figure 3.6

Binary means two perspectives

This type of association is called *binary* because it has two perspectives, one on each side of the association. You could say, for example, that a Patterned Wafer class (of the silicon, not the cookie, variety) has a binary association with the Die class. From the perspective of any given instance of a Patterned Wafer we can say that it IS IMPRINTED WITH many instances of Die. As the name implies, there must be at least one Die imprinted to make a wafer a Patterned

---

[3]I picked up the term "potato diagram" from my friend Chris Raistrick at Kennedy-Carter.

Wafer. Now take the perspective of a given instance of the Die class. A Die IS PRINTED ON exactly one Patterned Wafer. This is a binary association because there are two perspectives: IS IMPRINTED WITH 1..* and IS PRINTED ON 1.

Names and multiplicity on each perspective

One of the most important things to notice about a binary association is that each perspective has a potentially different multiplicity. The precise multiplicity is critical when it comes to generating efficient, bug free code. A precisely worded name on each perspective is required if you want to get the multiplicity correct. This is especially important when modeling less tangible classes.

All pairings of multiplicity expressions allowed in Executable UML are summarized in Figure 3.6 above. These expressions are organized into the unconditional (zero not possible) and conditional (zero possible) forms.

We call this type of association nonreflexive because it spans two different classes.

Reflexive binary associations

Use a *reflexive binary association* when you want to model a correspondence among instances of the same class.

Reflexive binary association: Correspondence among instances of the same class

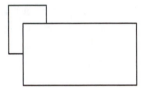

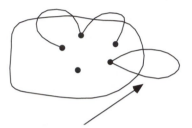

Seven asymmetric reflexive forms
1:1, 0..1:0..1,
1:1..*, 0..1:1..*, 0..1:0..*,
1..*:1..*, 0..*:0..*

Four symmetric reflexive forms
1:1, 0..1:0..1,
1..*:1..*, 0..*:0..*

Cycles (link to same instance) allowed unless the association is constrained to be acyclic

Figure 3.7

Two perspectives, one class

You can use a reflexive binary association, for example, to model a path followed by aircraft as they proceed from one location to the next through a series of Waypoints. A given Waypoint (Waypoint A, let's say) may or may not be VISITED BEFORE a different instance of Waypoint. Waypoint A may or may not be VISITED AFTER a preceding instance of Waypoint.

Asymmetric and symmetric perspectives

So we see that a reflexive binary association is just a binary association wrapped on the same class. A reflexive association may have two asymmetric perspectives, as is the case in the Waypoint example. It is also possible for both perspectives to be identical. Consider a model of adjacency among Territories on a map. A Territory BORDERS one or more other Territories. Unlike the VISITED BEFORE / AFTER association on the Waypoint class, the borders association implies no order and is completely symmetric. Symmetric reflexive associations have identical names and multiplicity expressions on each side of the association.

All pairings of multiplicity expressions that can be used in asymmetric and symmetric reflexive associations are summarized in Figure 3.7.

Cycles   One more thing: Reflexive associations may be constrained, if desired, to exclude cycles. Cycles permit an instance of a class to relate to itself. This topic is addressed on page 174.

Associations and links   It should be clear now that a *link* is an instance of an association between an instance of one class and:

a)   an instance of another class (non-reflexive)

b)   an instance of the same class (reflexive)

c)   the same instance (also reflexive)

Association classes

Use *association class* when you need to place attributes or behavior on a binary association or when you want to attach relationships to a binary association.

An association class is signified by a dashed line extending from the association class to the middle of a single binary association. Each link along a binary association generates one object in the association class.

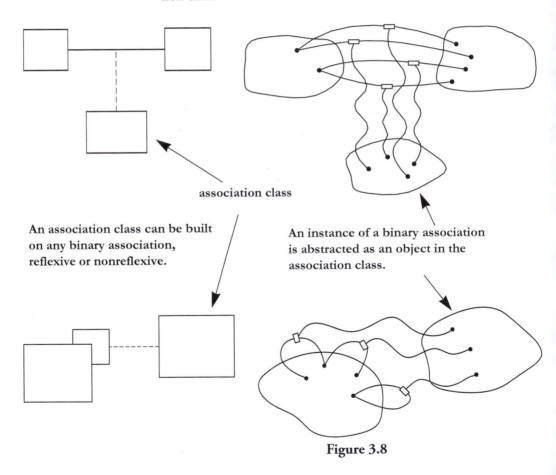

association class

An association class can be built on any binary association, reflexive or nonreflexive.

An instance of a binary association is abstracted as an object in the association class.

Figure 3.8

102

A home for inbetween attributes

Consider a symmetric reflexive association among computer Processors. A Processor IS CONNECTED TO zero, one or many Processors. Attributes like Location, IP_address and Primary_operating_system are clearly properties of the Processor class. But where do we put the Connection_speed, and Line_quality attributes? These are properties of a Connection between Processors. We attach a Connection association class to the IS CONNECTED TO association and now we have a home for our inbetween attributes.

An association may exhibit behavior

Even if we weren't searching for a place to hang a few attributes, we may still need the Connection class to house communication behavior like opening, negotiating, transmitting and closing, behaviors that clearly do not belong in the Processor class.

Dependency

The potato diagrams in Figure 3.8 show that each object in the association class arises from a link between objects in the *participating classes*. (A participating class is a class that participates in the binary association attached to the association class. If the association is reflexive, there is only one participating class.) This means that an instance of an association class cannot exist independent of a link. This should make sense since each object in an association class represents a link between objects in the participating classes.

The ability to transform any association into a class is an extremely useful feature.

Generalization

There are several uses (and even more misuses) for a *generalization* relationship. For now, though, let's focus on the positive. You can use generalization relationships to:

- Resolve a class definition where all instances share the same attributes, same behavior and conform to the same policies and yet don't really because of a few nagging exceptions. Instead of tacking some discriminator flag type attributes onto the class (which will unnecessarily complicate the state and procedure model control threads), generalization can come to the rescue.

- Model mutual exclusion. "An instance of A must relate to one instance of B or one instance of C, but never both at the same time, and never zero." Or perhaps, "An instance of X is always in either the Y mode or the Z mode, but never both at the same time."

- Discard any associations and attributes that become irrelevant for periods of time in the lifecycle of a class while retaining those attributes and associations that should always persist. From a reliability standpoint, it's bad policy to keep irrelevant data lying around in the naive hope that no one will try to look at it. Also, the model compiler is robbed of an optimization opportunity when the analyst specifies the retention of unnecessary data.

It is a common misunderstanding (promoted by some case tool vendors) that generalization is the same thing as inheritance. WRONG. Generalization is not the same thing as implementation inheritance. Generalization relationships may be translated by the model compiler using the inheritance features of a target object-oriented programming language. For that matter, some binary associations may be implemented using inheritance. This distinction is especially important when your models are translated into a language with no concept of inheritance (assembler, VHDL or C, for example).

Generalization relationships can be used in an implementation independent way that does not require any inheritance capability in the target programming language. The full power of generalization is made available to the analyst without any of the implementation artifacts.

To do this, Executable UML requires a couple of standard UML constraints on all generalization relationships. This also results in class models that are entirely consistent with the relational model of data. As is the case with the rest of the class model, set building blocks can be arranged to accomplish everything that can be done with implementation inheritance, but in a simpler, more powerful way, and without any of the drawbacks common in implementation inheritance. Let's see what we can do.

We can model nonoverlapping subsets of instances:

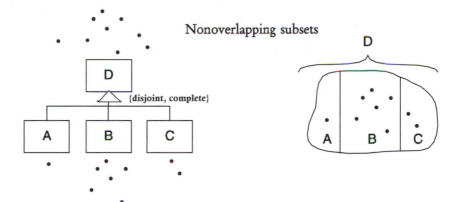

Figure 3.9

Or even sets within sets within sets:

Nonoverlapping, many-layered hierarchical subsets

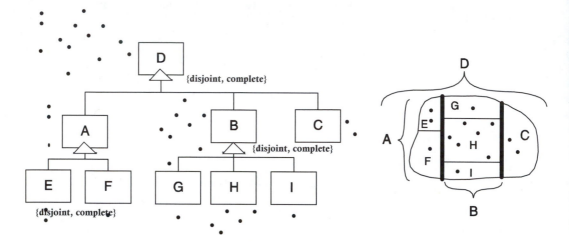

Figure 3.10

Multiple generalization relationships can model overlapping subsets.

Overlapping subsets

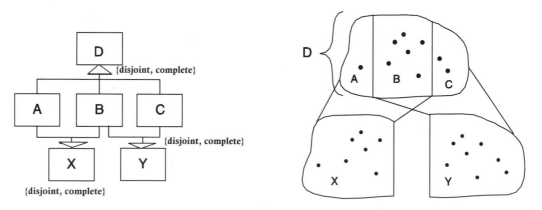

Figure 3.11

This type of model is covered in Chapter 9 on page 201.

Summary of Executable UML relationship types

That's it. We can model an enormous variety with just these four types of relationships. In other words, we will model the world in terms of classes that relate to one another, classes that relate to themselves, associations that are transformed into classes, and generalization, based on sets that encompass and intersect one another.

The following chapters use examples to explore these relationship types further.

Executable UML Relationship Types

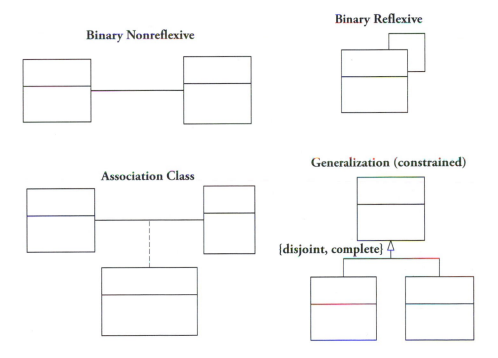

Chapter 4
Binary associations

An idea is a feat of association.

— Robert Frost

The fundamental concepts of the binary association are multiplicity, conditionality, naming and graphic representation. I will start off with some advice on how to think about binary associations so that you:

- don't get instances and abstractions confused

- build syntactically correct associations

- in general, avoid doing stupid things

In addition to listing all possible forms of binary association for easy reference, I will detail a few application examples. The nonreflexive form of binary association will be examined first with all its variations. Finally, we will review the reflexive form.

Don't get abstractions and instances confused

There's a lot more to modeling a binary association than drawing a line between two classes. In fact, notation is the least important aspect of Executable UML. It's what the notation represents, sets, elements and mappings, that's important. Difficulty with associations, especially among beginners, arises when classes and associations are confused with objects and links. Be careful not to confuse abstractions with instances.

How to keep it all straight

The best way to keep all this stuff straight is to draw your class diagram on one sheet of paper with UML notation and then illustrate scenarios involving specific instances on a separate sheet of paper (or on a whiteboard) in *non-UML* notation.[1] The class diagram notation is already well defined, but how do you illustrate instances of classes and associations? There are at least three methods that I like to use, which you will see sprinkled throughout this book: icons, potato diagrams, and tables. A brief description of each approach follows.

Icons

Represent class instances with icons. See Figure 3.1 on page 89 for an example. If you are using a drawing program, build up a clip art library for your project. This clip art, along with increasing skill using the drawing program, will make it possible for you to quickly produce these drawings. If you are drawing on a whiteboard or paper, use your imagination to come up with easy-to-draw[2] icons that clearly represent the intended classes. Links can be represented various ways. Try connecting lines, relative proximity or containment — one thing inside of another — to convey association.

The downside to the iconic method of instance illustration is that it takes time and effort. This is especially true if you don't have any clip art to work with. The time and effort, however, are rarely wasted. The process of illustrating instances almost always leads you to ask important questions about the application requirements. While I am carefully illustrating a scenario, critical abstractions

---

[1] This is heresy to many case tool vendors who, it seems, would prefer that you confine your thinking to the approved list of polygons and connecting lines. As you can see from the figures in this book, I rarely use UML notation to depict real-world instances. UML is great for formalizing abstractions yet pathetically limited when it comes to illustrating the real-world. Every good analyst must reach for ingenious abstractions while keeping both feet grounded in real-world examples. In fact, the best abstractions arise from meticulous study of many agonizingly detailed real-world examples.

[2] If you are lazy and have no drawing talent, like me, just use basic icons made up of simple shapes like circles and triangles.

often occur to me that would not have been otherwise apparent. Besides, you leave a trail of excellent documentation to support your models. I often paste these illustrations into the model descriptions. The illustrations are also indispensable when you present your model to colleagues.

Blobs, dots and arcs   If you want to sketch some example instances but don't like to create icons, then try a potato diagram. This approach won't crystallize the all the nuances of your application, but sometimes you just need a fast sketch.

Tables   Finally, there is the table approach demonstrated in Model 4.1. This method of instance illustration is useful when you want to make sure that you aren't breaking any of the table rules. If you can draw instances that conform to good tables, then you can be pretty sure that the corresponding model is syntactically correct.

Now let's see what we can do with binary associations.

Nonreflexive binary associations

Here again is a snapshot of the nonreflexive binary association:

Nonreflexive binary relationship: Correspondence between instances of two different classes

Three unconditional associations
1:1, 1:1..*, 1..*:1..*

Seven conditional associations
1:0..1, 1:0..*,
0..1:0..1, 0..1:0..*,
1..*:0..1, 1..*:0..*,
0..*:0..*

Figure 4.1

This potato diagram shows what a nonreflexive binary association looks like — two classes and a connecting line with a multiplicity expression on each side. The list of legal multiplicity expression pairs is organized into unconditional and conditional association groups. Finally, the potato diagram illustrates some links participating in a binary association.

Multiplicity

The number of instances that can participate on each side of an association is called the *multiplicity* of an association. The three forms of unconditional multiplicity in Executable UML are summarized below:

Verbal	Expression
one to one	1:1
one to many	1:1..*
many to many	1..*:1..*

Table 4.1

In an unconditional association, all instances on both sides of the association must participate in at least one association. Let's take a look at an example of each unconditional association form.

One to one

With one-to-one multiplicity, items from each side of the association are paired up. Here's an example:

APPLICATION NOTE

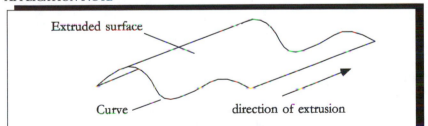

We have a curve that is moved linearly through space to form an extruded surface. An extruded surface cannot exist independently of its defining curve. A curve is created exclusively for the purpose of creating a surface.

The association between Curve and Surface must be 1:1.

Here is a model with some example instances:

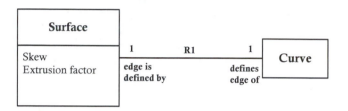

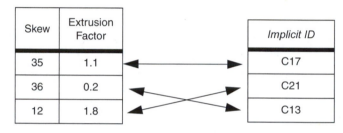

Model 4.1

As you can see from the tables, every instance of Surface maps to exactly one instance of Curve and vice versa. In the actual application, this meant that whenever a user wanted to create an instance of Surface, he or she would have to first select a spline from a library, specify extrusion factors, and then the Surface would be created. When a Surface was deleted, the Curve would vanish as well.

One to many

With one-to-many multiplicity, an item on side A of the association may reference one or more items on side B. But an item on side B must reference exactly one item on side A. Consider a new application example in which we have a semiconductor wafer with multiple die imprints:

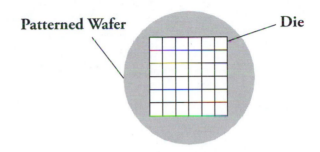

Figure 4.2

By definition, a Patterned Wafer has a number of Die patterns imprinted on it. The fabrication process guarantees that every Die exists on exactly one Patterned Wafer.

Here we see the association modeled:

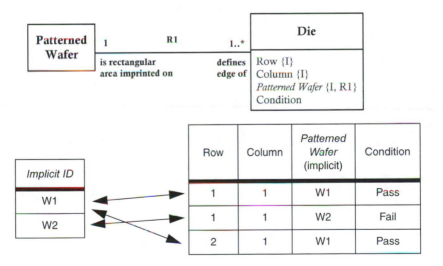

Model 4.2

The Die class in this example has a real-world identifier consisting of Row + Column + *Patterned Wafer*. (Italics indicate that the Patterned Wafer is a reference to the implicit ID of the named class). The compound identifier states that it is illegal to have two instances of Die at the same Row/Column intersection on the same Patterned Wafer. This has nothing to do with the multiplicity of the association — I just thought I'd point it out.

Many to many

With a many-to-many association, instances on one side of the association are linked to one or more instances on the other side and vice versa.

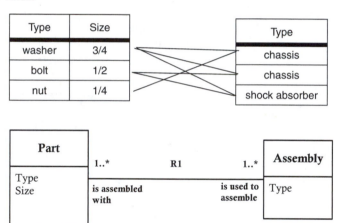

Model 4.3

Every instance must participate in at least one link since we have a 1 rather than a 0 on each side of the association. But is this really true in our example?

Model 4.3 says that an Assembly is built from at least one Part. That makes sense. Can we have Parts lying around that aren't used in any Assemblies? Intuitively you might say "Sure", but that's not what the model says. The class diagram clearly states that every Part is used in at least one Assembly. That's because "Part" doesn't mean a physical part in this model. Part is really a specification. Association R1 defines what kinds of Parts are necessary to build each Assembly.

As you can see, the validity of the multiplicity expressions depends on both the meaning of the association, which should be elaborated in an association description, as well as the meaning of the class names, which should be defined in the class descriptions.

It's frequently the case with many-to-many associations that you want to place an attribute on the association itself. Consider, for example, a Quantity_required attribute. A certain quantity of a Part is required to create a given Assembly. We can't place the attribute on Assembly, since it has a different value for each Part. We can't place the attribute on Part, since each Part is used in a different quantity depending on the Assembly. In fact, Quantity_required is an attribute of a Part Usage.

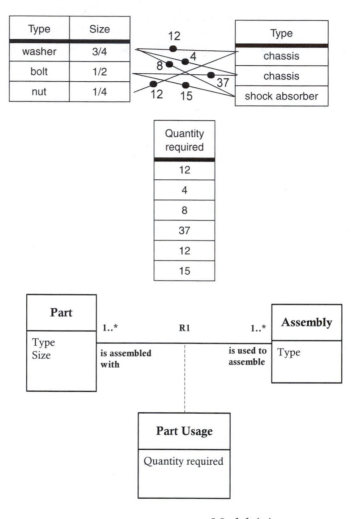

Model 4.4

For more about association classes, see Chapter 5 on page 125.

Conditional associations

In a conditional association, instances may exist on either or both sides of an association that do not participate in any links. In the following application example, we want to model the usage of cables plugged into sockets.

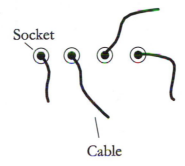

Figure 4.3

Only one cable can be accommodated by a socket, and only one socket can be attached to a cable. Both cables and sockets may be unused. Consequently, this is a 0..1:0..1 association — conditional on both sides.

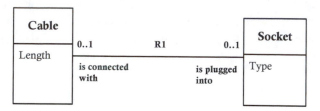

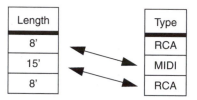

Model 4.5

As you can see from the table, one 8' cable is unplugged.

Here is a list of all conditional multiplicity expressions in Executable UML:

Verbal	Expression
one-to-one conditional on one side	1:0..1
one-to-one conditional on both sides	0..1:0..1
one-to-many conditional on the one side	0..1:1..*
one-to-many conditional on the many side	1:0..*
one-to-many conditional on both sides	0..1:0..*
many-to-many conditional on one side	1..*:0..*
many-to-many conditional on both sides	0..*:0..*

Table 4.2

Reflexive associations

A reflexive association works exactly like a nonreflexive association except that you have only one class. All principles of multiplicity and conditionality work the same way for nonreflexive and reflexive associations. Even so, the reflexive association can stir up a little confusion. It helps to draw an instance illustration and think through all the same rules that work for nonreflexive associations.

Let's review the snapshot of the reflexive association:

Binary reflexive association: Correspondence among instances of the same class

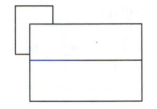

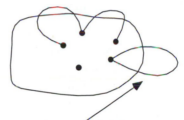

Seven asymmetric reflexive forms
1:1, 0..1:0..1,
1:1..*, 0..1:1..*, 0..1:0..*,
1..*:1..*, 0..*:0..*

Four symmetric reflexive forms
1:1, 0..1:0..1,
1..*:1..*, 0..*:0..*

Cycles allowed unless the association is constrained to be acyclic

Figure 4.4

This left side of Figure 4.4 shows what a reflexive binary association looks like — one class and a connecting line with a verb phrase and multiplicity expression on each side. Not all combinations of multiplicity and conditionality are possible. The potato diagram shows some possible links among the instances of the same class.

When to use a reflexive association

Reflexive associations are necessary when you want to model a correspondence among instances of the same class. Consider a script containing a set of commands to be executed in sequence.

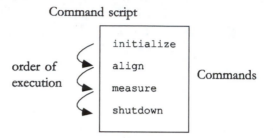

Figure 4.5

The order of command execution is an association among instances of the Command class. This can be seen when you take the perspective of two linked instances of Command. Take the second and third Commands from the top in Figure 4.5 — `align` and `measure`. The `align` Command IS EXECUTED BEFORE the `measure` command and the `measure` Command IS EXECUTED AFTER the `align` Command. Q: How many Commands can be executed after[3] `align`? A: One or zero. Q: How many Commands can be executed before `measure`? A: One or zero.

Consequently, we have a one-to-one biconditional (0..1:0..1) association on the Command class as illustrated below:

Associations among instances of the Command class

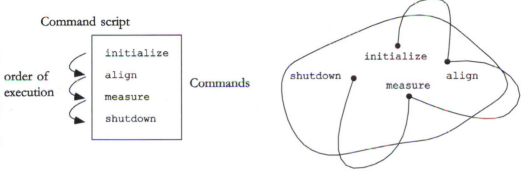

Binary association applied to a single class

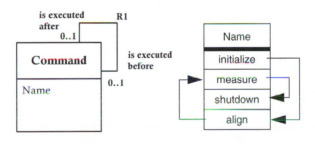

Model 4.6

As you can see in the table of Model 4.6, the instances aren't in any particular order. That's because the analyst can make no assumptions about the order of instances in a class. If instances must be sequenced, the analyst must specify this with an association.

---

[3] In a reflexive association, when we say "after", we usually mean "directly after". This should be spelled out in the association description.

Why a sequence can't be numbered

At this point you might ask, "Why not just add a Sequence_number attribute to the Command class?" You could, but then you would have to fluff up the procedure model so that it maintained the number order when Command instances are inserted, moved and deleted. That's a lot of error prone work best left to the model compiler. The R1 association captures the essential requirement: Commands are executed in a specific order. How the order is implemented is the model compiler's problem.

More examples

Well, that's it for the basics. I could write whole chapters on how reflexive associations work and how you can use them. In fact — I did. Part 3 contains several chapters on reflexive associations.

Chapter 5

Association classes

An *association class* is simply an association magically transformed into a class. You can amaze[1] your friends by performing this trick on any binary association. In Figure 5.1, the Person OWNS/IS OWNED BY Car association is formalized by the Ownership class. Now every link between a Person and a Car becomes an instance of Ownership. What was once just a boring association is now, in fact, a class, even though it's still an association. It's a wave, it's a particle — it's both!

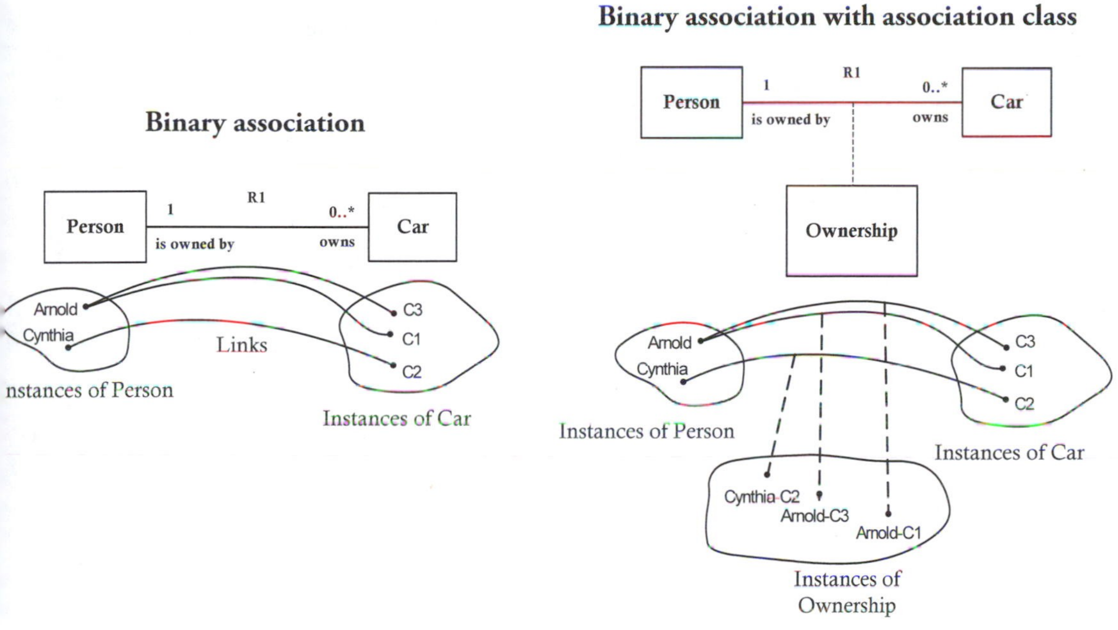

Binary association with association class

Binary association

Figure 5.1

So why would you do this to a perfectly good binary association? For one thing, you can put attributes on the association (by putting them in the association class). You can put a state model on the asso-

---

[1] Or annoy.

ciation (by sticking it on the association class). And you can connect relationships to your association by attaching them to the association class. Lacking any interesting application requirements, I'm quite happy with the left-hand side of Figure 5.1. But in this chapter we'll explore some examples where the need for an association class is compelling.

Let's start with this application:

APPLICATION NOTE

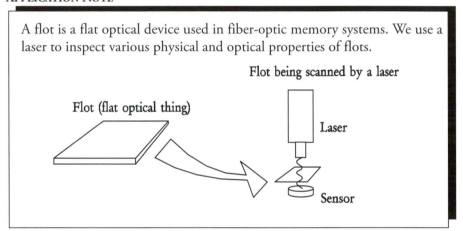

A flot is a flat optical device used in fiber-optic memory systems. We use a laser to inspect various physical and optical properties of flots.

Figure 5.2

We can model the fact that a flot is being scanned by a laser illuminator with a normal binary association:

Flot			**Laser Illuminator Station**
	0..1	R1 0..1	
Thickness Reflectance factor	is illuminating	is being illuminated by	Intensity Frequency

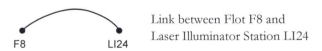

Link between Flot F8 and
Laser Illuminator Station LI24

F8   LI24

Model 5.1

Creating a binary link   In Model 5.1 an instance of Flot (F8) is linked to an instance of Laser Illuminator Station (LI24). These are all implicit ID's, by the way. That's all we have to do when there is no association class.

Creating an association class instance   When there is an association class, each link on a binary association generates an instance in the association class:

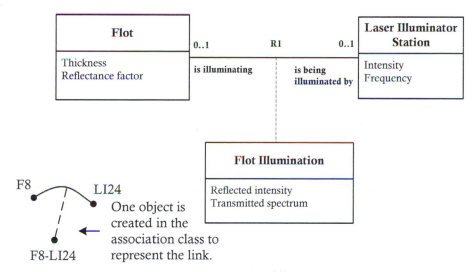

Model 5.2

In Model 5.2, an instance of Flot (F8) is associated with an instance of Laser Illuminator Station (LI24), just as before. But this time an instance of Flot Illumination is created. This new object requires values for the Reflected_intensity and Transmitted_spectrum attributes that describe the F8-LI24 link.

Why create an association class?

Why would you want to create an instance of a class each time a link is established in a binary association?

Three reasons:

[1] You want to assign attributes to an association

Some attribute values will be generated only when a link is established in the binary association. Here's an example:

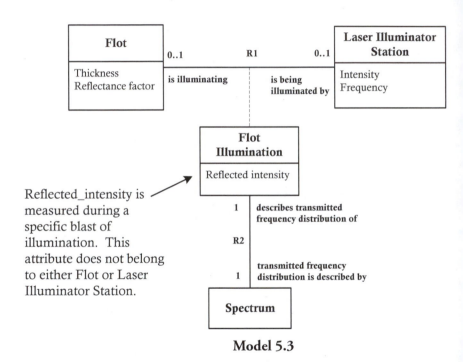

Reflected_intensity is measured during a specific blast of illumination. This attribute does not belong to either Flot or Laser Illuminator Station.

Model 5.3

Reflected_intensity is relevant only when a Flot is being Illuminated.

[2] You want to build a relationship to an association

In Model 5.3 we have effectively connected the R2 association to the R1 association! The Spectrum class may consist of numerous attributes and have relationships to other classes. All of this is created only when a Flot is illuminated. This capability of sprouting one or more relationships off of an association class makes it possible to model some extraordinarily complex associations. Like any class, an association class may participate as a superclass or a subclass in a generalization relationship. So whenever you think binary just isn't enough — you want ternary, or n-ary association capability — just start with one association class and branch out from there.

[3] You want to model the behavior or lifecycle of an association

Special behavior comes into play whenever a link is created in the binary association. This behavior has more to do with the association class than it does with the classes on either side of the association.

Where is the best place to describe the dynamics of the Flot Illumination test process? In the Flot Illumination state model! The life cycle probably goes like this:

INITIATING ILLUMINATION ➔ WAITING FOR LASER TO WARM UP ➔ ILLUMINATING ➔ WAITING FOR DATA COLLECTION TO COMPLETE ➔ SHUTTING DOWN LASER ➔ TERMINATING ILLUMINATION

Since the multiplicity of this association is one-to-one, you *could* cram all the attributes, associations and behavior into the Flot or the Laser Illuminator Station and end up with a syntactically correct class model. So what? The resulting model would be less descriptive and less extendable. The goal of analysis is to expose information — not to hide it!

Multiplicity with an association class

Okay, so you get one instance in the association class for each link created in the attached binary association. But would you ever want more than one instance in the association class for each link? Answer: yes. Can you represent this in UML? No. Is there a workaround? Happily, the answer is yes! I will show you how, but we're getting ahead of ourselves. Let's go one step at a time.

One association class instance per link

First let's review the simple case. In Model 5.2 we can clearly see that for each link between an instance of Flot and an instance of Flot Illumination Station we get exactly one instance of Illumination.

The multiplicity on R1 (0..1:0..1) has nothing to do with this fact. In Model 5.4 we change R1 to (0..*:0..*) by rewording the verb phrases to HAS ILLUMINATED / HAS BEEN ILLUMINATED BY, but it's still be the same story.

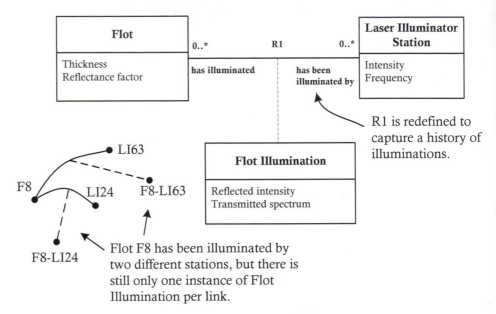

R1 is redefined to capture a history of illuminations.

Flot F8 has been illuminated by two different stations, but there is still only one instance of Flot Illumination per link.

Model 5.4

As you can see, you still get one association class instance per link, even though the multiplicity on the binary association is now many-to-many.

Many association class instances per link

Okay, let's take a look at an application where one association class instance per link isn't good enough.

APPLICATION NOTE

In a material transport system, parts must be delivered to work stations for assembly. (These work stations are called Assembly Stations). We need to track the progress of each part delivery as it makes its way through the factory. Depending on the location where a part is stored, it may be delivered by conveyor belt, automated guided vehicle, robot or through some combination. Parts are delivered in special purpose boxes. Every box has a unique barcode label.

If the quantity of a part requested exceeds the capacity of a single box, multiple boxes may be used to complete the delivery of the part order. These boxes will be routed through the factory independently.

Here is an example part delivery scenario:

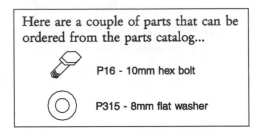

Here are a couple of parts that can be ordered from the parts catalog...

P16 - 10mm hex bolt

P315 - 8mm flat washer

Boxes of parts enroute to assembly site AS5

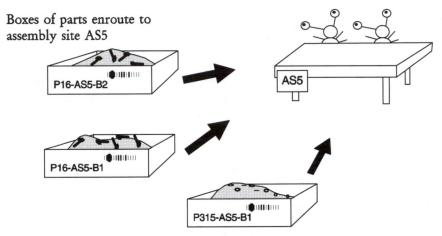

Figure 5.3

In this scenario, an order for part number P16 (10mm hex bolts) is being delivered in two boxes. A separate order for P315 (8mm flat washers) is being delivered in a single box. Both orders are on their way to assembly station AS5.

Now let's look at the class diagram for part deliveries:

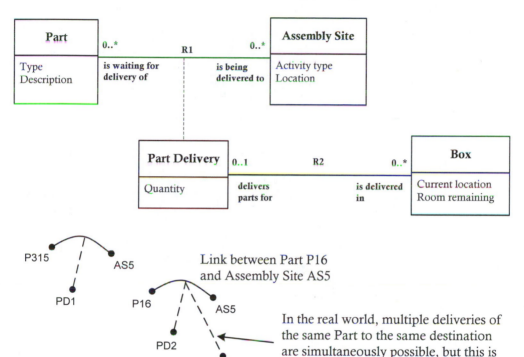

Link between Part P16
and Assembly Site AS5

In the real world, multiple deliveries of
the same Part to the same destination
are simultaneously possible, but this is
illegal in an association class!

Model 5.5

Let's say that at a specific point in time we want to dispatch one
delivery of 200 P16's (10mm hex bolts) to destination AS5 and, for
tracking and accounting purposes, another separate delivery of 150
P16's to the same destination. Model 5.5 won't permit this because
we are allowed only one instance of Part Delivery per Part-
Assembly_Site link! One workaround, coming up...

The workaround:
Approach 1

I know of at least two solutions depending on the specific application requirements. Here's the first approach:

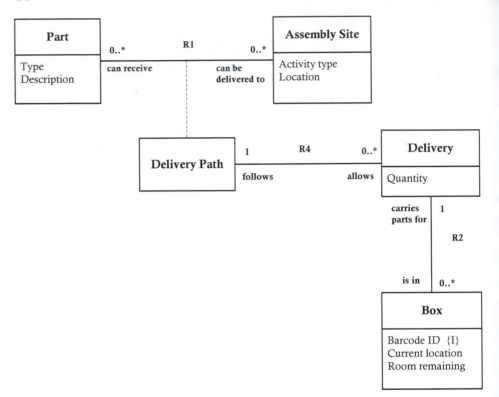

Model 5.6

Here's what changed:

* R1 was redefined as the CAN BE DELIVERED TO association.

* The association class was redefined in accordance with the binary association — now it is a Delivery Path. It may be known in advance that certain types of Parts are used at certain Assembly Sites. This information can be preconfigured into the known Delivery Paths.

- A 1:0..* association (R4) was added, which connects Delivery Path to Delivery. A Delivery Path may or may not have any active Deliveries at a given point in time. A Delivery is constrained to follow a legal Delivery Path only.

This first approach works fine if it makes sense to predefine all legal delivery paths. This would be the case if Assembly Sites were highly specialized so that we would want to ensure that only legal Part Types arrive at the relevant Assembly Sites.

The workaround: Approach 2

But what if each Assembly Site is continuously reconfigurable so that there is no point in making rules about what Part can go where? Every type of Part can go to every type of Assembly Site. It would be inefficient to model all the paths. No model compiler would save you from this kind of stupidity. In that case we go with the second approach:

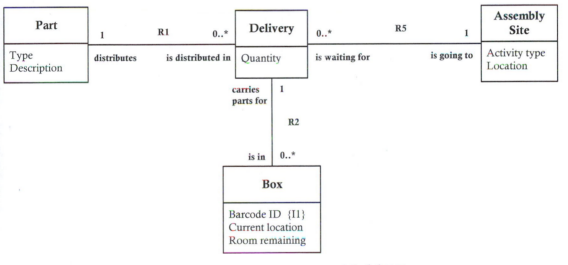

Model 5.7

Here's what changed:

- R1 was redefined as the 1:0..* DISTRIBUTES association.

- The association class was eliminated entirely.

- A 0..*:1 IS GOING TO association (R5) was added between Delivery and Assembly Site.

This solution seems like the easiest — why not use it? It all depends on the requirements (not the analyst's desire for less work!). The second approach (Model 5.7) is not smart enough to reject illegal Parts distributions. It will send parts *anywhere*. The first approach (Model 5.6) can verify that a Delivery Path exists before sending solder to the drilling station!

Conditionality with association classes

Why can't you specify a multiplicity expression on an association class, as shown in the illegal Model 5.8 below? Because it doesn't make any sense!

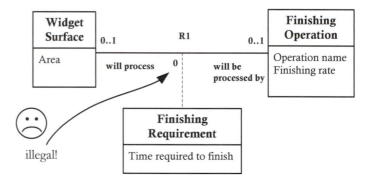

Model 5.8

Model 5.8 doesn't make any sense because instances of the association class represent links between objects in the participating binary classes. So if there is no link between Widget Surface and Finishing Operation there would be no instance of Finishing Requirement. You can express all the multiplicity and conditionality you need by placing expressions on the two sides of the binary association. Let's explore conditionality further with this application:

APPLICATION NOTE

In a factory, widget surfaces are prepared with various processes such as buffing, filing and sanding. These are called "finishing operations." Before a widget surface is prepared, a manufacturing engineer must select a set of predefined finishing operations. (For this example we don't need to worry about sequencing of operations.) Only those surfaces that will contact other machine parts must be prepared. These are called contact surfaces.

Conditionality on one side

By definition, all Contact Surfaces require at least one Finishing Operation. Since Finishing Operations are predefined, the WILL BE PROCESSED BY association is conditional on the Contact Surface side. We can model it as a 1..*:0..* binary with an association class, as shown:

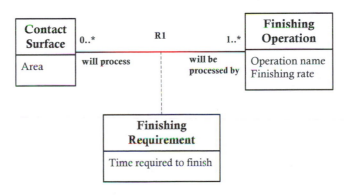

Model 5.9

Some example objects and links are sketched below:

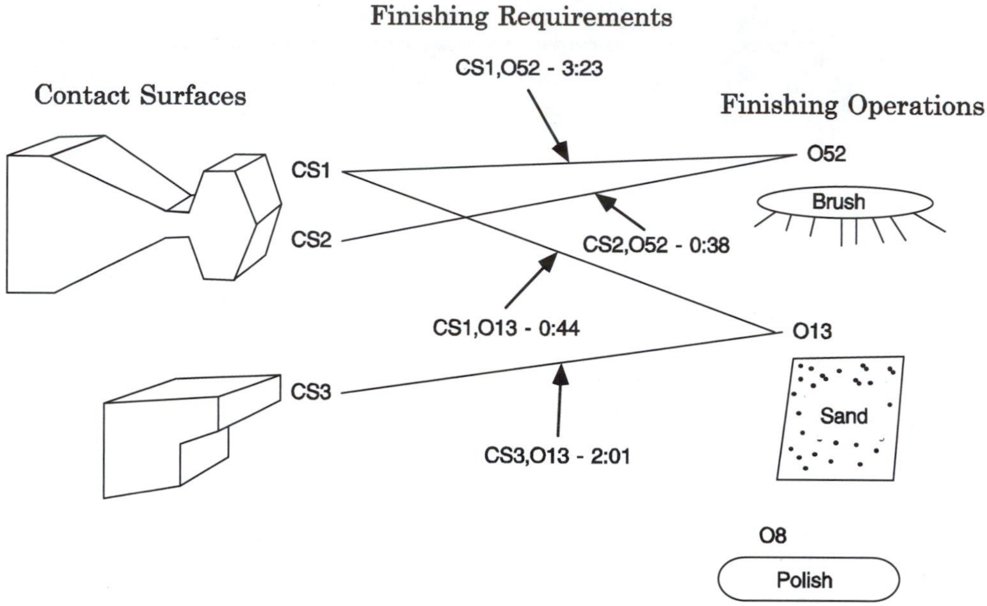

Figure 5.4

Model 5.9 says that each Contact Surface requires at least one Finishing Operation. But a Finishing Operation might be defined that is currently not required by any Contact Surface (O8 — Polish, for example). No problem; O8 just sits there. Since O8 does not associate with any instance of Contact Surface, no Finishing Requirement is created. But for every association class instance, there must exist a corresponding Contact Surface and Finishing Operation.

Conditionality on both sides

To explore conditionality further, let's make our model less precise. (Don't do this at home). The Contact Surface class is replaced in Model 5.10 with the more encompassing Widget Surface class. Any surface on a Widget, including a Contact Surface, is a Widget Surface. Consequently, we have to add another 0 to association R1 making it 0..*:0..*. Not all Widget Surfaces require Finishing Operations.

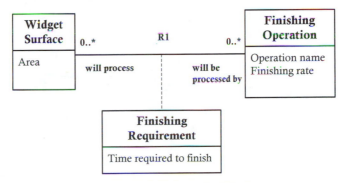

Model 5.10

Now our scenario needs to be revised.

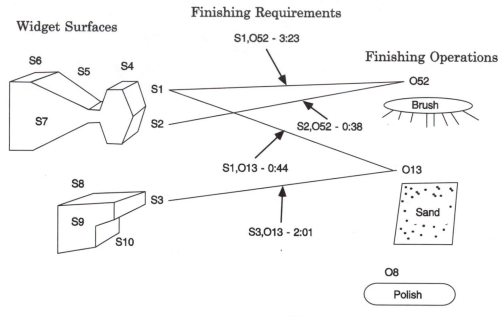

Figure 5.5

Even though the conditionality of the binary association has changed, an instance of Finishing Requirement must still exist for each association between an instance of Widget Surface and an instance of Finishing Operation. If a Widget Surface does not require a Finishing Operation, S9 for example, it just sits there, and no Finishing Requirement is created.

To sum up, when an association class is present, conditionality is tweaked using only the 0's on either side of the binary association. You can't create an instance of an association class without establishing a corresponding link between instances on both sides of the binary association. So it makes no sense to put a 0 on the dashed association class connector as was absurdly proposed in Model 5.8.

Frequently asked questions about association classes

Can more than three classes participate with an association class?

Can several classes all come together to create one big association class? In UML yes, in Executable UML no. UML notation allows for the specification of an n-ary association involving any number of participating classes and one association class like this:

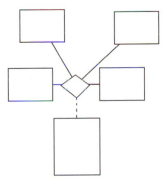

Relational theory does support this concept, but from an analysis perspective it is a recipe for disaster. The resulting model would most likely have several problems: The snarl of associations will be difficult to interpret. The model would fall apart as soon as any of the relevant application requirements change. The effort to bind all the associations together would probably cause subtle application policies to be overlooked. When presented with a three- or four-way association[2], I have never had difficulty finding an overlooked application issue that causes the whole mess to unravel.

You can model all the complexity you like without resorting to confusing n-ary associations. Just use decomposition techniques like we did to produce Model 5.6. There is just no point in hiding lots of interesting application requirements in a stupid diamond. The goal of analysis is to expose, not hide information.

---

[2] One client brought me a class model (at least that's what they called it) where almost all of the classes participated in one giant n-ary association. Essentially they were saying that everything related to everything else, sort of. Now let's write some code!

How do you name an association class?

You should try to make the name of the association match up with the name of the association class (and vice versa). If you end up with a nonsensical name for either the association or the association class, you may need to rethink it.

Chapter 6   Naming Associations

Lister: "To the lease holder of Kryten 2X4B 523P." That's your full name?

Kryten: Yes, but personally I don't much like the 2X4B. I think it's a jerky middle name. Still, it could be worse. I once knew an android whose middle name was 2Q4B. Poor sucker!

— Red Dwarf/Series III, The Last Day

Association names are important. Insightful analysis is difficult if not impossible without the discipline of precise naming. Yet most beginners use meaningless names like "contains", "has", "uses" and the laughably pointless "is associated with", when they bother at all, to name their associations. Vague and generic names betray an assumption by the beginner that the class model is simply an arrangement of data bound with association connectors.

Anyone who thinks that an association is simply a structural connection among data elements completely misses the point. To get our software to work correctly, we need to expose the rules and policies of our application. The best tool for this job in the analyst's toolbox is the precisely worded association. Without precise associations, critical policies slip through the cracks only to be caught by the state models or if-then laden procedure models or worse, nothing at all. A policy that eludes the analyst will result in one or more malevolent bugs in the delivered system.

We don't want to wait to discover elusive policies until after most of the code is generated because at that point the cost of a software change is considerably more expensive[1]. We usually don't want to defer rules to the state or procedure models for at least three reasons.

First, state and procedure models are often less powerful tools for the job. It's like using pliers to remove the lug nuts off a flat tire. Second, we want to minimize the number of control threads we have to integrate and test. The more tangled the control threads necessary to enforce the application rules are, the more complexity, the greater likelihood of slippery bugs, the harder to test, and the less reliable the overall system. And third, a rule captured in data can often be changed by updating values (as opposed to editing the model structure). This kind of change can be accommodated during run-time or through re-initialization. A rule buried in a procedure if-then statement or a state chart transition, on the other hand, necessitates compiling, debugging and re-integration. Yecch!

The best way to enforce a rule is to organize the class model so that illegal data simply cannot be accommodated. Then you don't have to write procedures to reject incorrect data since there would be no place to put it anyway. The logic built on a solid class model should never solicit or accept insidious data.

Of course, all this is easier said than done! So let's move beyond philosophical diatribe and get to a real example.

How NOT to model an association

I can demonstrate the value of precise names by taking a simple application requirement and building an imprecise model the way beginners do. Then I will sort out the mess by going back and doing it the right way.

----

[1] *Software Engineering Economics*, Barry Boehm, 1981, Prentice Hall, 0138221227. This is one of the first sources in the industry to point out the relationship between project phase and cost to fix a mistake, demonstrated in a graph in Figure 4-2 of Boehm's text.

First we start with an example application requirement:

APPLICATION NOTE

A medical ultrasound scanner station operates with hundreds of parameter settings. A complete collection of parameters with initial value settings can be stored in a preset file. The capabilities of the ultrasound scanner depend entirely on what preset file has been loaded. An operator may load one file to configure the scanner for a cardiology exam or a different file to set the station up for an ob-gyn exam. Upon power-up, the scanner automatically loads values from whichever preset file has been designated as the station default.

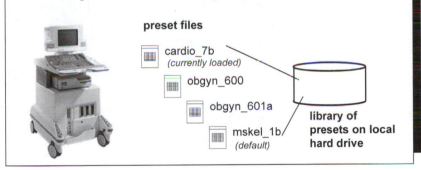

Taking the sloppy approach advocated in many UML books, we might start with something like this:

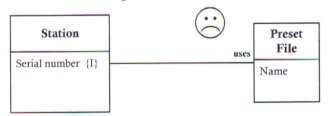

Model 6.1

So far we see that there is some association between Station and Preset File. The mistaken procedure most novices follow is to 1 — draw the association, 2 — give it a vague name on only one side, or none at all, 3 — establish the multiplicity and 4 — get confused about the conditionality[2] and just make the associations conditional on both sides to accommodate maximal indecision. Names are so hard to think about, so we'll just say that a Station "uses" Preset File. Let's see how that plays out.

How many Presets might a Station use? Lots. Depends on what we mean by "use" but let's not worry about that for now. A Preset can be used by only one Station since it is local to the Station's hard drive. So we add the multiplicity:

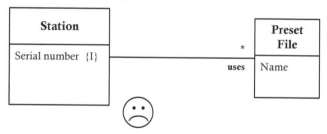

Model 6.2

In UML the multiplicity expressions * and 0..* mean the same thing: zero to many. In practice, I find that the casual modeler can't remember whether * means 1..* or 0..*. Then again, the casual modeler probably doesn't care. It seems that a Station is always using a Preset File, but just in case, why not throw in a zero for flexibility? And since "uses" is vaguely defined, let's stick to our casual theme and leave multiplicity on the other side unspecified.

Now, intelligent reader, I'm sure that *you* would never do anything so sloppy, but I find something like this on just about every new project I visit — so there is nothing contrived in this example. Honest, I'm not making this stuff up!

---

[2]Whether or not there is a 0 in the multiplicity expression.

Does the model we've drawn support the requirements as stated? We can test the model by asking some key questions and see if they can be answered:

- Which Preset File is now controlling the Station?

- How do we ensure that only one Preset is controlling the station at a time?

- Which file is loaded upon power-up?

- Which files cannot be deleted?

The model may answer some of these questions (depending on the meaning of "using"), but it certainly doesn't address all of them. There is no clear way, for example, of distinguishing the default Preset File from the one that is currently controlling the Station.

Enough slop. Let's get the job done right.

Find and state the rules   When we model associations, we model **rules**. It is premature to lay out the associations until you are clear on the rules.   This is where UML executable or otherwise, cannot help you. You need to research your application using good analysis detective skills. Sometimes you can lift rules directly from a requirements document, but it is rarely this easy. Most of the time the analyst must read between the lines, fill in the missing pieces and divine the hidden policies. You must unjumble the narrative, interrogate the experts and figure out what is really going on. Try itemizing the rules in plain text before you begin crafting the associations. Later, you can compare your model with the list of rules to verify that each rule is accommodated.

Let's reread the application note and give it a try:

1. At any given point in time, a Station is using the parameter values from exactly one Preset File.

2. There is always exactly one Preset File designated as the default for the local Station.

3. Any Preset File may be designated as the default file for the local Station.

Don't try to model all the rules at once. That way usually leads to confusion. Break the problem down and account for the rules one at a time. Let's start with Rule 1.

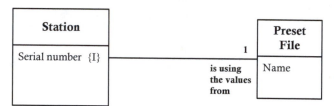

Model 6.3

Rule 1 Every binary association has two perspectives. Name and set the multiplicity expression on each side carefully. We start with the perspective from the Station. A Station (imagine any single instance of Station) IS USING THE VALUES FROM (at any given time) exactly one Preset File. Now that we have a specific name on this side of the association, the multiplicity and conditionality become obvious. It's clearly one, unconditional.

Now we consider the other side:

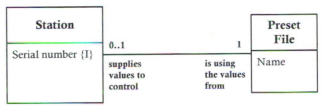

Model 6.4

A Preset File (imagine any single instance of a Preset File) may or may not (at a given time) supply values to one Station. If an instance of Preset File has been selected, it is supplying values for the local Station. If it hasn't been selected, then it isn't.

The name on the left side of the binary association is simply the reverse perspective. So why bother stating it? Because saying (and writing) the phrase forces you to think it through and consider the implications. This is the only technique I know that ensures the multiplicity and conditionality is set correctly.

When I see a model where the associations are named on only one side, I can usually think of a boundary case that disproves the conditionality or multiplicity on the unlabeled side. I do this by, you guessed it, labeling the unlabeled side of the association. You'd be surprised how many times I've discovered paradigm shattering bugs and earned my consulting fee with this boneheaded simple step. So it's not enough just to say the phrase out loud to yourself. Lack of precise labels is clear evidence of sloppy thinking. If you're going to go to all this trouble, you might as well write everything down on the model. Remember that the model is supposed to expose the rules. (We'll leave it to the code to hide all the rules.)

Rules 2 and 3   Now we proceed to the rule that says that a Station powers up using a designated Preset File. This is a distinct association:

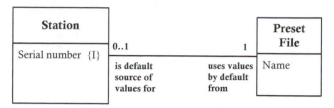

Model 6.5

The names have changed, but the multiplicity and conditionality is the same as the association in Model 6.4. Is it really the same association? NO! When we ask the question: "For this Station, which Preset File is the default?", we may answer File A. When we ask the question: "For this Station, which Preset File is currently supplying values?", we may answer File B. So we need to model two separate associations:

Station	0..1 R1 1	Preset File
Serial number {I}	supplies values to control is using the values from	Name
	0..1 R2 1	
	is default source of values for uses values by default from	

Model 6.6

And now we see the value of the names. The R1 and R2 names clearly distinguish the two associations. Eventually we may write a procedure which navigates a specific association, for example:

```
select one myDefault related by self->PFILE[R2];
```

It's critical that the correct association be specified in any procedure that traverses an association.

Expanding the problem   All this time we've assumed that the Preset Files are on media local to each scanning Station. That's how it worked on the project that inspired this example, but let's extend the application requirements so that we can put our precise association skills to the test.

Updated requirements:

APPLICATION NOTE

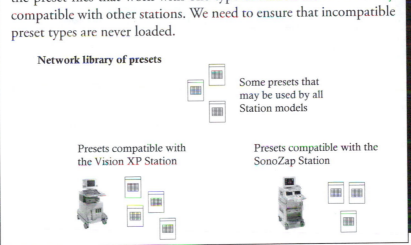

Some customers purchase a server option where multiple scanning stations access a single server. In this case the preset library will be available for loading by all networked stations. The problem is that the preset files that work with one type of station aren't necessarily compatible with other stations. We need to ensure that incompatible preset types are never loaded.

Network library of presets

Some presets that may be used by all Station models

Presets compatible with the Vision XP Station

Presets compatible with the SonoZap Station

Do we need to add yet another association "can be loaded by" (R3) between the Station and Preset classes?

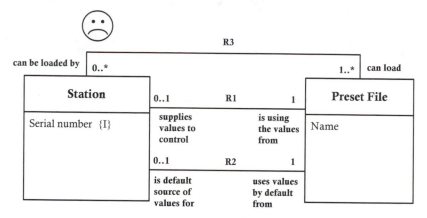

Model 6.7

This model is no good because a rule has slipped through the cracks. The Preset Files that may be used by a Station depend on the design of the Station, not the serial number of the Station. In other words, all Stations built to the same design — the same model — have access to the same presets.

The use of the term "type of station" should alert us to the need for a specification class. We can then restrict a Station so that it can select only from presets configured for compatible models.

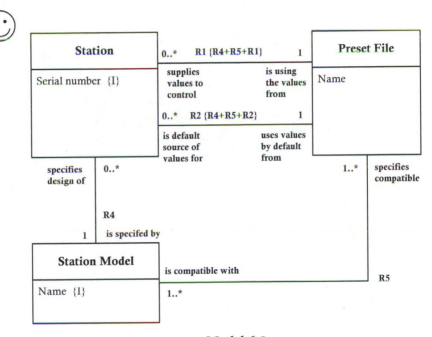

Model 6.8

The final result (Model 6.8) solves the problem with two associations R4 and R5 and a specification class, Station Model. Model 6.8 is not as minimal as Model 6.7, but being minimal is not our only goal. If it were, we could have just stopped at Model 6.1! Our primary analysis objective is to model the world (the rules and policies) accurately and that's what we've done with Model 6.8. Let's closely examine each of the new model components, starting with R5.

R5 — is compatible with

Any given Station Model specifies one or more compatible Preset Files. This is clear from the requirements. But here's what may not be clear. There must be at least one Preset File compatible with each Station Model, otherwise we would not have a complete Station design. A Station cannot operate without a complete set of parameter values. What if the network comes up and all of the Preset Files for a given Station Model have been damaged or misplaced? Then we have a serious error in our system! The class model tells us what is legal in our application.

Wait — we're not done with R5 yet. We have to look at the other side. A Preset File may be compatible with more than one Station Model. Again, this is clear from the requirements. But can we have a Preset File that does not work with any Station Model? Maybe it's an experimental Preset File? Maybe in the lab, but not in our hospital! If there is a Preset File loaded on our network it must be compatible with at least one known Station Model. Why? Because I'm the product manager and I say so![3]

R4   Every Station has its design characteristics specified by exactly one Station Model. There is no such thing as a Station without a blueprint. Many Stations may conform to the same Station Model specification. But is it possible to have a Station Model that does not specify any existing Stations? Sure. At any given moment the network may have the resources to accommodate a Station that has not been plugged in.

R1 and R2   Since the Preset Files are on a network, rather than the local drive of a single Station, the multiplicity of associations R1 and R2 changes. The same Preset File may supply parameter values to more than one Station. In practice, I probably would have anticipated this kind of change (all embedded systems participate in networks these days) by making it 0..*, even before the requirements were extended to include a network. You'd be surprised by how much flak I take for

---

[3]Figuring out whether an association is conditional or unconditional is NOT a matter of modeling expertise. No matter how good you are at Executable UML, no matter how experienced an analyst you may be, decisions like this are made by the product managers or application experts. We analysts just capture the decisions in our models. To get good decisions we need to do our homework (covered in Part 2) first.

doing things like this: "But we only have one Station". "Right, but that's just the way it is now...". "No, our requirements are frozen, we only have one Station. The presets are on the hard disk." "It is now, but...", "Our requirements are frozen", "well, okay...".

Notice also the {R4+R5+Rx} constraints on R1 and R2. I'll describe what this means here, but a thorough explanation of the constraint notation can be found in Chapter 7.

Loops and constraints

Whenever we have a model loop, R4-R5-R1 and R4-R5-R2 we need to consider constraints. Let's start with R4-R5-R1. When a given Station, station_A for example, loads a Preset File (R1), it can't just select *any* Preset File. It has to select a Preset File that has been designed to work with this model of Station. The only Preset Files available for linking on R1 are those that are accessible through the set of objects selected by traversing station_A->R4->R5. That would be the set of Preset Files compatible with station_A's specified Station Model. So {R4+R5+R1} defines a constrained loop. It is the entire loop that is constrained. We could have placed the constraint with any association in the loop, but R1 is the point where we do most of the selecting, so that's a good place to draw attention to the loop constraint.

A similar constraint applies when the default is set on R2. Only Station Model compatible presets may be selected as the default. So the {R4+R5+R2} loop is also constrained.

Verb phrases vs. role names

There are two ways to name a perspective on a binary association, verb phrases and role names. A role name is used in the following example:

Establishing a Role

Model 6.9

We read this as: A Person is the owner of zero or more Cars. So the Person class plays the role of "owner" with respect to Car. Consequently, the owner role is adjacent to the Person class. The multiplicity expression is adjacent to Car since it refers to the number of Car objects that may participate in the association.

Alternatively, we can use a verb phrase as shown:

Using a Verb Phrase

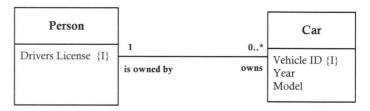

Model 6.10

This reads as: A Person owns zero or more Cars. The role "owner" is implicit and the target action "owns" is adjacent to the Car class because Car is the direct object (English grammar terminology) of the phrase "Person owns".

Verb phrases are better

So far, the difference appears academic. Why not just go with the currently popular style of using role names? Because it's stupid[4].   To be more specific, it's easier to expose precise rules with verb phrases. Role names, on the other hand, tend to be vague and redundant. Let's look at some examples.

An association isn't precise unless there's well reasoned multiplicity and conditionality specified from each perspective. Well reasoned multiplicity and conditionality are not possible unless the perspective is clearly named. Again and again I've watched students and beginners struggle with multiplicity expressions. Is zero a possibility? Is it one or many? Without a precise name it is almost impossible to set the multiplicity correctly. So for each side of an association you must first name it and then set the multiplicity and conditionality.

How easy is it to name an association on both sides with the role naming style? Look at the Person Car example again — what is the role of the Car with respect to the Person? In other words, what is the opposite role of "owns"? It's tempting to say "is owned by", but that's the verb phrase style and we're not doing that now. We need a role name. Hmmm. Is it "ownee", "asset", "property"?

Model 6.11

---

[4]As is so often the case in the software field, "popular" and "stupid" go hand in hand.

This reads as: A Person "is owner" of zero, one or many Cars. Car is an "asset" of exactly one Person. Okay, well, that doesn't seem so bad once the work is done. The minor mental gymnastics necessary to think up the opposite side of owner seems unnecessary. Once you have "owns", the opposite perspective "is owned by" is obvious. No thinking required! The extra step of searching through your mental dictionary to come up with "asset" sheds no additional light on the problem.

Let's try another.

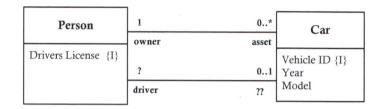

Model 6.12

It's easy enough to say that a Person driving a car is the driver. But what is the name of the other perspective? "Drivee", "piloted vehicle", "driven car"? If we go with "driven car" we are redundant since we already know it's a car by the name of the Car class.

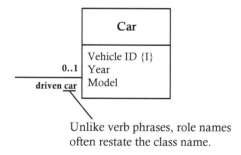

Unlike verb phrases, role names often restate the class name.

It seems to me that it is much easier to use verb phrases "drives" and "is driven by". We can be more specific and say "is driving" / "is being driven by", or perhaps "has permission to drive" / "may be driven by" — depending on what rule is relevant to our application.

So not only are verb phrases easier to think up, they can be so much more expressive. They can express subtle gradations of a rule. Restricting yourself to role phrases is like having only 8 crayons in your box.

But as long as we stick to simple examples like Car / Person, Dog / Dog Owner and so forth, you may still be tempted to go with the popular convention and just live with a little pain. But now let's put the toy problems aside and tackle a realistic model with many subtle gradations. Yes, let's take another look at Model 6.8, and see what would happen if we had used roles instead of verb phrases.

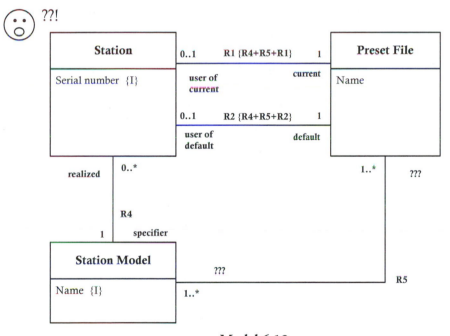

Model 6.13

Okay, this just looks stupid. Maybe I'm just not very good at thinking up role names. But I don't think it's just me. I visit lots of projects and everyone seems to be having the same problem. Not only is Model 6.8 easier to understand, it was easier and faster to build. So I don't care what's "popular", I refuse to slog through the mud. Verb phrases are the best way to construct precise associations.

Practical tips

Here are two practical tips that will make it easier to model precise associations:

- Use a verb phrase on each side of every binary association. Don't slack off and name only half the association.

- Specify the multiplicity and conditionality on each named side. Make sure you have a precise verb phrase first, otherwise you are wasting your time.

If you find yourself getting confused about the multiplicity and conditionality, especially on a reflexive association, use this formula to think it through:

> <class name — singular> <verb phrase — conditional or unconditional> <multiplicity> <class name — singular or plural> AT A GIVEN POINT IN TIME

Here are some example applications of this formula to some of the associations used in this chapter:

> A Person is driving one Car at a given point in time.

> A Car is or is not being driven by one Person at a given point in time.

> A Person owns zero, one or many Cars at a given point in time.

> A Car is owned by exactly one Person at a given point in time.

> A Preset File is the default source of values for zero or many Stations at a given point in time.

A Station loads parameter values from exactly one Preset File at any given point in time.

And when this simple formula doesn't help me, I draw a picture! Whatever it takes to nail down the rule is okay. Remember that most confusion results not from an inability to model, but from inadequate supporting analysis. When you force yourself to craft precise associations you almost always find that you don't really understand the application as well as you thought you did! Discovery of your ignorance is infinitely preferable to the alternative. When you realize that you don't know enough about the application to finish your model, go back to the experts and get more information, write a technical note, collect and reorganize data or do any other activity that will yield the information you need.

What about aggregation and composition?

These next few paragraphs are for those familiar with the UML class diagram symbols for aggregation and composition. These are the hollow and solid diamonds that can be drawn on the ends of an association. You may be wondering why they aren't discussed in a book on class modeling. That's because this is a book on 1) precise class modeling, 2) implementation independent modeling and 3) modeling with Executable UML.

Insufficient precision

The aggregation and composition diamonds are both ambiguous and imprecise compared to the alternative, specific verb phrases. We can say, for example that A Patterned Wafer IS IMPRINTED WITH AN ARRAY OF Dies. Or we can say that a Car RIDES ON Axles. These phrases accurately describe the real-world. These phrases force the developer to think about the rules and policies that govern these associations.

If we use diamonds instead, we are reduced to inane phrases like A Patterned Wafer IS COMPOSED OF Die. Not really! Patterned Wafer CONTAINS Die is no better. How about a Car CONTAINS Axles — not in any vehicle that I've seen! These childish approximations of reality can lead to dangerous bugs. If I say that a Runway IS AN

AGGREGATION OF Landing Paths, I miss the reality that a Runway IS ORIENTED ALONG ONE Forward Landing Path and one Reverse Landing Path. (A plane be directed to land in the north direction or the south direction, for example). The class model should bring out the fact that simultaneous landings on opposing paths of the same strip of asphalt are not permitted. The concept of "orientation" is more likely to lead you to that solution than "aggregation".

Then why are diamonds popular in the general UML community? Good question. As far as I can tell, a nonsensical phrase like "Car contains Axles" could be justified in a couple of ways.

Justification 1: Coding instead of analysis

First, the goal of the modeler may be tilted more toward making a statement about the code to be written rather than about a real-world rule or observation. In that case, coding and not analysis is being performed. Certain features of object-oriented programming languages are being hinted at. It is perfectly acceptable for a Car data structure to *contain* a data structure to accommodate Axle data. But a key principle of Executable UML is that coding decisions should be made separately from analysis decisions. No assumption is made that an object-oriented programming language is targeted. In practice, I know that the model compiler together with model coloring will supply sufficient coding hints. It's my responsibility as the analyst to faithfully model the real (or hypothetical or simulated) world we intend to monitor and control.

Justification 2: Sloppy thinking

Second, the modeler may be a sloppy thinker. Perhaps because he or she intends to solve all the real problems in the code, in which case, why bother modeling at all? Or maybe the modeler is slapping down as many and varied symbols as possible in an attempt to impress someone in upper management. You will find one of these fools on almost every project. Oh my — look at all those pretty diamonds!

Seriously though, it's not that I hate diamond symbols. They do look pretty. But they aren't useful unless we all agree on the meaning. If a black diamond means "is composed of" and I really do want to say Particle IS COMPOSED OF Quarks, then a black diamond is just as good as the phrase. But what is so special about that particular phrase? I rarely have a need for it. Then again, I'm the sort of crazy person that thinks that a Car rides on its Axles. If we're looking for symbols to replace phrases I would like to vote for symbols to replace "is specified by", "constrains motion of", "intersects", "is a conduit for", "partitions" and the list goes on! A class model would be quite unreadable with so many varied icons.

Fortunately for all of us, I'm a practitioner, not a methodologist. I don't invent the symbols I just use'em. Executable UML does not employ the UML aggregation and composition diamonds so that's that.

Verb phrases are all you need I do argue that this is a good thing since verb phrases give you much greater expressive power than those flakey diamonds.

Further reading: For an enlightening example of the ambiguity of the aggregation and composition concepts, see page 80 of UML Distilled by Martin Fowler.[5]

Summary

A good model precisely and completely captures the real-world rules and policies in the domain of interest. We prefer to expose these rules in the structure of the class model rather than bury them deep in the state and procedure models. Class diagrams slapped together using associations with vague, incomplete or missing names do not model critical rules. Precisely worded and defined associations, on the other hand, build strong class models resistant to nasty bugs. These are usually boundary condition bugs that don't get noticed until very late in the development process or in the delivered system.

So, as I said at the beginning of this chapter, names *are* important!

---

[5] UML Distilled, Martin Fowler, Addison-Wesley, 1997, ISBN 0201325632

Chapter 7

Loops and constraints

What is a loop?

A *loop* is a path of one or more contiguous relationships that originates in one class and leads back to the same class. Here is an example of loop involving three associations (R3+R2+R1):

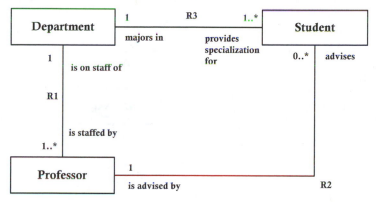

Model 7.1

And here is a simple loop involving only one association (R4):

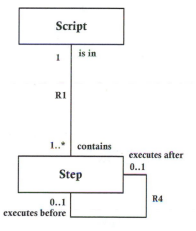

Model 7.2

When you begin modeling loops it is easy to make two kinds of modeling mistakes: *redundant loops* and *imprecise loops*. These mistakes may result in missed requirements, easily corruptible data, excessively complicated models and elusive bugs in your software.

Mistake 1: Redundant loops

Can you spot a redundant loop? Are there any in the following model?

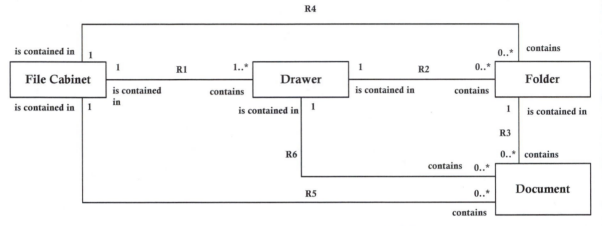

Model 7.3

I'm guessing that you'll take one look at Model 7.3 and recoil in horror at the pointless excess. But which associations should be omitted? And why?

To figure this out, let's start with a bare bones model lacking any loops. Then we'll see if we need to add anything.

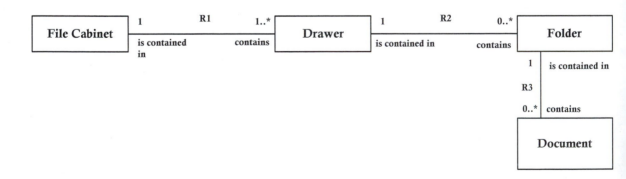

Model 7.4

There, now we're de-looped. Model 7.4 models the physical containment hierarchy from a File Cabinet on down to a Document. Given an instance of Document, not only do you know what Folder it's in, you also know what Drawer and what File Cabinet it's in. All you have to do is navigate the associations. Given an instance of Drawer you can find out what Documents it contains. Just traverse R2, get all of the Folders, then for each Folder, traverse R3 and get all of the Documents in the Folder. So as far as containment goes, no loops are necessary. The associations R4, R5 and R6 in Model 7.3 are redundant and should be omitted.

Considering speed of access

What about speed and convenience of access? Our system may need to frequently ask the question, "What File Cabinet contains this Document?". Rather than answering this question by traversing R3->R2->R1 every time, couldn't we put R5 back in the model so we can take a shortcut?

We could. We would then have to write procedures to update two links every time we create or refile a Document. If you only did this in one place, it wouldn't be so bad. But you know what's going to happen once you get started down this road, don't you? Before you know it you're second guessing every access direction and you're modeling loops and redundant procedures everywhere. I've seen it done on real projects involving hundreds of classes. It isn't pretty.

Don't optimize for fast access in the class model

Of course we do want to optimize everywhere we can for fast data access, but the class model is the wrong place to do it. The model compiler should be smart enough to optimize frequently traversed chains of data navigation. (The analyst may have to color the high traffic association chains to make this possible.) When the model compiler generates data structure code, it can generate extra pointers, hash tables and any other mechanisms it needs to optimize data access. The model compiler can scan the class and procedure models and any added coloring to choose the correct optimization mechanisms. In fact, the analyst's well-intentioned class model optimizations, such as redundant associations, can result in fatter, slower generated code. I've seen this happen several times and come to the conclusion that the best optimization an analyst can offer is a minimal formalization of the essential requirements. The less gunk the model compiler has to sift through, the better.

A nonredundant loop Now let's extend our file cabinet application requirements a little so that we do need a loop. Consider the following model:

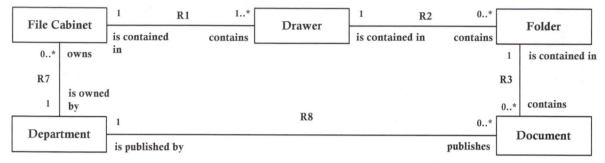

Model 7.5

Do we really need association R8? Given a Document, couldn't we just locate the publishing Department via R3->R2->R1->R7? No, we can't. This chain of navigation would lead us to the Department that OWNS the File Cabinet that contains our Document. But this is not necessarily the Department that PUBLISHED our Document.

The R8 association is necessary because it expresses a fact not already expressed. Since PUBLISH means something different than CONTAIN, it is not redundant — just another reason why it is so important to always name both perspectives on every association!

Mistake 2: Imprecise loops

When you tie both ends of a loop together you can easily miss- specify the constraints that determine which instances are allowed to interconnect. Consider a university that requires Students to choose an advisor among

Professors who work in the same Department as the Student's declared major. Does the following model satisfy this requirement?

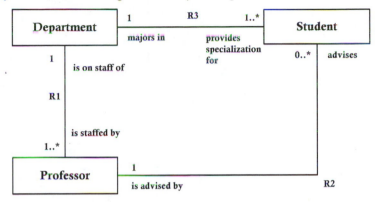

Model 7.6

As drawn, Model 7.6 places no restriction on the Student's choice of an advising Professor. This is easier to see if we populate our model with some example instances.

Unconstrained Loop

Student may select major and advisor independent of one another.

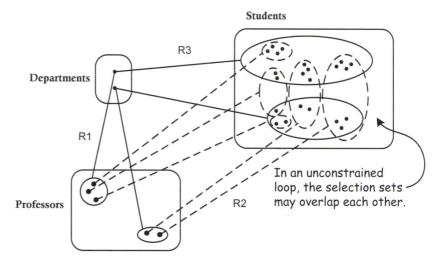

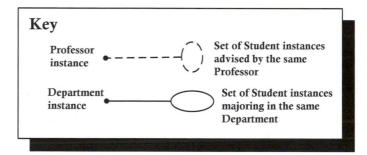

Figure 7.1

In an unconstrained loop instances may be linked across one association without regard to links along other associations. Model 7.6 works for a university where a Student may select an advisor without regard to whether or not the selected Professor is on the staff of the Student's major Department. But that doesn't match the requirement at our university!

We need to constrain the loop to get the following result:

Constrained Loop

Student must select advisor on staff of same Department as declared major.

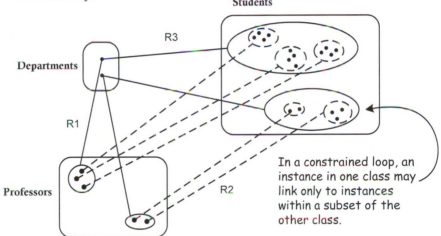

Figure 7.2

In this constrained loop, an instance of Student may link across R2 to a subset of Professor instances. The subset of allowable Professor instance selections is defined by links along R1. This would also work if Professors do the selecting. In that case an instance of Professor could link along R2 to one or more instances of Student within a subset defined by an existing link across R3.

In fact, you can start anywhere you like in the loop and the constraint holds. Let's consider an unlikely case just to prove the point. Say that an instance of Professor, Phillip, plans to advise a particular Student, Terrance, in the physics department. So we start with an instance of Professor and we want to link to an instance of Department across R1. If Phillip wants to be Terrance's advisor, he must be hired in the Department selected by tracing the opposite way around the loop R2->R1.

How do we express this constraint on the class diagram? First we must define the loop. We can do this with an expression like R1+R2+R3. Secondly, we need to say that the loop is of the constrained variety.

Model 7.6 is annotated below to reflect the constraint on the loop.

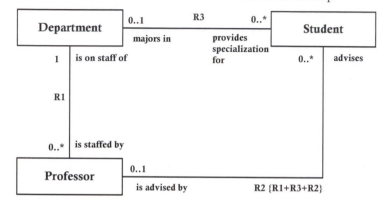

Model 7.7

In Model 7.7 we see that the loop has been defined and placed inside {} braces to indicate the constraint. Since there is no obvious place on a loop to hang this constraint, we just hang it on one of the associations in the loop, R2 in this case. It would be perfectly legal and mean the same thing if we had placed the constraint on R1 or R3 instead.

Nonetheless, we choose to put the constraint on R2 because, most likely, that's where potential links will need to validate themselves against the constraint before being created. Professors will be hired by Departments prior to taking on Students. Students may select majors prior to selecting advisors. Students with declared majors will then be restricted when they go looking for potential advisors. Of course, nothing in the class diagram prevents a Student from first selecting an advisor and then a major. If you think this is more likely to happen, then put the loop constraint on R3. The choice of where to hang the constraint is an issue of clarity. As long as you put it on one of the paths in the loop you're okay.

Enforcement of the constraint

The constraint notation on the loop is nothing more than that. Notation. In Executable UML, notation is must have a deeper meaning to result in real code. In my project experience so far, we have expressed constraints in the procedure models in proprietary[1] action language. The procedure that creates a link along R2 or R3 would have to ensure that only valid instances were linked.

In the near future, we anticipate the use of statements written in OCL (Object Constraint Language). These statements could then be processed to generate the required action language or target code.

Unconstrained loops are not necessarily bad

There is nothing wrong with an unconstrained loop as long as it accommodates the requirements precisely. If our university changes its rules so that a Student may choose any Professor as an advisor, regardless of major, then Model 7.6 becomes the correct model. The analyst must understand the application in enough detail to specify the correct level of constraint on all loops.

Now let's take a look at more examples of loop constraints. We'll examine a simple loop involving only one association and then look at a more complex pattern involving multiple loops.

---

[1] See list of Executable UML tool vendors in the "Where to learn more" section at the back of this book.

Simple loop Imagine we model a scripting language where a Script consists of sequentially executing Steps.

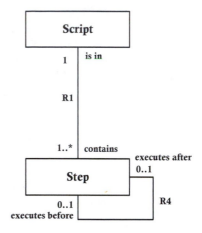

Model 7.8

Should the R4 loop be constrained? In the unconstrained case any instance of Step could be linked to execute before or after any other instance of Step. But that wouldn't make sense, since execution order is defined local to each Script. In other words, Steps are ordered within a single Script. We wouldn't want the "Power Laser OFF" step in the "Laser Diagnostic" script to be followed by the "Align Platform" step in the "Scan Wafer" script followed by the "Power Laser ON" step in the "Laser Diagnostic" script.

Step execution is ordered *within a script*

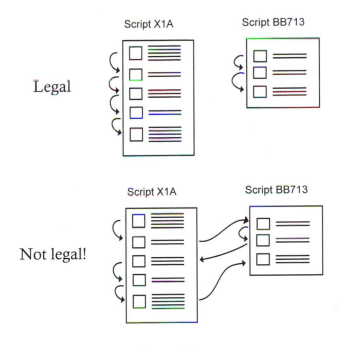

Figure 7.3

So the constraint on R4 is this: "An instance of Step may execute after or before another instance of Step in the same Script". Furthermore, an instance of Step must execute after a step other than itself.

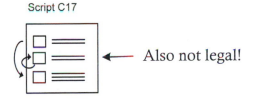

The necessary constraints can be illustrated in a set diagram:

Two constraints on Step to Step linkage

A Step may link to another Step other than itself
within the same Script.

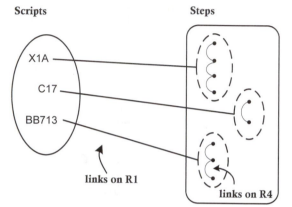

Scripts

Steps

Constraints on R4

Subsets constrained by
links on R1.

Links are acyclic.

X1A

C17

BB713

links on R1

links on R4

Figure 7.4

We can see from Figure 7.4 that links along R1 partition the set of Steps
since every Step belongs to exactly one Script. When a link on R4 is created, it originates from one instance of Step and terminates on another
instance of Step in the same R1-partitioned subset.

The notation in Model 7.9 below places the appropriate constraints on R4.

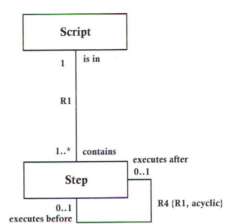

Model 7.9

As a matter of style, when more than one constraint appears on an association, I proceed from the general to the specific. A link along R4 may connect to the subset defined by an existing link on R1 and then only to those instances in that subset that do not include the origin instance.

Summary

A loop is a contiguous path of associations that originates and terminates on the same class. A reflexive association is the simplest case of a loop.

Two modeling errors are common when it comes to modeling loops: redundant loops and imprecise loops.

Redundancy is bad. You should omit associations that close a loop without adding any new information. Each association must capture rules or facts about the application not previously modeled.

The correct level of constraint on each loop must be specified. When both ends of a loop come together, there is some level of constraint on what instances may link together. In the unconstrained case, any instance in one class may link to any instance on the other side of the association (on any association in the loop) without regard to any other existing links in the loop. In the constrained case, other links must be taken into account to determine which instances are eligible for linking on any given association in the loop.

The following constraints have been introduced in this chapter:

- Loop {concatenation of all associations in the constrained loop}. For example, R1 {R1+R5+R6} indicates that R1 is part of a loop, R1+R5+R6, which is constrained.

- Reflexive {an attached association}. For example, R1 {R2}, where R1 is a reflexive association and R2 is a nonreflexive association attached to R1, indicates that links on R1 must start and end on instances linked to the same instance across R2.

- Reflexive {**acyclic**}. For example, R7 {acyclic}, where R7 is a reflexive association, says that an instance may not link to itself across R7.

Remember that, in Executable UML, notation has to be backed up by semantics. All notational elements, whether graphic, text or both, must be backed up by an unambiguous formalism. Constraints on associations can be specified either in the action language of the procedure models, or in a corresponding OCL expression. If you think of a constraint not expressed in Executable UML, write the corresponding OCL expression. Then you can invent your own constraint name (such as "acyclic") to put between the Rx {} brackets.

Constraints are important. If the class model does not reflect selection constraints, subsequent procedure models will often ignore or misrepresent the constraint as well. Eventually the bug will be detected and fixed but at excessive cost. More to the point, the process of building a tightly constrained class model causes the analyst to ferret out detailed project requirements right up front.

Chapter 8

Generalization: the basics

All generalizations are dangerous, even this one.

— Alexandre Dumas

Generalization is one of the most abused and misunderstood concepts on the class model. Most of the confusion stems from a perverse desire to use implementation inheritance, á la C++, to solve analysis problems. This is like migrating from Assembler to C and wanting to shoehorn the JUMP instruction into the for-loop construct. Another type of confusion occurs when the underlying instance sets are misunderstood. And even if both of those problems are avoided, it is still easy to spin a tangled web of relationships (generalization and otherwise) that obfuscate rather than expose the true application requirements. It is easy to sweep the annoying dust of reality under the mat of a generalization hierarchy. Having made plenty of these mistakes myself, I appreciate the need to cut through all this confusion. I hope the next two chapters help!

Generalization is not inheritance

In Executable UML, generalization is similar to, but not the same as, program language inheritance. This is because the needs of the analyst are different from those of the programmer. Analysts want the power of generalization without the needless complexity of implementation inheritance. Furthermore, the analyst cannot assume that the target programming language features inheritance. Most of my projects are real-time distributed and embedded systems that, for efficiency and custom platform reasons, must target multiple languages. A mixture of Java, C++, C and assembler is not uncommon. So there is no point in constructing generalization relationships intended to map, one for one, to C++ class hierarchies. Generalization relationships should be easily translatable and optimizable to any target programming language. At the same time, we need the full power of generalization to specify complex requirements.

Analysis goals

The goal of the analyst is not to render complex, exception-ridden requirements as a complex, exception-ridden model. Our goal is to analyze. That means we strive to understand what is really going on inside those snarled knots of requirements complexity. This involves a lot of thinking, but the payoff is worth it. Instead of a one-for-one mapping of requirements to model elements we decompose the requirements into orthogonal building blocks that can be assembled in various ways to account for the full range of application complexity. Generalization must support this process.

Generalization for analysts

Remember the definition of a class from Chapter 1? A class is the abstraction of a set of real-world things such that all things in the set:

- have the same characteristics

- exhibit the same behavior

- and are constrained by the same rules.

There are times when this definition seems impossible to satisfy. You often encounter real-world entities that all appear to be the same in some respects with minor nagging exceptions. In an air traffic control application Aircraft are all the same, sort of. Without generalization one type of real-world entity, an aircraft N14579Q let's say, is represented by one class in the class model: Aircraft. Generalization allows us to use multiple classes to represent a single type of thing in the real-world. It may be convenient sometimes to think of a helicopter as an instance of Aircraft: they all fly around, but sometimes (like when you are trying to land one) it may be more useful to think of a helicopter as a Rotary Wing Aircraft: they take off and land vertically. There is only one real-world entity — the helicopter N14579Q, but it manifests itself *simultaneously* as a member of the Aircraft set and the Rotary Wing Aircraft set.

Let's first take a look at how this aircraft example could be modeled in Executable UML using a generalization relationship. Then we will explore the underlying relational semantics to ensure that our modeling language is on firm, translatable ground. Finally, we will explore several application examples to get a feel for what we can accomplish with generalization.

Terminology   But first, let's get our terms straight. The UML standard specifies three types of relationships relevant to class models — association, dependency and generalization.The generalization relationship is sometimes referred to as a specialization relationship or a generalization-specialization relationship. For consistency's sake, I will try to always use the term *generalization relationship*.

An example of generalization

The best way to see how generalization works is to look at an example. Here's our application:

APPLICATION NOTE

Planes enter a landing pattern and then land on a runway. The Aircraft category determines the type of runway (pavement quality/ minimum length). Helicopters, on the other hand, take off and land on helipads. The landing pattern for a helipad is completely different than that of a runway.

All instances of a class must share the same characteristics, behavior and rules. Planes and Helicopters have Altitude, Airspeed and Heading and Position attributes. They take off, fly and land. But Planes land and take off from runways while Helicopters use helipads. It's tempting to sweep this minor distinction under the rug and just create an all, inclusive Aircraft class. But then we would be in danger of building a system dumb enough to tell a plane to land on a helipad or assign a helicopter to a wide circular landing pattern. Small distinctions are still important distinctions.

Everything we do in an Executable UML class model is based in sets, so let's organize our problem accordingly. Imagine several instances of Aircraft which may be in our airspace at a given point in time:

What's in our airspace right now?

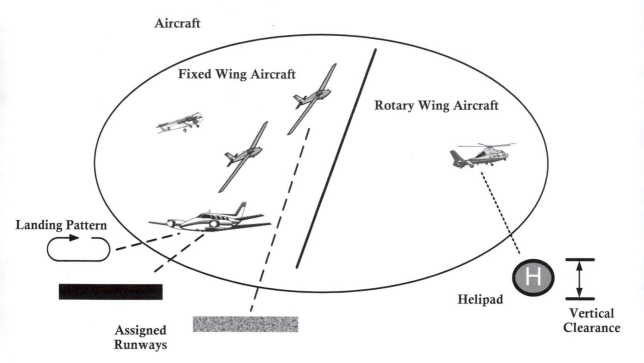

Figure 8.1

We have drawn a superset containing all instances of Aircraft regardless of type. This set has been partitioned into non-overlapping, mutually exclusive subsets. Each subset represents a type of Aircraft, Fixed Wing or Rotary Wing[1].

We can now abstract a generalization relationship to accommodate the set partitioning in Figure 8.1:

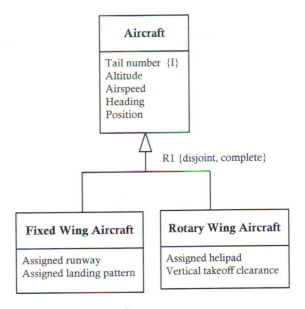

Model 8.1

Corresponding instances

Model 8.1 says that *each* instance of Aircraft is either a Fixed Wing Aircraft or a Rotary Wing Aircraft. An instance of a class corresponds not to a real-world entity but to a single set membership. In Figure 8.1, each real-world entity has two simultaneous set memberships, one in the superset and one in a subset. Consequently, whenever a plane flies into our airspace we must create two instances, one Aircraft and one Fixed Wing Aircraft. Whenever a helicopter leaves our airspace we must delete both the Aircraft instance and the corre-

---

[1] I decided to stick with this common aircraft terminology to keep our scope limited. On a real project I would be tempted to name the subsets "Vertically/Horizontally Docking Aircraft" to account for Harrier style jump jets. Then the issue of landing mode vs. aircraft type comes into play and the fun is only beginning. Since my publisher would like to see a manuscript this month, let's just say that Version 1 of our system excludes multi-landing mode aircraft!

sponding Rotary Wing Aircraft instance. Helicopter N14579Q is an Aircraft. It's not two Aircraft, it's not half of an Aircraft, it's always one whole Aircraft.

Generalization in Executable UML is based on the same relational theory that supports all class model relationships. We can easily represent the contents of a generalization relationship using tables:

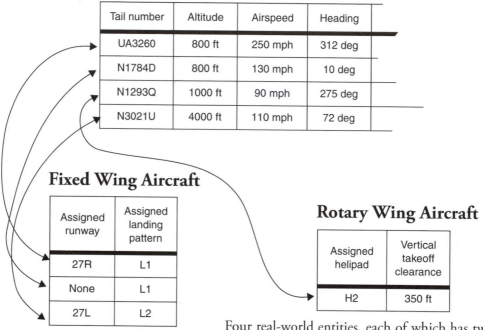

Aircraft

Tail number	Altitude	Airspeed	Heading
UA3260	800 ft	250 mph	312 deg
N1784D	800 ft	130 mph	10 deg
N1293Q	1000 ft	90 mph	275 deg
N3021U	4000 ft	110 mph	72 deg

Fixed Wing Aircraft

Assigned runway	Assigned landing pattern
27R	L1
None	L1
27L	L2

Rotary Wing Aircraft

Assigned helipad	Vertical takeoff clearance
H2	350 ft

Four real-world entities, each of which has two simultaneous set memberships, making a total of eight instances. A superclass and subclass instance pair must be created and deleted as a single unit.

Table 8.1

Expose the rules, thinking required

This points out a nice feature of Executable UML. The modeling language forces you to sort out the requirements. If you want to include aircraft that are neither fixed wing nor rotary, then you have to come up with a different classification scheme. Maybe you need to separate out the concept of landing mode from aircraft. Maybe you need to define a third subclass. There are many possibilities. What you cannot do in Executable UML is be wishy-washy. You can't say that there might be subsets not yet known. You can't say that there may be subclass instances that might not be Aircraft.

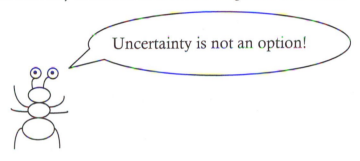

Uncertainty is not an option!

Generalization rules in Executable UML

Let's summarize the rules of generalization learned from our air traffic control example. Figure 8.2 illustrates the correspondence between sets and classes in a generalization relationship:

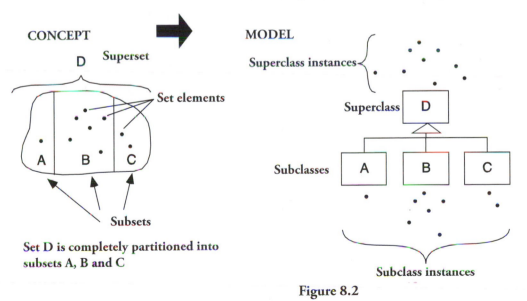

Figure 8.2

185

The left-hand side of Figure 8.2 illustrates the underlying set concepts. On the right we see how these concepts are realized in a generalization relationship. The rules are summarized below:

Set partitioning   Set: A superset is completely partitioned into nonoverlapping subsets.

Model: The superclass models the superset, and each subclass models a subset.

Set membership   Set: Each element of a subset (A, B or C) is simultaneously a member of the superset D.

Model:

- Each subclass instance from A, B or C has exactly one corresponding superclass instance in D.

- Each superclass instance in D must have exactly one corresponding instance in ONE of the subclasses (A, B, or C).

- If you create an instance of D, you must also create an instance in A, B or C. If you create an instance in A, B or C, you must also create an instance in D. If you delete an instance of D, you must also delete the corresponding subclass instance. If you delete an instance in A, B or C, you must delete the corresponding instance in D. (All of this activity is handled in the state and procedure models.)

- The cardinality of the union of the subclass instances always equals the cardinality of the superclass instances.

Notation   The generalization arrow always points toward the superclass and away from the subclasses. The superclass corresponds to our superset and the subclasses correspond to the partitions. Each generalization relationship in Executable UML carries the following standard UML constraint pair: {disjoint, complete}. This constraint pair ensures that each instance in the superclass corresponds to exactly one subclass instance and vice versa. Since this is the case on all generalization relationships in Executable UML we leave {disjoint, complete} implicit to minimize chartjunk.

Specific and general associations

Generalization does more than just sort attributes into common and specific classes. Associations may also be classified as general or specific.

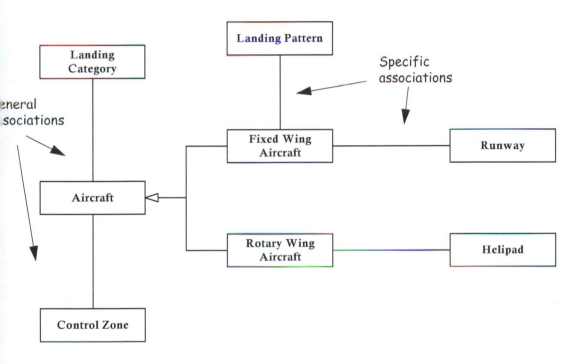

Model 8.2

In Model 8.2 we see that Landing Patterns may only relate to Fixed Wing Aircraft. Landing Categories and Control Zones, however, are relevant to all Aircraft regardless of type.

Specific and general rules

And now for something really amazing that you can do with a class model! Generalization can be a powerful tool for expressing complex rules. Consider these rules in our Air Traffic Control application:

- Every Control Zone is continuously monitored by an Air Traffic Controller.

- An Air Traffic Controller cannot monitor any Control Zones unless he or she is logged into a Duty Station.

- To avoid overworking a controller, we need to monitor the time accumulated since the most recent break.

Check it out:

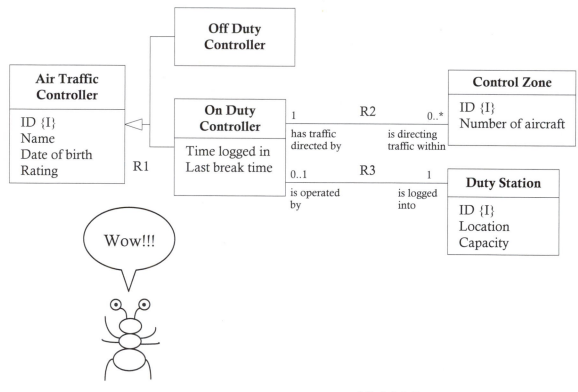

Model 8.3

Many rules are enforced

There's more going on in Model 8.3 than you might realize at first glance. Note that an instance of Air Traffic Controller (ATC) may or may not be On-Duty. When an Off-Duty Controller migrates over to the On-Duty class, he or she must log into a Duty Station. If no Duty Stations are available, the instance won't be able to migrate and will remain Off-Duty. And an Off-Duty Controller can't link up to a Control Zone. When an On-Duty Controller quits for the day, he or she must hand off all Control Zones to someone else since R2 is unconditional.

Storage efficiency can be optimized

We see that Time_logged_in and Last_break_time need only be monitored while an ATC is on duty. When an instance of On-Duty Controller migrates to the Off-Duty class, those two attribute values are thrown away — exactly what we want. But other attributes like ID, Name, Date_of_birth and Rating persist as long as an ATC exists in the system.

Generalization is one tool the analyst can use to create models that require a minimum of storage resources. The model compiler can see that certain data items (variables, pointers, etc.) can be deallocated safely at specific points in time. Of course, the model compiler has many performance trade-offs to manage and may choose an implementation that keeps all the data around anyway. But the analyst can use generalization to avoid specifying the needless retention of data.

Framework for the dynamic models

That said, the class models themselves don't actually *enforce* any rules. The state and procedure models do that. But the class models do establish a constraining foundation for the dynamic models. Rules are nicely exposed so that they can be reviewed by the application experts before a lot of time is wasted developing unconstrained state and procedure models.

But what about the empty Off-Duty class?

Oh yeah, that. Three choices. One: save it as a placeholder to hang future behavior, associations or attributes. Two: leave it there anyway, knowing that the model compiler is smart enough to not generate code to maintain the separate subclass. Three: okay, if it really bugs you, do this instead:

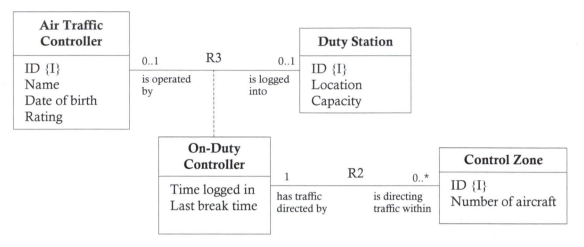

Model 8.4

In fact, if I knew that I had no use for the Off-Duty Controller class, I would prefer the simplicity of Model 8.4. It enforces all the rules captured in Model 8.3. Even though R3 is now conditional on both sides, it is still true that an On-Duty Controller must be logged into exactly one Duty Station. If this isn't obvious, go back and study the "Association classes" chapter! And we can also see that only an On-Duty Controller may direct traffic within a Control Zone.

The lesson to be learned here is that, wonderful as generalization relationships are, you can also do amazing things with association classes! So always try to find the right tool for the job. To help you in this effort, let's explore more examples.

More examples

There are two situations where the generalization relationship is necessary:

1. "Exception to the rule" style complexity

2. "This or that, but not both" — mutual exclusion

We'll explore one example of each.

Using generalization to tackle complexity

The following application presents a problem in which a number of general rules are stated along with some important exceptions. We have an analysis goal and a modeling goal. The analysis goal is to formulate a small set of concepts and rules that take into account both the general rules and the specific exceptions. The modeling goal is to formalize these concepts and rules into a class model. First, let's take a look at the application.

APPLICATION NOTE

We are creating a user interface for a diagnostic medical scanner.

A variety of parameters, like operator name, scan frequency, focal depth, and power setting, can be input and edited using a joystick and/or a keyboard. We want to prevent the entry of illegal values, although for some parameters it doesn't matter what you enter. String parameters, for example, can be assigned any arbitrary ASCII string. Numeric parameters, on the other hand, must be real numbers, which may or may not be constrained.

In the unconstrained case, a continuous range of numeric values is acceptable within a virtually[1] infinite range. To avoid a divide-by-zero condition, a zero value is illegal for some numeric parameters. Another example is the Frequency Scale parameter, which can take on all numeric values other than -1 and 1 (don't ask me why).

Due to the nature of this medical device, we don't ever want to force the user to resort to the keyboard for data entry. In fact, we must do whatever we can to make the joystick the preferred method of data entry. Since the magnitude of legal numeric ranges varies considerably, we will let the user specify a joystick increment speed for each numeric parameter. Furthermore, the user may want some values to wrap around when the joystick hits the upper or lower range limit, or the user might want to stop incrementing when a limit is reached.

Some numeric parameters specify discrete settings. In this case only integers may be entered. The filter setting, for example, must be an integer in the range from 1 to 5.

There are also some toggle settings. The Invert Video parameter must be either True or False. Question: what do we do about the Background Texture, which has three values: Smooth, Rough or None?

The parameter names and editing constraints are configured by the system developers for each application parameter.

---

[1] Well, to the extent that the implementation platform can accommodate us. The application does not specify or require a limit.

The first step is to account for all these rules, along with any unstated but anticipated rules, using as few concepts as possible. After some analysis, we end up with a technical note that defines a scheme for defining parameter domains. Here is the key illustration taken from that note:

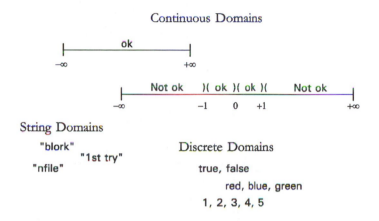

Figure 8.3

The different types of parameters have been grouped according to editing constraints. Since there is virtually no constraint on the entry of string values, string domains constitute one group. Continuous parameter domains can be constrained by marking off ranges on a number line. A variable joystick increment speed will be associated with this type of parameter. Finally, we define discrete parameter domains as an ordered list of acceptable values. The list order represents the sequence in which values are displayed when the joystick is pushed in either direction. Discrete domains account for toggles and small lists of numeric and nonnumeric values. A long list of integers (0 to 9999) would be handled using a continuous parameter domain along with a precision modifier, set appropriately.

Now we can build a generalization relationship that formalizes these different parameter domains:

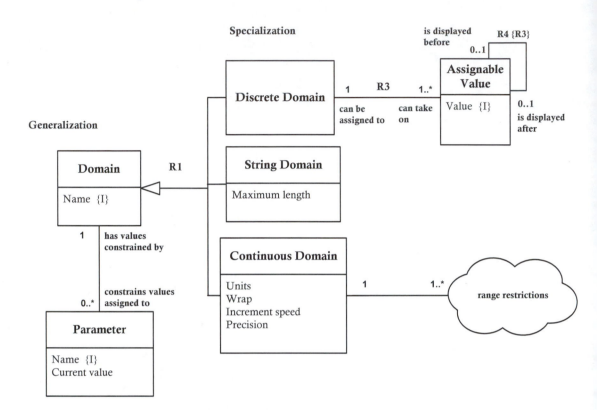

Model 8.5

This model says that every Parameter is defined by a single domain which must be Discrete, String or Continuous. A Discrete Domain consists of a list of values that can be assigned to a Parameter. No restrictions are placed on a String Domain. Our model takes into account a number of properties (Units, Wrap, Increment Speed and Precision) that apply only to continuous parameters. But we have yet to model the actual mechanism for restricting illegal number ranges. (And we won't, since that takes us beyond the scope of generalization relationships[2].)

_____

[2]And, no, it's not because I haven't modeled it — I have!

To better visualize how the generalization solution works, let's look at some example instances:

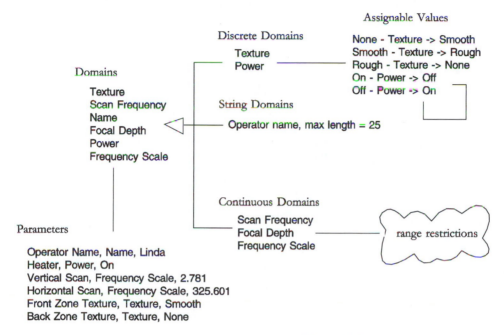

Figure 8.4

As you can see, all the cases mentioned in the application note are handled (or can be readily handled) by Model 8.1. First we had to separate the concept of a Parameter from the concept of a Domain. The Domain class represents a set of rules for assigning values. The Parameter class represents a control value that is constrained according to the rules of a Domain. The Texture Domain, for example, permits the assignment of the values None, Smooth and Rough. The Front Zone Texture and Back Zone Texture Parameters are constrained by the Texture Domain. In Figure 8.4, the Front Zone Texture Parameter is currently set to Smooth while the Back Zone Texture Parameter is set to None.

All Domains are the same in that they constrain one or more Parameters. But each of the three types of Domains uses different rules to constrain the set of legal values. Discrete Domains specify an enumeration of Assignable Values. These Assignable Values are organized into a display sequence so that when a user moves the joystick or hits an arrow key, the next sequenced value will be presented. String Domains simply constrain the length of the entered string.

Continuous Domains are defined in terms of a system of range restrictions hinted at, but not modeled.

When to specialize

Use specialization when:

- You have a class where behavior is the same for all instances, but there are some minor (and sometimes major) exceptions.

- Certain attributes change or lose meaning as a class changes state.

- Certain relationships are systematically formed or broken as a class changes state.

When to generalize

Use generalization when:

- One or more attributes with the same name keep popping up in seemingly disparate classes.[3]

- One or more associations (referential attributes) with the same name keep popping up in seemingly disparate classes.

Now let's take a look at a completely different way to use the generalization relationship.

----

[3] Warning: If the resulting superclass has an open ended list of subclasses, then you may be encountering a service domain boundary. In an animation application, for example, coordinate attributes X, Y kept appearing in numerous classes. Initially, we abstracted a superclass where we promoted the ubiquitous coordinates. But we ended up with about 30 subclasses and the promise of dozens more as the requirements expanded. Instead, we renamed the superclass as "Movable Entity" and put it in a newly defined service domain titled "Coordinate System Management". This service domain knew about matrix hierarchies, perspective transforms, coordinate axes and so forth. We then colored any classes in the application that required motion services to be instantiated with corresponding Movable Entities in the service domain.

Using generalization to model mutual exclusion

The generalization relationship breaks a set into mutually exclusive subsets. This concept comes in handy when you are faced with application requirements that call for an EXCLUSIVE OR type of situation.

APPLICATION NOTE

A scanner has a sensor that acquires a lot of data. This data is fed through various processing stages that are implemented in hardware. Due to application requirements and the way the hardware is designed, you have to make careful choices about how you route the data.

Here is one example: You can feed the data through one of the high-frequency analyzers or you can feed it through a decimator. To increase bandwidth, it is sometimes necessary to use multiple frequency analyzers or decimators in parallel. But it is extremely important to never perform both decimation and high frequency analysis simultaneously.

Let's take a look at the classes involved:

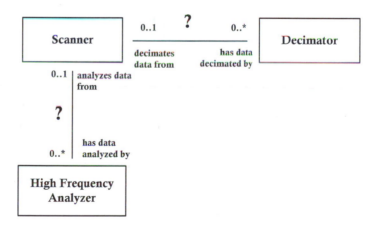

Model 8.6

There is no way that any combination of binary associations and classes can express the desired application rules. We can model a

Scanner connected to many Decimators and High Frequency Analyzers, but we can't exclude the possibility of being hooked up to a combination of the two.

That's where the generalization relationship comes in:

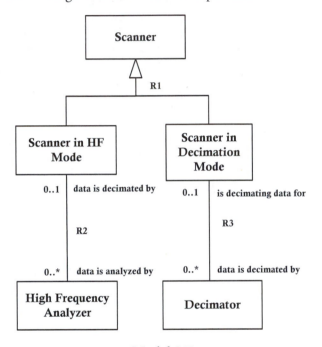

Model 8.7

As you can see, a Scanner must now be placed in one of two modes before linking up to any data-processing hardware. This makes it impossible to mix High Frequency Analyzers and Decimators in the same Scanner output path.

More exclusion   For a different type of problem that requires mutual exclusion, see Chapter 15 on page 303.

Frequently asked questions about generalization relationships

When should a class be specialized according to its states?

Normally, the states of a class appear in a state model, not the class model. But sometimes you need to create a separate subclass for each state or primary state in the superclass's state model. Model 8.7 is a perfect example. You should do this only when:

- One or more associations are relevant in some states but not in others.

- One or more attributes are relevant in some states but not in others.

So when a class's rules or data structure change from one state to another, subclass only those states or modes necessary to reflect the change. If it's only the data values that are changing, you don't subclass according to the states.

Chapter 9 Advanced generalization relationships

We reviewed the plain vanilla generalization relationship in the last chapter:

But there are even more powerful things you can do with generalization as shown below:

Generalization Patterns

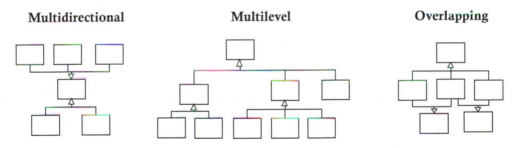

Let's examine what these patterns mean and study some cases where they are useful as well as some cases where these patterns can be troublesome.

Multidirectional generalization

First let's jump right into an example application.

APPLICATION NOTE

In a submarine computer game we need to model how torpedoes are carried and deployed on simulated submarines. A limited number of torpedoes is initially loaded onto a submarine. These torpedoes are stored safely in racks until they are needed for battle. When ordered by the captain, a torpedo may be loaded into an empty torpedo tube. The tube is flooded and then, when the order is given, the torpedo is fired. At this point, the torpedo is ejected from the tube and the torpedo swims under its own power toward a designated target.

The torpedo lifecycle is illustrated below:

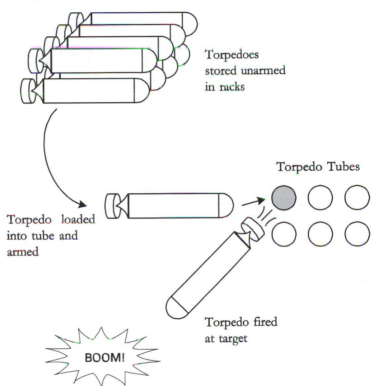

Figure 9.1

Notice that the association between a torpedo and a tube is only meaningful when a torpedo is in its LOADED state. It stands to reason that there might be attributes that are meaningful only in certain torpedo states. Consequently, it is a good idea to specialize Torpedo according to its primary modes of operation.

Here's a first cut at a model.

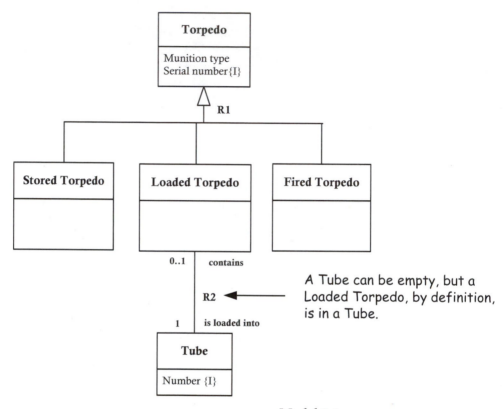

Model 9.1

Now let's complicate matters.

APPLICATION NOTE

Two torpedo designs are used aboard submarines in this game.

The first type of torpedo is guided by a virtual wire that is reeled out of the back of the torpedo as it swims toward its target. Commands and data are sent back and forth along this wire until the spool runs out. At this point the wire is cut. If the torpedo has not found its target by then, it commences a descending spiral search pattern until it either hits something or runs out of fuel. Often the torpedo will be detonated just prior to running out of wire to minimize the risk of having the torpedo hit the sub from which it originated.

The other type of torpedo is smart. It has no wire and is entirely self-guided. As the torpedo is loaded, a search program is selected and target parameters are downloaded into the torpedo.

If it weren't for the specialization of Torpedo in Model 9.1, we would be able to draw this alternate model:

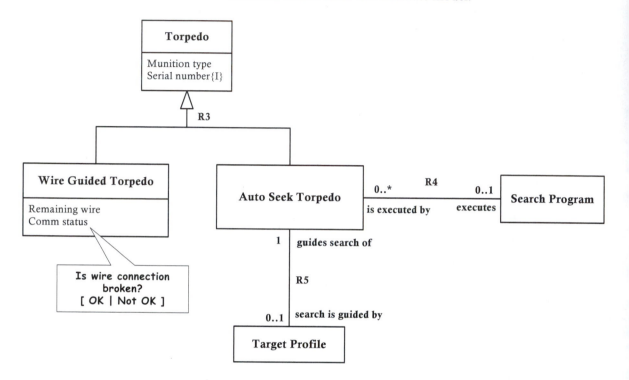

Model 9.2

This model specializes Torpedo according to guidance procedure. We have accounted for the amount of remaining wire and whether or not the wire is broken. Auto Seek Torpedoes are more complex. It will take more than a couple of attributes to define the guidance heuristics. Association R4 models the selection of a Search Program that guides an Auto Seek Torpedo. The content of the Search Program is the subject of another subsystem or problem domain. R4 is conditional on the many side since a single program is fairly standard and may be in use by any number of Auto Seek Torpedoes, including zero at any given moment. A Target Profile is more specific, however. Each Target Profile is created specifically for a given

Auto Seek Torpedo. The details of the Target Profile are also beyond the scope of this example.

This specialization works fine, but how do we account for the application facts originally captured in Model 9.1?

We would like to combine Model 9.1 and Model 9.2 to get the following model that simultaneously specializes in two directions:

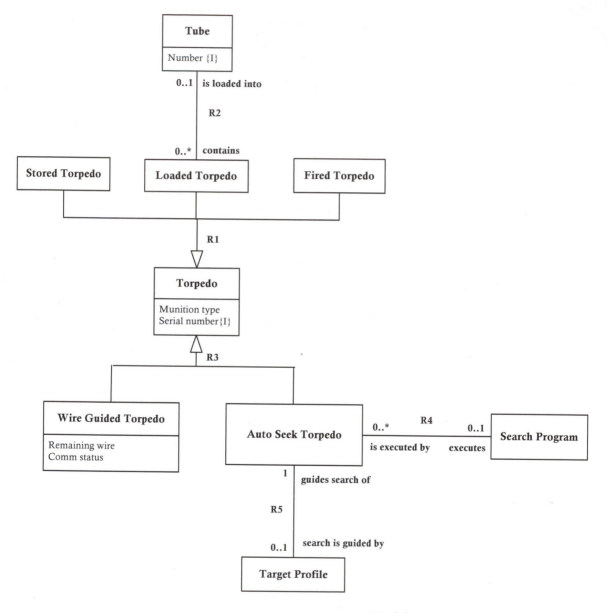

Model 9.3

Is multidirectional generalization legal?

Can we get away with this? In other words,

- Is this kind of two-way generalization legal?

- If so, does the model say what we want it to?

When we aren't sure about model syntax, we have to examine the underlying instances and table rules. We know that a normal generalization relationship formalizes the partitioning of a set (see "Set partitioning" on page 186). A two-way generalization, as shown in Model 9.3, partitions the same set of example instances in two independent ways, as shown below:

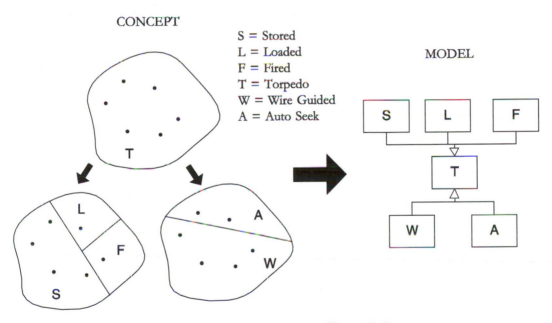

CONCEPT

S = Stored
L = Loaded
F = Fired
T = Torpedo
W = Wire Guided
A = Auto Seek

MODEL

Figure 9.2

Notice that every instance has exactly three set memberships: (T), (A or W) and (S, L or F).

It is easy enough to draw a set partitioned more than one way, so we ought to be able to specialize a class more than one way. So we've dealt with the question of whether two-way generalization is syntactically correct. Yes, you can do it. But, as we shall see, this is not always a good idea.

Why multidirectional generalization is often a bad idea

The crux of the problem lies in this principle of the multidirectional generalization pattern:

> Each specialization on the superclass is totally independent of the other specializations.

Sooner or later a previously overlooked or newly introduced requirement may negate this independence. In fact, it's going to happen in our submarine application. Consider the following overlooked requirements:

1. Associations R4 and R5 are conditional because they don't apply when an Auto Seek Torpedo is in storage.

2. A number of Wire Guided attributes need to be added, such as Desired_heading, Desired_speed, Actual_heading and Actual_ speed, which apply only when a Wire Guided Torpedo is Fired.

The two generalization directions are no longer independent. The Desired Heading attribute is relevant only to Wire Guided Torpedoes. (An Auto Seek Torpedo determines its own heading.) We are tempted to place Desired_heading in the Wire Guided Torpedo class, but then our model would say that all Wire Guided Torpedoes have a Desired_heading. But only a Wire Guided Torpedo that has been Fired can be commanded. We can't place Desired_heading in the Fired Torpedo subclass because then it would apply to both Fired and Auto Seek Torpedoes, which is not what we want.

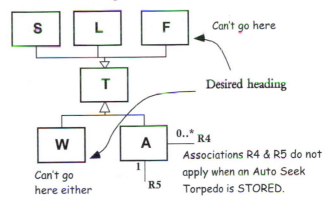

Figure 9.3

Furthermore, associations R4 and R5 can be made unconditional, but only for Auto Seek Torpedoes that are either Loaded or Fired, but not Stored.

The two-way generalization forced us into a modeling corner that we can escape only by totally abandoning the multidirectional generalization approach. Instead, we can generalize in multiple levels.

Nonetheless, multi-directional generalization is useful if you can prove to yourself that the specialization criteria for each direction are independent of one another.

Multilevel generalization

Everything that we wanted to model with a multidirectional generalization can be accomplished using multiple levels instead. Here the torpedo model is recast as a multilevel generalization:

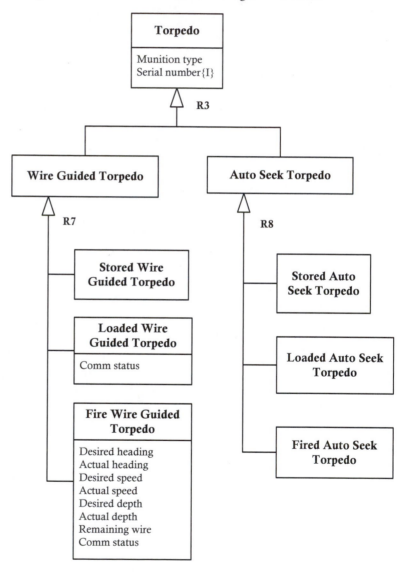

Model 9.4

Let's go back and look at sets of instances. The multidirectional and multilevel subset partition schemes are compared below:

Multidirectional partitioning   **Multilevel partitioning**

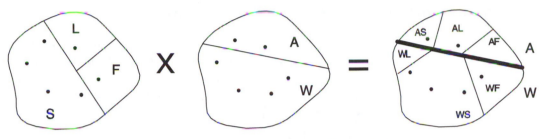

Figure 9.4

With multilevel partitioning, the set of Torpedoes is first partitioned into Auto Seek and Wire Guided Torpedoes. Then each of these subsets is further partitioned into Stored, Loaded and Fired Torpedoes. You can see that we don't lose anything in the translation. In fact, we pick up a few sets that we didn't have before.

Better precision

The advantage of this approach is that we can be much more specific about torpedo capabilities. With the multidirectional Model 9.3, we could make statements about a Torpedo of a particular type OR a Torpedo in a particular operating mode. The multilevel Model 9.4, on the other hand, can make statements about a particular type of Torpedo in a specific situation. For example, Model 9.4 says that a Fired Wire Guided Torpedo has some special command parameters (Desired Heading, Speed, etc.) that are not relevant to any other torpedo type in any other mode of operation.

Better adaptation to future requirements

Of course, not all the subclasses have special characteristics. A Stored Wire Guided Torpedo has no special attributes or relationships. Will any develop in the future? Well, that's just the point. Any newly discovered attributes or associations are more likely to have a place to go. Model 9.4 will adapt more easily to new requirements than Model 9.3.

Questions that probe deeper

More importantly, Model 9.4 forces us to ask probing questions about the application that are more likely to be overlooked with Model 9.3. Are Stored Wire Guided Torpedoes organized the same as Stored Auto Seek Torpedoes? Can you send any commands to an Auto Seek Torpedo once it is fired? Can you download any parameters in advance into a Loaded Wire Guided Torpedo?

Overlapping superclasses (selective generalization)

In all the fuss over torpedo specialization, we created some loose ends. What happened to associations R4 and R5 from Model 9.3? And whatever happened to R2? Thanks to the new classes added in Model 9.4, there is now more than one place for each of these associations to connect. This can be fixed by generalizing.

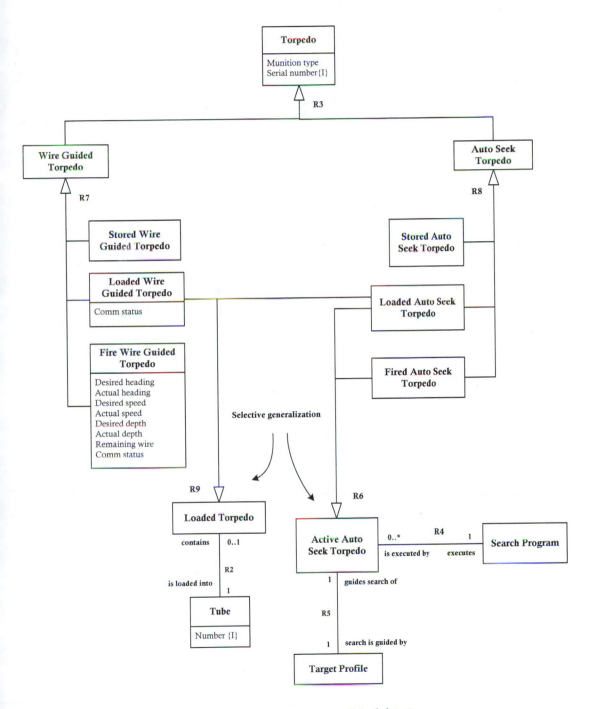

Model 9.5

Two new superclasses have been created that join together some of the Wire Guided and Auto Seek Torpedo subclasses. The Loaded Torpedo class represents the union of all Loaded Wire Guided and Loaded Auto Seek Torpedoes. A Loaded Torpedo, by definition, must be in a Tube. Consequently, R2 is now unconditional on the Tube side.

Since associations R4 and R5 apply to both Loaded and Fired Auto Seek Torpedoes, they are connected to the newly created Active Auto Seek Torpedo class. The superclass definition allows us to make R4 unconditional on the Search Program side and R5 unconditional on the Target Profile side.

Overlapping sets   Let's see how some generic instances might be grouped:

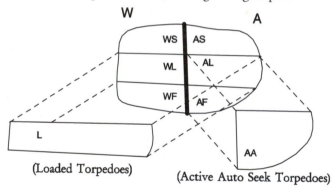

Figure 9.5

The two new classes, Loaded Torpedo and Active Auto Seek Torpedo, are designated as sets L and AA. Set L is the union of sets WL and AL, while set AA is the union of sets AL and AF. Note that sets L and AA overlap on AL. So membership in AL necessitates simultaneous membership in five sets: T, A, AL, L and AA. In our model, this means that an instance of Loaded Auto Seek Torpedo must always have corresponding instances in Torpedo, Auto Seek Torpedo, Loaded Torpedo and Active Auto Seek Torpedo to formalize the set memberships.

Now we have the powerful ability to break down any set into non-overlapping subsets, at multiple levels, and then to unify those subsets in any combination that we need.

The only problem is that the Comm Status attribute appears in both the Loaded and Fired Wire Guided Torpedo classes. We can take the generalization a step further to produce the following model:

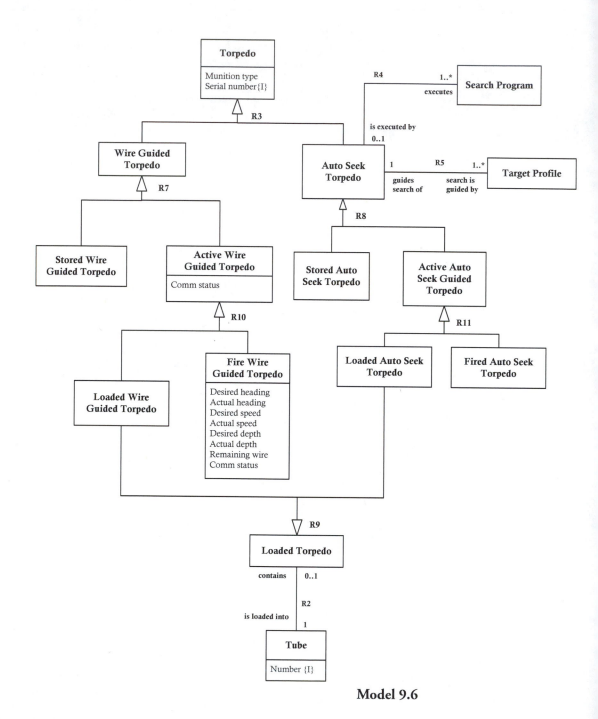

Model 9.6

Eliminating duplicate attributes

As you can see, that's quite a change just to accommodate one troublesome attribute, leading me to the following two points: (1) No matter what the situation, you can always come up with an arrangement of generalization relationships that eliminates duplicate attributes, and (2) Just because you can eliminate duplicate attributes doesn't mean you should. Remember that the goal is to arrive at the simplest complete executable model set (class + state + procedure models). It's okay to perfect the class model if it leads to simplification in the state and procedure models. If not, move on.

The danger of generalization hacking

Don't waste time with minute details

It is important to do thorough analysis. If you collect attributes one by one, rearranging your subclasses each time to achieve optimal generalization, then you may be thrashing with your model forever. It's normal to sketch out a variety of relationship and class combinations, some of them quite unwieldy, before settling on a concise, yet stable result. (By stable result I mean a model that can incorporate minute requirements changes without being completely rearranged like a trailer park in a tornado.) It is a common mistake to try to achieve this stability by hacking a model to death, rather than by investigating the application properly. Nonmodeling analysis activities (see Chapter 10, "How to avoid model hacking" on page 231) may lead to some insight about the application that would do more to simplify your work in a few minutes than another week of class shuffling.

How to avoid thrashing

For example, let's say that Model 9.5 generated a lot of questions about torpedoes. I wouldn't waste another minute trying to produce Model 9.6 just to get the Comm Status attribute into the same class. Instead, I would first get my questions answered. I would conduct interviews, draw informal diagrams to confirm my understanding, and search every scrap of documentation and requirements relating to torpedo features that I could find. Only then would I go back and try recasting my model. By then the Comm Status attribute might have become a moot point. Maybe there was yet another type of torpedo — not in use, but planned — that had not been considered.

Maybe I would have discovered other attributes or concepts that would lead to a very different model. Then, again, maybe I wouldn't find anything new. In that case, I would go ahead and produce Model 9.6. Let your understanding of the application fuel the model tweaking and not the other way around.

How to organize generalization levels

Going back to Model 9.5, let's consider a question that hasn't been addressed yet. We specialized Torpedo into Wire Guided/Auto Seek and then into Stored/Loaded/Fired. But couldn't we have done it the other way around? Why not first specialize Torpedo into Stored/ Loaded/Fired and then specialize each of these classes into Auto Seek and Wire Guided?

From a table/set/class model perspective, there isn't much difference between the two approaches. But if you move along to the state models, there is a big difference that favors the approach used in Model 9.5.

Subclass migration

Subclass instance behavior can be classified in these ways:

- Migrating subclasses
- Nonmigrating subclasses

Migrating subclasses Both ways of generalization are employed in our torpedo example. Consider the Wire Guided Torpedo:

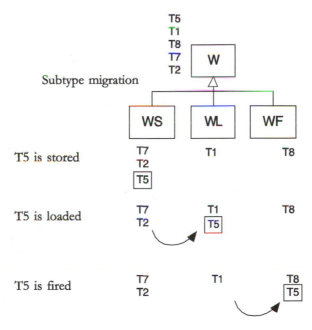

Figure 9.6

An instance of Wire Guided Torpedo starts out with a corresponding instance of Stored Wire Guided Torpedo (WS). When the Torpedo is loaded into a tube, the instance of Wire Guided Torpedo stays in place, but its corresponding instance in WS moves to Loaded (WL). In other words, the WS instance is deleted and a new corresponding instance is created in WL. Eventually, the WL instance hops over to Fired (WF). This is what is meant by subclass migration.

Nonmigrating subclasses Now contrast this subclass behavior with a nonmigrating subclass on Torpedo:

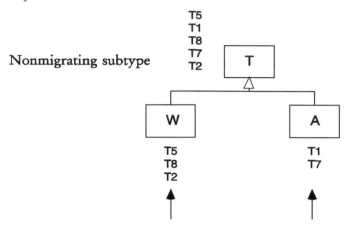

Nonmigrating subtype

Once created, instances stay put

Figure 9.7

When a Torpedo is created it is either an Auto Seek or a Wire Guided Torpedo. End of story. One cannot be converted into the other — in this application anyway.

Now let's take a look at all the migration that occurs with each arrangement of specialization levels:

Easy migration

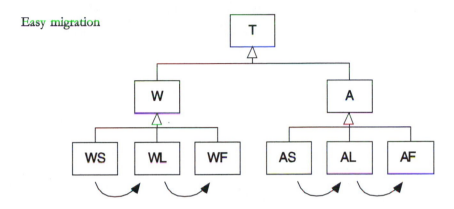

Awkward migration

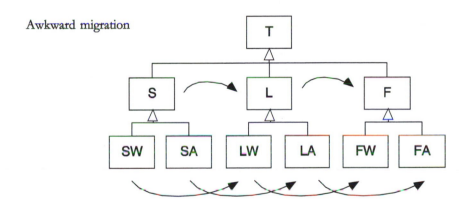

Figure 9.8

As you can see, we won't have to create and delete so many instances if we go with the first approach. It is a good idea to specialize in such a way that you simplify dynamic behavior.

When to specialize a class according to its states

In the Torpedo models introduced in this chapter, we specialized a Torpedo for two different reasons. The Wire Guided/Auto Seek specialization allowed for different Torpedo guidance behavior. The Stored/Loaded/Fired specialization accounted for different Torpedo operating modes. The Wire Guided/Auto Seek specialization seemed to jump right out of the application description. But what about the Stored/Loaded/Fired specialization? The need wasn't so obvious.

Look for states where relationships and attribute relevance changes

The behavior of every class in a class model can be characterized by a state model. But we don't specialize every class according to its states. So why did we specialize Wire Guided and Auto Seek Torpedoes according to their STORED-LOADED-FIRED states? We did it because there were associations and attributes that were relevant only in certain states. In fact, the state model for a Wire Guided Torpedo probably has more than just the STORED-LOADED-FIRED states. Other states might be INITIALIZING-ARMING-RESETTING. In fact, the state model for Wire Guided Torpedo must either move the subclass instance or generate events that result in the migration of the corresponding subclass instance in the STORED-LOADED-FIRED states.

Don't overdo the hierarchical thing

If you end up with a generalization relationship with many levels, like this one:

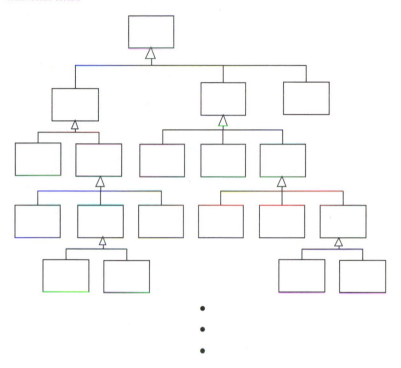

then you are probably doing something terribly wrong. A structure like this is inherently unstable. The deeper the hierarchy, the more likely there is an attribute or relationship somewhere that breaks the hierarchical pattern. Odd combinations of attributes and classes conspire to subvert the hierarchy and complicate the state models.

If you are presented with a suspiciously hierarchical model like the one here, look for common behavior, attributes or relationships in the subclass extremities that aren't properly generalized in a single superclass. For example, you might find an attribute with the same name throughout subclasses on the leftmost and rightmost sides of the tree. This will lead you to join some of the subclasses into a superclass, thus creating more of a layered structure.

An example of bad generalization

You can get into a lot of trouble when you specialize the wrong class.

APPLICATION NOTE

Let's say, for example that we are building a system that tracks defective braces. The brace may be defective because it is bent, sheared or cracked. When it is bent, it has a bend angle. When it is cracked, we are concerned about the crack depth.

Here is a first stab at a model of brace defects:

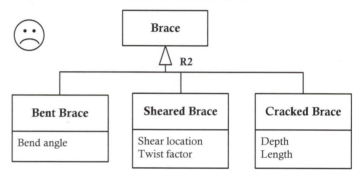

Model 9.7

This model says that:

A Brace may be a Bent Brace, a Sheared Brace or a Cracked Brace.

But what if a Brace is both sheared and cracked? You can't create two instances in the Brace class with each defect because one Brace is one Brace — not two!

And what instance do you create when you have a Brace that is not defective? Let's review the application rules:

• If a Brace is normal, it is not sheared, bent or cracked.

• A Brace may be bent, sheared, cracked or some combination.

Since a Brace is either normal or defective, this idea could be specialized. But defects don't necessarily exclude each other — so a subclass doesn't seem appropriate.

The key is in the use of the word "defect". A Brace can be normal, or it might have some combination of defects, which leads us to this model:

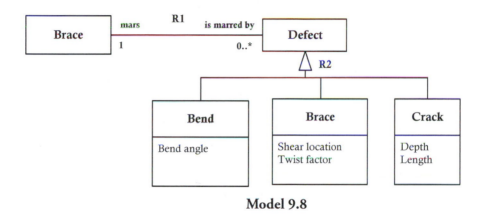

Model 9.8

This model says that a Brace has zero, one or many Defects. A Defect may be a Bend, a Shear or a Crack.

So with Model 9.8 we handle the case when a Brace is normal. A normal Brace has no Defects. That's why R1 is conditional. In addition, this model correctly allows a Brace to have multiple Defects of the same or different types.

Summary

In this chapter we have examined the multidirectional, multilevel and overlapping generalization patterns in Executable UML. These patterns are summarized as follows:

Multidirectional generalization - A class participates as a superclass in more than one generalization relationship. Each generalization relationship is specialized using completely independent criteria.

Multilevel generalization - A class is specialized according to one criterion; then some or all of the subclasses are further specialized.

Overlapping superclasses - Some subclasses from one or more different generalization relationships are brought together to form another superclass.

These patterns make it possible to model general rules about a class while also exposing varying levels of exceptions and local degrees of commonality.

Remember that all generalization relationships in Executable UML are constrained as {disjoint, complete}. To minimize clutter, these constraints are omitted from the class diagrams.

How to build useful models

2

Chapter 10

How to avoid model hacking

The formal nature of Executable UML is no guard against developing bad modeling habits. As with any skill, bad habits are easily acquired, impede your progress and are difficult to throw off. I would like to warn you about the worst of these: model hacking.

We are all familiar with the code hacking syndrome. That's where you root around in a mass of code that doesn't quite work. Rather than step back and rethink the underlying design, it is tempting to make just one more minor adjustment to the code, recompile and then see what happens. If it doesn't work, then you repeat the cycle repeatedly until the code seems to work. We all hack, but as experienced programmers we know how dangerous and unproductive this process can be. Hacking yields quick and dirty fixes. It does not lead to sophisticated systems that are reliable, extendable, or maintainable.

In fact, that's *why* we do analysis. Question: Now that we are building models, are we immune to the hacking syndrome? Not a chance! It's just as easy to get mired in a tar pit of ugly models as it is to get whipped up into an endless code hacking frenzy.

Let's take a look at how model hacking occurs, review its symptoms and then see how hacking can be avoided — or at least minimized.

Model hacking is exactly the same as code hacking without the benefit of a compiler.[1] Actually, it's worse since you are working at a higher level of abstraction so instead of shooting yourself in the foot with a gun, you now have a canon. When you are introduced to the tools provided by a modeling language, it's natural to want to immediately apply them to some problem. The next thing you know, you're sketching rectangles and connectors like crazy. You reflect on those estimates you heard about analysts producing an average of one class per day — sometimes less. Obviously, that must apply to people less intelligent and industrious, because *you* have just drawn dozens of classes in under an hour.

The symptoms of model hacking

Unfortunately, you are headed for trouble. Sooner or later one or more of the following problems arise:

- You can't tell if your model is capturing the rules you set out to formalize.

- You have a hard time convincing anyone that your model is correct and appropriate to the problem at hand.

- Past some number of classes (4? 7? 10?) additional classes and

---

[1] Just for fun, I'm retaining this footnote from the 1996 edition: "Advances in model translation technology are rapidly eroding this distinction." Fast forward to 2001: Correction: The distinction is now no longer relevant — we *have* model compilers! Excellent!

relationships add annoying redundancies and inconsistencies to your initially pristine model.

- You find it excruciatingly difficult to model some concept that should be simple and intuitive.

- People nod politely when you explain your model, but you can tell that they don't really get it.

- You (consequently) get no useful feedback on your work.

- You dutifully model rules given to you by application experts only to find out later that the "experts" were wrong.[2]

- You have no idea whether your model is complete — or ever will be.

So what's causing all this trouble? Is it a deficiency in Executable UML? — No. Operator error? — Yes! All the problems listed are classic symptoms of model hacking. Too much effort has been expended on building and revising models while essential analysis activities are being ignored.

The difference between modeling and analysis

That's the real problem. It is easy to confuse modeling with analysis. It took me years to appreciate the critical distinction between these two activities. Modeling is the process of formalizing an idea using elements of a language. Analysis, on the other hand, encompasses many tasks:

- Finding, collecting and organizing data (very unglamorous)

- Brainstorming

- Presenting and reviewing alternative concepts (not necessarily models)

- Sketching out informal ideas on the whiteboard (or cocktail napkins)

- Generalizing, simplifying, abstracting

- Arguing

---

[2] Wrong = incomplete, oversimplified, half-baked — to name a few.

- Skillful interviewing (the expert system people have some interesting methods)

- Taking and publishing good technical notes

And, oh yes...

- Modeling

Focus on the analysis   The frustrations I listed earlier do not result so much from bad modeling skills, as they do from inadequately performing the nonmodeling analysis tasks. Unfortunately, the schedule pressure to produce a complete model of 30 objects in four weeks causes panic. This panic results in 80% of your time hunched over a class model that will never be any good. Spend 60%-80% on the nonmodeling analysis tasks in the previous list, and you will produce a more clear, concise and useful class model.

Productive Analysis Time Allocation

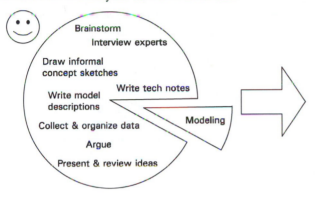

Steady progress, solid models, close match to application requirements, models build upon one another nicely

Time invested in analysis pays off

Material can be interpreted and used by those not well versed in the modeling language

Unproductive Analysis Time Allocation

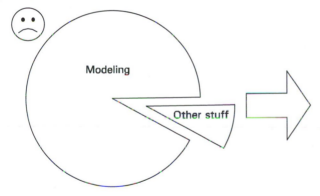

Lot's of models generated quickly

Models never validated, difficult to integrate models and most of the work never reaches implementation

Analysis paralysis inevitable

Nothing generated of value to those not well versed in modeling language

Figure 10.1

Draw informal sketches The best way to focus the nonmodeling analysis tasks is to produce informal sketches and instance based scenarios. Let's see how this works using an application example.

APPLICATION NOTE

We have a set of robots, lights, and roller coaster conveyors we want to control in an amusement theme park. Different sets of controls are available for each of these things. Lights have intensity, on/off status, color, filter type, and 3-D position. The track car has a 1-D position and a speed. During a show, each of these controllable objects can have its characteristics changed in a preprogrammed way. To program a light, for example, the desired 3-D position, intensity, and filter at a handful of intermediate points are specified. If t is time, at $t = 0$ the light will be at a certain x, y, z with an intensity i and a filter level f. At $t = 2.4$ it will have different values for some or all of x, y, z, i and t. Using a smooth interpolation algorithm, the values between the times $t = 0$ and $t = 2.4$ will be computed and used for control while the show is running. On the other hand, the light might not be used at all and remain stationary and powered down for the entire show.

We want a way to program the intermediate values for all the controllable classes so that they can later be driven in real-time.

Before getting to the informal sketches (don't look at Figure 10.2 yet), imagine that the class diagram in Model 10.1 has been presented to you as a solution and that you are (pick one):

a)   the manager

b)   an application expert

c)   the analyst (returning to your model after four weeks in the Caribbean)

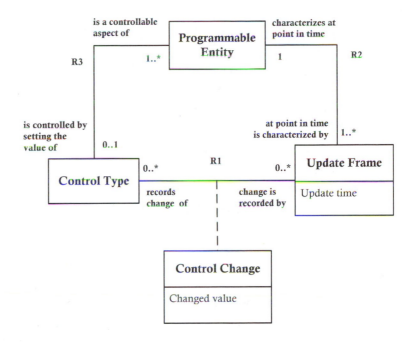

Model 10.1

Does Model 10.1 compare different approaches to representing control changes? Does it show you how the scenario in the problem description might work? What does the model say? Let's see, a Programmable Entity is controlled by setting the value of one or more Control Types. A Programmable Entity at a point in time is characterized by one or more Update Frames. (Yawn) You can tell that the model is syntactically correct, but is it the right model?

My point is this: It doesn't matter how much modeling experience you have; when you are presented with a new model, you don't see the application. All you see are boxes, lines and names that you don't understand. Especially if the model is large, complex and, ugh, poorly laid out.

Now look at the informal sketch I have drawn in Figure 10.2.

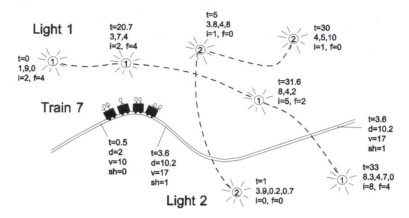

Figure 10.2

The sketches in Figure 10.2 might seem a bit cryptic, but don't they easier to relate to the application description than all those boxes and lines in Model 10.1?

Formal models versus informal sketches

Let's compare the two approaches.

A class model:

- is an abstraction of all cases, not just the one you think about most of the time

- can be integrated with other modeled concepts, all using a uniform language

- yields an unambiguous interpretation

- can be mapped directly to an implementation

- forces specific policy decisions

- imposes a vocabulary on the problem

Whereas an informal sketch:

- lets you use whatever symbols you like

- can be read and understood quickly by anyone familiar with the application

- is less work to produce than a model, so you can compare and discard approaches more economically

- describes a problem in terms of real examples rather than abstractions, thus keeping you in touch with reality

- is not necessarily object-oriented

I draw informal sketches prior to modeling as I collect and verify facts about the application. Then I model what I have sketched. When I get bogged down in modeling confusion, I go back to sketching. These sketches usually focus on specific instances and data values. I illustrate the normal cases as well as the odd, but legal boundary cases. If I can't sketch a problem, then I either need more data, a better concept or just more coffee.

In order of importance, I draw informal sketches to:

Think: You can't model what you can't sketch.

Collect Information: A good sketch elicits better feedback from more people than does a bunch of obscure UML symbols.

Communicate and Verify: Your illustrated technical notes will keep colleagues informed and off your back while they wait for your completed models.

Document: We all know the value of documentation. By the way, you can paste some of your sketches into the class descriptions. Notice that I listed documentation fourth in importance.

The process of informal sketching helps you to focus on the critical nonmodeling analysis tasks, which will aid you immeasurably in producing good models. Not only that — it's much more fun than model hacking.

The entire analysis process is summarized (and admittedly oversimplified) as, ahem, an informal sketch on the next page.

How to build a class model

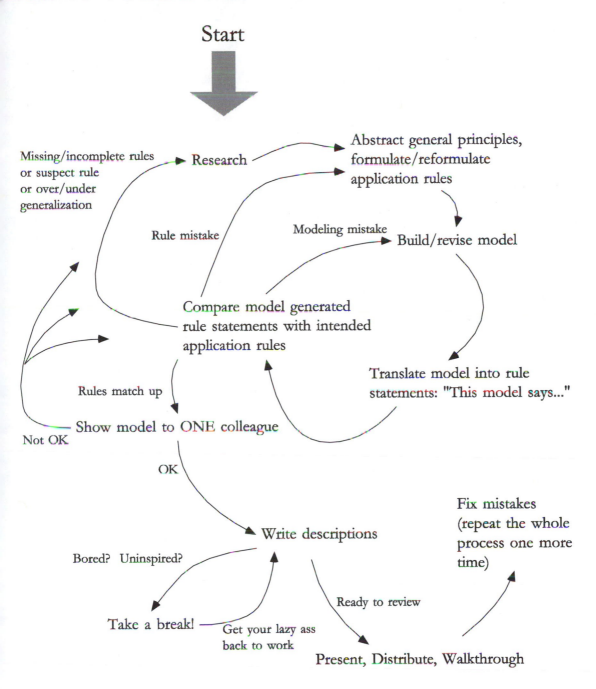

Start

Missing/incomplete rules
or suspect rule
or over/under
generalization

Research

Abstract general principles,
formulate/reformulate
application rules

Rule mistake

Modeling mistake

Build/revise model

Compare model generated
rule statements with intended
application rules

Translate model into rule
statements: "This model says..."

Rules match up

Show model to ONE colleague

Not OK

OK

Write descriptions

Fix mistakes
(repeat the whole
process one more
time)

Bored? Uninspired?

Take a break! Get your lazy ass
back to work

Ready to review

Present, Distribute, Walkthrough

Why write model descriptions?

Chapter 11

The network of classes and relationships laid out on a sheet of paper is NOT a class model. It's just a class diagram. That would be like mistaking an outline for a whole book. The real work is in the text and drawings that constitute the model descriptions. (If you doubt this, I invite you to download the official UML specification[1] and meta-models and try to interpret them without the benefit of the 500 pages of descriptions.)

I don't know how many times I've been handed a class model with skimpy or nonexistent descriptions. As an experienced modeler I can verify the model syntax (Are the constraints specified properly? Are the association classes formalized correctly?) and the syntax is generally in good shape. But modeling skill won't tell me what each of the classes, attributes and relationships mean. The authors of the model must explain their work to me verbally. As soon as the explanation starts, the authors invariably become aware of missing attributes, incorrect relationships and all manner of ambiguity, uncertainty and handwaving. Happens every time.

It's this process of explanation that forces a closer examination of what the authors previously considered to be pretty much complete. What I find interesting is that this scenario plays itself out only when the descriptions are deficient. Whenever I am handed a model with complete descriptions, most of the errors in the model tend to be minor syntax issues. But even the most subtle application requirements are well addressed.

---

[1] Download from the OMG (Object Management Group) website at www.omg.org.

The ant says it best.

If you want to build correct, translatable class models, write those !#$!! descriptions!

How do you write good descriptions?

The following three chapters provide detailed guidelines for writing class, attribute and relationship descriptions that yield useful class models. If you like building things, but hate writing — like me — then you are probably still wondering why the descriptions are worth all the bother.

When I started building class models, I didn't pay much attention to the model descriptions. But as I developed more and more models on more and more projects, I experienced many ugly setbacks that hampered productivity and resulted in wasted time. Many of these setbacks could be traced to flawed model descriptions.

The only real way to learn how to write good descriptions is to experience the consequences of *not* writing them! You need to know precisely why you are writing the descriptions and how you are going to use them later on. Unfortunately, this experience takes time to accumulate. Hopefully, the advice in the next few chapters will reduce the amount of experience you need to acquire to produce effective class models.

Five reasons to write model descriptions

The following reasons are ranked in order of importance from the perspective of the analyst, not the model reviewer.

① INCREASE THE QUALITY OF YOUR MODEL

Documentation is not the primary reason for writing model descriptions. If it were, I would get to them sometime after I organized that junk drawer under my kitchen phone.

The most important reason for writing model descriptions is to improve the technical quality of the concepts you are modeling. True, that is the same reason for writing technical notes. But technical notes and model descriptions each contribute to the quality of a model in different ways.

The goals of technical notes and model descriptions are different

A technical note may collect information, propose or compare concepts, and explore scenarios. But when you produce a model description, you are taking a stand on a single approach that you define in detail. It is okay for a technical note to be full of loose ends. The model descriptions, on the other hand, must demonstrate that the model is internally consistent.

The informal technical notes generate the raw concepts that are refined to produce the formal model descriptions. Yet I always end up copying or referencing subsets of the technical note text and diagrams in the model descriptions.

Don't get cocky

As you develop experience building class models, it is easy to get cocky. I don't know how many times I have had discussions, written technical notes, and sketched out a model that I characterized as "being pretty much complete" — except for a little documentation. I always find it hard to believe that I am going to learn anything substantially new by writing a bunch of descriptions. All manner of rationalizations bounce around in my head, like: "Sure, I always nag other engineers to write complete descriptions, but *I've* been modeling for years. This model is based on principles learned from an earlier project. I know what I am doing and I have this subsystem all figured out. Oh, well — I'll just get this little documentation task out of the way...".

But there is something about the process of writing model descriptions that makes you consider subtle policies and boundary conditions that you missed in the technical notes. With a 25-class model, I end up discovering at least five to ten holes in my thinking. By "holes" I mean cases I didn't consider, questions I didn't ask, policies that need to be established, and behavior that wasn't obvious.

The activity of model description is a crucial thinking process. If you want to produce useful, well thought out models, you have to write good descriptions.

② MAGNIFY YOUR EXPERTISE (AVOID LOOKING STUPID)

It's easy to become an authority when you write good model descriptions. The creation of class model descriptions is the analyst's equivalent of writing code (well, the data structure code anyway). Watch what happens after you wallow around in the details of your model for awhile. When you are in a conference and someone brings up one of the issues relevant to your subsystem, you will suddenly find yourself answering questions and resolving issues with a precise vocabulary and an extremely clear understanding of the problem that will amaze, if not intimidate, your colleagues.

Of course, anyone can read your descriptions and approach your level of expertise. Your goal is to share rather than monopolize information. But you always develop more intimacy with subsystems you write about than with those that you merely review.

③ AVOID HAVING THE SAME ARGUMENT OVER AND OVER AND OVER

My team was plagued with a series of déjà vu experiences on an early project. There was a technical issue that took a lot of effort and argument to resolve. We thought we had killed the issue, but it kept coming back to life like Schwarzenegger[2] in that Terminator movie. Not only did we end up revisiting the issue every couple of months, but we kept arriving at the same conclusion! Had I written relevant class and relationship descriptions more thoroughly, I am convinced that we could have avoided this situation. To appreciate how this happened I will have to fill you in on the application a little.

The video effects application

We were building a system that allowed a postproduction video engineer to create a special type of animation called an effect. An effect consisted of animated entities, each of which was characterized by one or more independently editable parameters. One type of entity was a light source with four parameters: intensity and x, y, z location.

Here is a diagram of how different values could be assigned to these parameters over the course of a 3-second effect.

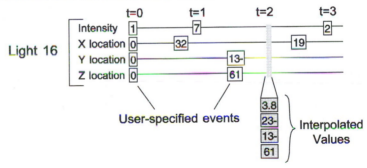

Figure 11.1

Each parameter had its own time line containing some number of events. When the operator pressed the RUN key, the effect would

---

[2]Not too many UML authors can say they have a reference to Schwarzenegger in their bibliography.

start playing at t=0 and run until the end, 3 seconds later in this case. As time progressed, every parameter would be assigned a new value. This was important because the hardware that implemented the light source needed to be fed a new set of legal values every 1/60 second.

If the current time happened to coincide with the time of an event, the parameter would assume the specified value. At t = 2.5, for example, the value 19 would be assigned to the X Location attribute. When the current time was between events, some type of interpolation would occur. At t = 2, Intensity would take on some value between 7 and 2 (3.8 in this case).

The resolved issue that wouldn't die — "I'll be back."

So that's the background — here's the issue. To satisfy the hardware requirement, it was argued (Argument 1) that a parameter time line should contain a default event at t = 0 and t = end of effect. (Every parameter is assumed to have a default value.) The user would not be allowed to delete the terminal events. In this way we could ensure that the hardware would be fed a legal control value for a parameter at all times during an effect.

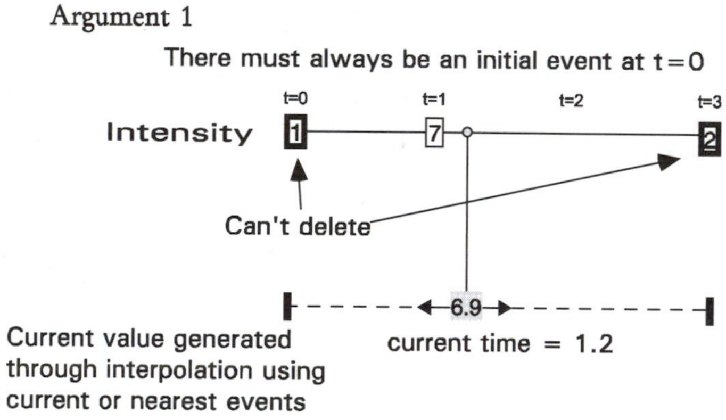

Argument 1

There must always be an initial event at t = 0

Figure 11.2

But the counterargument (Argument 2) was that this rule placed an inconvenient restriction on the user. The user should be allowed to create or delete any events he or she wanted. It was argued that the two-event rule established a scenario analogous to the rule that prevents a user from deleting the first paragraph of a document in a word-processing application. (Naturally, the counter-counterargument was that most word processors prevent you from deleting the first page, something users don't seem to complain about.)

Argument 2 proposed that we simply feed the hardware the default parameter values whenever the running effect time did not lie between two events.

Argument 2

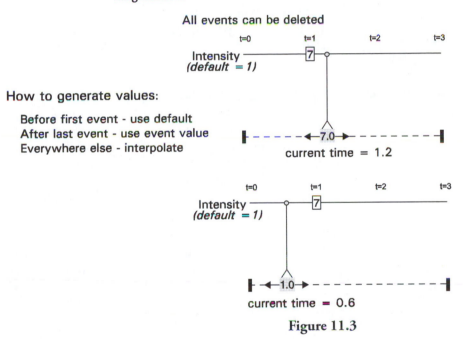

Figure 11.3

But a more fundamental fact killed Argument 1. We were building a second generation product. It was important to ensure that the new product would have the same animation behavior as the first-generation product. Some of the interpolation methods would generate different intermediate values over the length of a parameter time line depending on whether or not there were terminal events.

A decision was made

Each argument had its pros and cons. Either rule would have worked. But we had to make a decision, so we went with Argument 2 primarily because reverse compatibility and simplified event editing were such compelling issues. We decided that the slightly increased complexity of the parameter value generation would not slow us down significantly.

But none of these reasons or an analysis of the competing arguments made their way into the model descriptions. In our rush to complete the models, we didn't take the time to document the reasoning behind our decision. The issue was decided and we moved on! How many similarly complex issues are handled in this manner on your project?

How the issue resurfaced

Over a period of 12 months spanning analysis and design, several people who weren't involved in the early decision joined the project. We had the event rule discussion with the new analyst. We had it with the user interface guy. We had it with the second user interface guy (who rethought all the policies established by the first user interface guy). We had it with one of the designers. Each time we could only remember some, but not all, of the reasons for choosing our event editing approach. We remembered only that we had chosen an approach after much careful thought. We wanted new people to just accept our position without questioning it. Unfortunately, intelligent people always question assumptions. Each time the issue came up, I would try to find documentation of our first discussion. The following class description was the best I could find:

Excerpt from the class description of Parameter Time Line:

A Parameter Time Line is a function of time that determines values for Event-controlled Parameters. Events, which are points in time with associated Control Values, are the means by which the Parameter Time Line function is defined. These points, together with the following rules, define the function:

Before the first Event, the value of the Parameter is the default value defined by the Parameter Specification.

After the last Event the value of the Parameter is the Control Value of the last Event.

If there are no Events on the Parameter Time Line, the value of the Parameter is the Parameter Timeline.Default Value.

As you can see, this description simply states the decision we reached. It does not document the reasoning behind the decision. While it is important to answer the *what* questions, it pays off in the long run if you carefully answer the *why* questions, also.

④ COMMUNICATE WITH FELLOW ENGINEERS

Fellow analysts, application engineers, implementer, user interface designers and others need to understand your models in detail. If subtle but important aspects of your models are misunderstood by these people, you are in for lots of frustration and wasted time.

To make your models meaningful to other people you must write good model descriptions (see ants).

Figure 11.4

Communication through good model descriptions pays off in many ways.

Save time

Good descriptions minimize the time you have to spend explaining and justifying your model. This is time you should be using to develop new ideas. Of course, even the best descriptions require some explanation. But good descriptions will elevate the technical level of discussions about your work.

Improve progress in other subsystems

Your models may induce progress in adjacent subsystems. Details on the edges of your subsystem, like the features of a weird jigsaw puzzle piece, may guide fellow analysts toward a solution in another part of the domain.

Get quality feedback

One of the best ways to increase the quality of your work is to solicit feedback. When you hand your model to a reviewer, you are looking for profound insights, not spelling errors. But without good descriptions, a reviewer cannot think about a problem in enough depth to provide useful comments. A walkthrough of a class model without descriptions is a waste of time.

Control the implementation

It is likely that someone else will end up implementing some or all of your models. This happens even if you plan to do all the work yourself. Once implementation starts, there is always more analysis to be done. If you are a good analyst, your talent will continue to be in demand. It is therefore likely that someone else may guide your models through implementation while you generate the extra needed analysis. The descriptions you wrote will save time and steer the implementer clear of misunderstandings that would otherwise eat up lots of your valuable time.

Now put yourself in the position of an implementer (assuming you are doing hand translation here, but you really should be using a model compiler!), who we assume is familiar with Executable UML. You are given a class model by an author you know to be bright, but not infallible. As you implement, you find yourself wanting to change one of the associations from 1:1 to 0..1:0..1 to make your job easier. You look up the relationship description. It doesn't make much of a case for keeping the relationship unconditional. The author is out sick for two days. You decide to change the model (or at least deviate from it in the implementation). You don't realize it yet, but this change introduces potential error states in some of the behavior models. Later on you make changes to fix that problem. As more and more of the model unravels, you refer to it less and less.[3]

The moral is this: Regardless of how badly you want to be involved in the implementation phase, write your descriptions with the assumption that someone else will do the implementation. Otherwise, you can be certain that your models won't be implemented as correctly.

---

[3] Unless, of course, you are using a model compiler to generate the code. In that case, you will simply end up perverting the original models.

⑤ COMMUNICATE WITH YOURSELF

If you are working on a problem every day, it may seem silly to document it for your own purposes. You are already intimately familiar with the problem, so why bother writing it down? It's not like you are going to come in to work tomorrow and forget what you were working on. Even if you are a little fuzzy on some details, you can surely resurrect the details after a half hour or so. So how could it be worthwhile to spend a week writing up the descriptions when you are the only person working on the project?

When you are up to your elbows building a subsystem, it is hard to imagine that you might end up putting that subsystem on the shelf for a number of months. But on every project it is necessary to put work aside at some point.

You might find that the subsystem you are working on is much larger than you thought (not unlikely). You decide to focus on one aspect of that system and set the rest aside for a while. The part you decided to focus on takes longer than anticipated to complete (likely). The next thing you know, a couple of months have gone by and there you are picking up the loose ends of the remainder of your system.

Priorities change all the time

Maybe management changes priorities and you find yourself working on a completely different subsystem. All that work you put into your current subsystem ends up on the shelf for 4 months.

Maybe there aren't enough analysts to complete all of the work. You finish your subsystem. You move on to the next subsystem, and then another. Your first subsystem sits on the shelf for 6 or 7 months and now it is time to implement.

The point is that there are many scenarios where you could end up putting your partially or fully complete subsystem in cold storage for a few months. When you go back to finish that subsystem or integrate it into the other subsystems or implement it, what would you rather find? If the subsystem is even remotely interesting, you will find it contains classes that appear superfluous. What's that doing here? There will be relationships that aren't there for some reason, but you can't remember why. There are attributes that have some special significance that you forgot about. Next thing you know, you are spending weeks (that you don't have) redoing, retracing and making the same mistakes that you made originally.

Summary

Well, there you have it. Any chimpanzee can scribble out a bunch of UML gunk and claim to have completed a class model. But well thought out analysis that yields:

- simple yet precise solutions to complex application requirements

- fundamental building block concepts that readily support future extensions

- decisions that stand up to the inevitable challenges posed by newcomers to the project

- a robust design that stands the test of time

doesn't pop out of a four-hour-lock-yourself-in-a-room-with-a-whiteboard-and-coffee-pot-gee-aren't-I-bright thinking frenzy. You have to hunker down and spend a few days — ugh — writing (and drawing). It's the only way to produce results that you and your colleagues can build on.

The next three chapters proceed from these (hopefully) motivating principles by showing examples of how to write useful class, attribute and relationship descriptions.

Chapter 12

How to write class descriptions

Here are some specific guidelines for writing class descriptions.

Describe meaning — not syntax

We've all had the experience of trying to understand a chunk of program code written by someone else. If we are lucky, the programmer interspersed his or her code with useful comments. The comments are useful when they provide clues about how major components of the program work together. Useful comments give us insight into the thinking that generated all the code.

But of course, we are rarely so fortunate. Instead, we find comments like the following:

```
GprogQZ= ++CurrX->zur; // Increments pointer and saves it
```

So much for insight. The comment educates you about the syntax of the programming language rather than the meaning of the code.

But now we've graduated from Implementation to Analysis. The production of models puts us on the path to superior documentation, right? Sadly, that's not the case. It is just as easy to write useless documentation for models as it is for source code.

I'll show you what I mean with the following application:

APPLICATION NOTE

We have a device that measures surface texture by dragging a tiny sensor across the surface of a flat sample. Typical samples are devices that must have smooth surfaces, like a flat display panel, mirror or wafer. The acquired data is a profile that consists of a series of height samples.

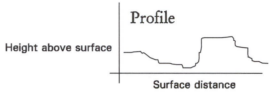

As a profile is collected, we would like to analyze the data using a variety of filters and functions. We want to make it easy to build data analysis programs for the incoming stream of data.

Using a graphical interface, an operator can access a library of data processors (functions and filters), that can be assembled into a data analysis pipeline. The output of one data processor is connected to the input of one or more data processors with a straight or branching pipe. An example pipeline is shown below:

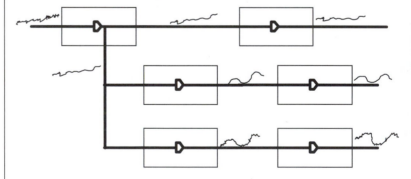

Each pipe contains data output by some data processor. The contents of each pipe may be stored or displayed.

Now let's take a look at part of the class diagram for this application.

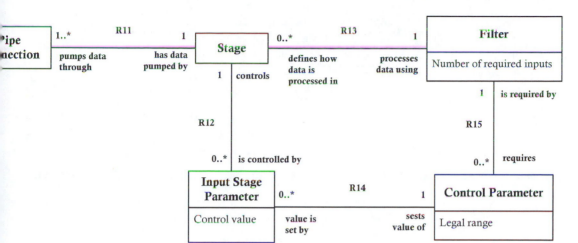

Model 12.1

Is it completely apparent how this model formalizes the pipeline diagram? Probably not. Some classes may appear superfluous. Maybe something is missing. Without descriptions, it's hard to tell. Here are a few notes that might help: The Pipe Connection is an association class. It formalizes the association between two connecting Pipes (not shown). The Filter class represents an algorithm that uses certain Control Parameters to produce an output profile by taking some characteristic away (a frequency band, for example) from an incoming profile.

It isn't apparent why the Stage class is required. Why not just attach Filter directly to Pipe Connection, collapsing R11 and R13 into a single 1:1..* association? To find out more, let's consult the Stage class description.

Stage (STG)

A Stage pumps data through a Pipe Connection. It processes data using a Filter. Note that a Filter can be applied at more than one Stage. A Stage is controlled by one or more Input Stage Parameters.

This description isn't any more helpful than the code comment at the beginning of this chapter. It doesn't say anything that isn't already obvious on the class diagram. If all the descriptions are going to be like this, you would be just as well off without them. The description on the next page is a lot more useful.

Stage (STG)

The term Stage refers to a stage of processing. A Stage is a place in a Pipeline where data is processed. Consider a Pipe containing data that we want to process:

Let's say that we want to reduce the noise in the signal by filtering out a band of high frequencies.

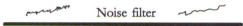

To do this we need to select a frequency filter from our library of filter functions, create a stage, split the pipe, and then insert the stage.

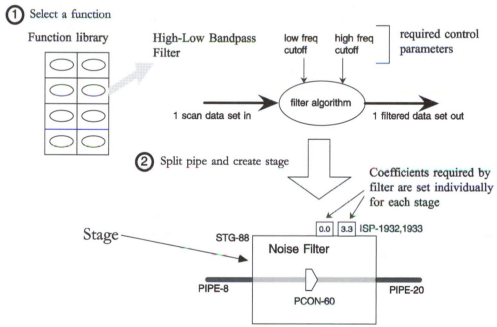

A Stage brings together all the elements you need to process data at a specific point in a Pipeline. It is important to understand the difference between a Filter and a Stage. A Filter is an algorithm. It specifies a function (Bandpass Filter). It specifies the need for two Control Parameters (low- and high-frequency cutoff) and the need for a single pipeline profile (input and output). A Stage, by contrast, represents the usage of a filter, with a specific purpose (Noise Filter) at a specific location (PCON-60) using specific Input Stage Parameter values (0.0, 3.3). Whereas a Filter may be referenced repeatedly and in more than one Pipeline, a Stage designates the usage of a Filter algorithm at a single Pipe Connection.

Here are the critical features of this improved class description:

1. It defines *what* the class is.

2. It explains *why* the class is a necessary concept.

3. It explains *how* the class works.

4. It reinforces the abstraction with diagrams and specific application examples.

5. It makes reference to other parts of the model, which the reader must investigate to understand how all the pieces come together.

Of course, I wouldn't expect the whole model to make sense without a complete set of class, attribute and relationship descriptions. In fact, even the Stage class won't make complete sense out of context, but hopefully you get the idea.

The most important thing to remember is this:

It is a waste of time to *merely* restate what is already obvious on the model.

Use both drawings and text

Use drawings to communicate

In the olden days — before desktop publishing became accessible to everyone — it wasn't always worth the effort to make pictures an integral part of documentation. Lack of artistic talent was another reason for relying exclusively on text to communicate. But those days are gone.

The tools are readily available for anyone, regardless of artistic talent, to interweave drawings with text. Why? Certain concepts are easier to communicate in a drawing than in a paragraph. Here is a classical demonstration of this principle: Try describing a spiral

using only words. Even if you can concoct a terse mathematical description, how many of your colleagues will instantly understand it? You can get the idea across a lot faster — to a wider variety of people — with a simple sketch. Naturally, the opposite is also true. There are many cases where text is superior to a diagram.

Usually some combination of text and diagrams yields the most useful descriptions. If you want to become an effective analyst, you must become skilled in the use of both technical drawing and word processing software.

Use drawings to analyze

Drawings aren't just for communication. The process of drawing, just like the process of writing, causes you to examine concepts in detail. But the process of drawing directs your attention to details different from those that you would notice while writing. Two weeks into a new project involving a semiconductor test machine, I discovered a critical safety error that no one else knew about. This all came about while I was producing a detailed diagram of how a robot arm moved around in an inspection chamber for a class description.

The diagram I was drawing incorrectly illustrated a mode of operation in which the human operator would have had his or her hand in the way of the robot arm while the robot was rehoming itself. One of the application engineers was explaining why my illustration was wrong when he realized that this particular scenario might actually be possible. After further investigation we found out that the bug really did exist.

Illustrate physical classes

It may not seem to be worth the time to illustrate physical classes. After all, physical classes are usually familiar to project members. If you are building a controller for a robot arm, it's not like you've got people on the team wandering around that don't know what the robot looks like. Even if some team members haven't seen the arm, they could just walk into the lab and take a look for themselves. If there aren't any robot arms in the lab, surely there is a picture in an operator manual somewhere.

Nonetheless, I've always found that it is worth the time to draw and describe most of the physical classes relevant to a domain. The process of drawing causes you to focus on details that are usually neglected. Drawings also go a long way toward clearing up confusion over terms. (This is especially important when you didn't realize that there was any confusion!)

Here's an application where a drawing of a common, well-known physical class (that no one wanted me to bother drawing) proved extremely useful.

APPLICATION NOTE

On one project we had a thing called a "stage," which served as a moveable platform for semiconductor wafers. People would use terms like "you put the wafer on the stage and move it to the load location," "you can rotate the stage," "you apply vacuum to the stage to hold the wafer down," "you can move the stage around manually," and so on. Frequently the term "chuck" was used instead of "stage". So you might "apply vacuum to the chuck." But there were odd differences. You "found the center of the chuck," but you never "found the center of the stage". The chuck had a diameter, but the stage didn't.

I resolved all this confusion by drawing and labeling pictures of the chuck and stage devices in the respective class descriptions. Here is the one for the chuck class:

Chuck (CHK)

A Chuck is a short, wide, metallic cylinder designed to support a Wafer during inspection within a Station. A typical Chuck has a diameter of 20 cm and a height of 2 to 3 cm. Small holes in the Chuck surface allow a vacuum to be applied to the underside of a Wafer to hold it firmly in place.

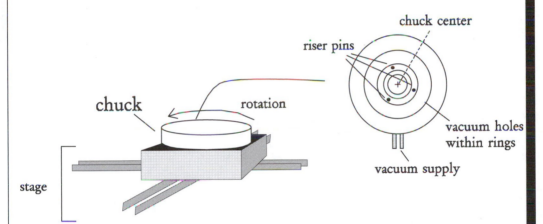

The Chuck rides on a Stage that can move the Chuck along multiple axes (see the Stage object for more about this). There are at least three different sizes (diameters) of Chuck to accommodate gross differences in Wafer size (15, 20 and 30 cm). When a new Chuck is mounted in a Station, it's a big deal — a technician has to recalibrate all the alignment parameters — a time-consuming process. Consequently, once a Chuck is installed, it tends to stay there.

Illustrated class descriptions of physical classes pay off in two ways. They resolve ambiguities in terminology and they highlight subtle physical features that otherwise would have gone unnoticed.

Illustrate soft classes   Soft (nonphysical) classes must also be illustrated. When you draw a physical class, you try to accurately render well-known and little-known but relevant features. Keen observation is the key to drawing physical classes. Soft classes, on the other hand, demand creativity. You may need to invent symbols. It can be a challenge sometimes to devise a useful way to visualize a nonphysical concept.

Here is a description of a soft class:

Step (STP)

A Step is a position within a Script where an Activity Specification may be attached. The only purpose of a Step is to establish the order in which Activity Specifications are normally executed. In an Archived Script acquired data is associated with the Step.

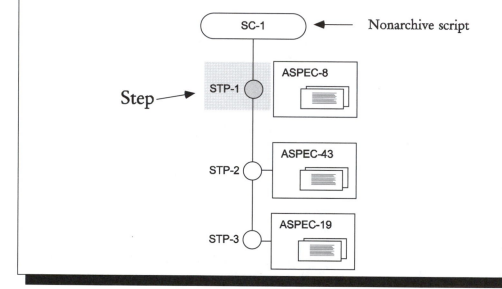

In this example, I invented symbols and labeled them with unique identifier values. The identifier value format is specified in the attribute descriptions of each class.

The process of drawing nonphysical classes almost always reveals holes in your thinking. (If not to yourself, then possibly to others!)

Use terminology appropriate to the problem domain

If you are modeling within the application domain, stick to application terminology. If you are modeling within a service domain, stick to terms that make sense in that domain. For example, the terms "software" and "computer" shouldn't appear in descriptions within most application domains.

☹ A Pause is a point in time specified so that the software knows when to stop an animation.

☺ A Pause is a point in time where a running animation will stop temporarily.

It is okay to refer to "the system" (as long as the system is defined as a class somewhere).

☹ Only one Session can run at a time on the computer.

☺ The Scanning System can run only one Session at a time.

Refer to other model elements in the same problem domain

You often need to explain a class in terms of how other classes, attributes and relationships are used. Here is an excerpt from a class description that explains how semiconductor wafers are transported.

> Once a Wafer is processed, it is moved according to the Transport Area's Active Route. The IS VISITED BEFORE association is used to find the first Process Site to visit that doesn't have a corresponding Completed Pass.

But don't overdo it. Explain just enough to put the class in context. The state and procedure models are the best place to describe dynamics in detail. Here is an example of overkill.

> Once a Wafer is processed, it is moved according to the Transport Area's Active Route. Get the Substrate.Current Location ID. Find the Transport Area that contains this Current Location. Get the Transport Area.Active Route.

Find the last Completed Pass associated with this Route. Select it and find the Completed Pass.Process Site ID. Use the IS VISITED BEFORE association to access the Process Site.Next Process Site ID.

Yechh!

This example is thorough, but it tightens down the bolts way too soon. One little change in the class diagram or state charts and you have to rewrite the whole paragraph.

Describe behavior

Some classes don't do much of anything. A specification class, for example, has a lifecycle like this: Create self and sit around and get referenced.[1] The description of a class like this mostly describes the nature and utility of the class, rather than it's behavior.

But many classes have interesting behavior. It would be hard to describe the landing gear of an aircraft in an embedded control system, for example, without describing some of the primary states of the gear — retracted, retracting, extending, locked and so forth.

Here is a soft class in a document version control system that requires a more detailed description of its behavior.

---

[1] Nowadays most software architectures and model compilers provide facilities to make pre-existing instances available without the need for explicit "create self" procedures. The analyst designates the relevant classes through coloring and lists the required instances ahead of time. The instances are put in place prior to model execution. So our specification class example would not require a state chart.

Document in Revision (DIR)

A Document in Revision is a checked-out Document Version. Only a Document in Revision can be edited.

When an Internally Controlled Document is checked out by a Reviser, an instance of Document in Revision is created. Only one Document in Revision may be created for a given Document. In this way, two Revisers of a Document cannot get their hands on the same Document simultaneously.

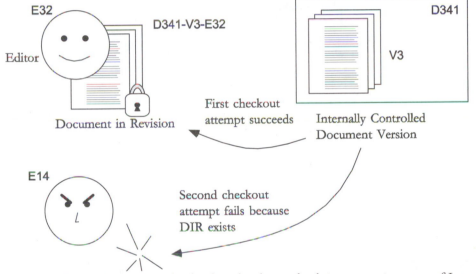

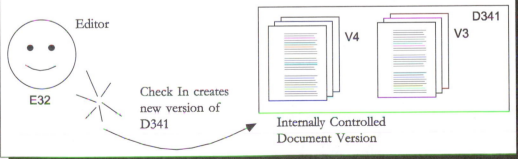

When the Reviser checks the edited copy back in, a new instance of Internally Controlled Document Version is created with an incremented Version Number. At this point the Reviser relinquishes control of the document and the instance of Document in Revision evaporates.

Don't describe detailed behavior

Don't waste time describing anything in the class model that would be better addressed in the state and procedure models. Statements like "then it sends an event to class X" and "this class communicates with class X" don't belong in a class model.

If you incorporate details of the dynamics in a class description, then your information will go out of date when you make changes in the state and procedure models. It's hard enough keeping the dynamic models up to date without having to keep coming back and changing the class model.

The situation you really want to avoid is where you spend so much effort describing what a class does that you forget to explain what the class means and why the class is required in the first place. Just because a class can be ascribed behavior doesn't mean that it is helpful or necessary.

Don't be wishy-washy

Avoid watering down your descriptions with wimpy qualifiers like "generally," "usually" and "probably". Tentative descriptions keep you from learning anything new. It is better to use definite terms like "always," "never" and "must". When you are wrong, these words are 400,000-volt cattle prods that spark useful feedback from your otherwise laconic reviewers.

Imagine for a moment that you are an application engineer with a expertise in the operation of an optical device inspection machine, the Flot-O-Scan 3000. Here is something you know about how flots[2] are inspected:

APPLICATION NOTE

Flots are usually loaded into the inspection station in batches using a cartridge. Sometimes flots are loaded one at a time, using the manual feed tray. There is also an entry port at the rear of the station that can be used to manually load a single flot for diagnostic purposes.

Now read this phrase taken from the Flot Handler class description:

☹ A Flot is usually loaded from a Cartridge.

This statement is too wishy-washy. Maybe the analyst knows about the other two ways to load flots and maybe he or she doesn't. Either way, this type of statement will not catch the application expert's eye.

Contrast it with a more direct statement:

☺ There are only two ways to load a Flot into the Flot-O-Scan. A Flot can be loaded one at a time using a Tray or in batches using a Cartridge. A Cartridge is used most of the time.

If you want the most up-to-date correct information, you must display your ignorance prominently. The direct statement (smiley face) is clearly false, and you can be sure that the application expert will

---

[2]Flot = flat optical device (see Figure 5.2 on page 126).

straighten you out (assuming he or she actually reads it, but that's a different problem).

Display your ignorance prominently.

Of course, you can always intersperse your descriptions with parenthesized questions like: (Is there any other way to load a flot?). But that only works when you know that you might be wrong.

How long should a class description be?

It depends on the class. Most classes take a page to describe, while others can be nailed down in three or four sentences. Some classes are so interesting that it takes two or three pages.

How much explanation is necessary?

Sometimes it is difficult to know just how much needs to be explained when you are writing a class description. You have to assume that the reader is already knowledgeable to some degree about the technology on your project. If you are describing a robot arm, you don't have to write 20 pages on kinematics, although it might be helpful to cite any texts that are particularly relevant in an introduction to the class model.

To set the right level of explanation, it helps to picture some typical readers of your model. These are the most common reader profiles (not necessarily in order):

- Someone newly transferred or hired on to the project

- Other analysts

- Application experts

- Members of the design/implementation team

- You (3 to 6 months later after you've returned from working on something else)

Assume that your reviewers are skeptical. If you make a nonintuitive abstraction, defend the reasoning behind it.

Summary

A class description must answer the what, why and how questions. The process of answering these questions benefits the analyst as much as the reviewers.

Ninety-nine percent of the time a class description is read because the reader of your model got confused looking at a symbol on the class diagram. Write/draw your description with this scenario in mind. Your description should help remove that confusion as quickly as possible. So:

- Use both text and drawings to define a class.

- Don't merely restate what is obvious on the class diagram.

- Use supporting examples.

- Make clear, decisive statements.

- Describe the essential behavior of a class, but don't describe state dynamics or collaboration in any detail.

Chapter 13 How to write attribute descriptions

When you point to an attribute on a class diagram — any attribute, there are a number of questions that typically come to mind: What does this attribute mean? Why is it in this class? Why is it necessary? What values can be assigned to it? To answer these questions, you simply pick up the model description document attached to the diagram, look up the relevant class and read the attribute description. It should look something like this:

meaning and purpose

elapsed travel time

name

This is the amount of time that has elapsed since the Torpedo entered the FIRED state. This value is used to determine when to detonate the Torpedo or when to decide that the Torpedo should be considered lost and removed from the game.

Domain: A positive real number of seconds.

domain of values (data type)

Figure 13.1

The three key parts of an attribute description are demonstrated in the example above: The attribute name, a description of the meaning and purpose of the attribute and a description of the domain of values that may be assigned to the attribute. The domain of values is often characterized in terms of a nonimplementation data type (more about that later).

You would be amazed how many times the process of writing a simple attribute description like this will throw your entire world view question. So to save yourself some pain, start writing these early in the modeling process when it's easier to shake things up. Most people wait until it's too late and have to settle with a needlessly awkward system.

To guide you along, I've filled this chapter with numerous examples of attribute descriptions. The key to writing useful descriptions is not writing style so much as attention to detail. Make sure that all of the key questions are answered.

The details of interest depend on whether you are writing about a descriptive attribute (such as a dimension, color, maximum load, stall speed and so forth) or a naming attribute (such as license number, barcode and the like). But for each.

Meaning and purpose of an attribute

For most attributes you probably think that the meaning is so obvious from the name that there is no point writing anything. I mean, if you have an attribute like Valve_state, then there's not much to say. Except of course whether this is a commanded or a detected value. But, hey, that's something. The problem is that you most likely have been steeped in your model for so long that you can't think of any questions or issues that someone might raise. So if you have total writer's block, find someone across the hallway and try a quick verbal explanation of the attribute and it's class. If any issues come up, and they probably will, fold those into the relevant descriptions!

Clarify the meaning of the attribute

Always look for subtle issues that most people would miss. It is often impossible to divine the precise meaning of an attribute solely from its name. Clear up the specific meaning.

Submarine.Current_heading

This is the direction in which the Submarine is pointed (the Submarine may or may not be moving). Note that a Submarine that is applying reverse engines will have a Current Heading that is 180 degrees from its actual direction of motion.

Subtleties like this, the distinction between heading and direction of motion, are the most important items to capture in any kind of model description.

Some attributes merit a complete essay. But there is a way to make the job easier.

Use pictures

Sometimes it is easier to illustrate attributes than it is to describe them in words. You'll see what I mean with the following description of a collection of attributes that define the path taken by a laser scanner:

> If x1 is the left edge of the leftmost unit region that is covered at least partially by the infinite horizontal strip of height Scan Sweep Length with its top edge located at y = Ystart, and x2 is the right edge of the rightmost unit region satisfying the same criteria, then the width of the strip is given by | Xend - Xstart | = Acceleration Distance + (x2 - x2) + Deceleration Distance.

Whoa! My brain hurts. I think it's time to go check my e-mail or something.

A picture like this makes the attributes easier to understand.

Strip attributes

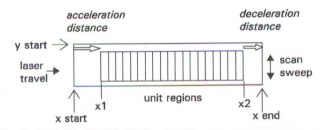

Figure 13.2

Ah, yes. Now I feel much better.

Of course, you should augment the picture with some text and math, but my point is that pictures add a lot to attribute descriptions — so use them.

Status attribute   There are a few things to keep in mind if you are describing an attribute that reflects the current status of it's class. Let's start with an example description:

> Submarine.Pilot_mode
>
> A Submarine may be controlled by either intermittently adjusting Dive, Rudder, and Engine settings or by establishing a Desired Speed, Heading, and Depth and switching the Submarine to auto-pilot mode. In autopilot mode, the game continuously adjusts the Dive, Rudder, and Engine settings as necessary to maintain the specified control setpoints.
>
> Domain: [manual | autopilot]

If a class has a state model, the current state is the set of states in that class's state model. Since the attribute domain is already defined by the state model, you don't need to document it yet again in a written description. In fact, Current_state should never appear as an attribute on any class since the software architecture maintains a current state data for all state machines.

Published status   Furthermore, it's a bad idea for one class to know the current state of another class. It leads to nasty control coupling which complicates maintenance and testing of the models. State based coordination should be mediated through event collaboration or through *published status*. A class may (in rare circumstances!) publish a control value for reading and/or manipulation by another class. In my case study book[1], for example, I use a class called "Door" in an elevator application that publishes a boolean state named "Locked". This published state is set by the Cabin class and both referenced and set by the Door class. It's used to resolve a potential race condition so the Door won't open itself while the Cabin is moving. Still the Cabin knows nothing about the detailed Door states and vice versa. Only the published status is shared.

---

[1] Leon Starr, *Executable UML: A Case Study*, Model Integration, 2001, ISBN: 0970804407

Current state — the lifecycle

Coming back to the issue of Current_state, you may want to define the overall lifecycle of a class. This is best done in the class description. Here's an excerpt of the Torpedo class description which describes not all the specific states but the overall lifecycle:

> Torpedo
>
> A Torpedo is created when it is loaded aboard a Submarine as a Stored Torpedo. A Stored Torpedo is prepared for use by loading it into a Torpedo Tube. The Stored Torpedo becomes a Loaded Torpedo at this point. This operation takes time since it requires the cooperation of a sometimes inexperienced or possibly hung-over crew. When a Loaded Torpedo is fired, it becomes a Fired Torpedo. The Fired Torpedo will rapidly hunt for its target or become lost. In either case the Fired Torpedo meets its end and is removed from the game.

The specific states could be shuffled around on the state chart, but the lifecycle should emerge unscathed.

Discovered identifier attributes

A discovered identifier is one that was already in use before you started the class model and, more to the point, is under the control of an external authority like a manufacturer or some organization. If you are modeling parts sold in a catalog, for example, you might use the manufacturer's catalog number combined with the manufacturer code as a unique ID.

Part	0..*	R1	1	Manufacturer
Catalog number {I} Manufacturer code {I, R1}	manufactures	is manufactured by		Manufacturer code {I}

Model 13.1

Since you are relying on some external source to ensure that the identifier values are unique. So you must justify the use of this outside source in the description.

Part.Catalog_number

A Manufacturer is responsible for assigning a Catalog Number to each Part that they sell. We haven't run across any cases where a Manufacturer duplicates a Catalog Number for the same Part. It is still possible that a duplication could occur, say a 4cm self-sealing stem bolt sold under two different Catalog Numbers. In this case, we would treat each Catalog Number as a separate Part even though each Catalog Number corresponds to the same product.

Part.Manufacturer_code (R1)

The Part is built by this Manufacturer. Since two Manufacturers might use the same Catalog Number, we need to add the Manufacturer code as part of the identifier.

In the Manufacturer class:

Manufacturer.Manufacturer_code

We assign a unique ID to each Manufacturer. This is usually the first three letters of the Manufacturer name. If two Manufacturers have the same three letters at the beginning of the name, then we will change one of the letters to make it unique.

The point is that you have to: (1) describe why the source is a good choice as identifier or partial identifier (you must explain the rule or policy that guarantees uniqueness) and (2) explain any meaning behind the identifier (if one exists). One way to do this is by taking a case where you could end up with duplicate IDs and then explaining how that situation is avoided. In fact, that's the real purpose of an identifier, to prevent illegal duplicates.

This practice often leads you to discover weaknesses in an existing identification scheme.

Domains and data types

Attribute domains vs. subject matter domains

A *domain* is a set of legal values that may be assigned to an attribute. I sometimes refer to this as an "attribute value domain" to distinguish it from a "subject matter domain"[2]. (In this chapter, assume I'm talking about attributes when I use the word "domain" unless I specify otherwise.)

The real number and integer domains are easily understood since they have standard definitions in mathematics. But you can feel free to invent any domain you need, however, such as "the colors red, blue and green" or "an integer between 1 and 10 inclusive", or even "any zipcode recognized by the United States post office".

Data types

If you want to use a domain for more than one attribute, it is convenient to give it a name. The domain "an integer between 1 and 10 inclusive" might be referred to as the topTen data type. In Executable UML a *data type* is, thus, a name for a commonly used attribute value domain. Example data types could be primaryColors, zipCode and so on. Data types come in two flavors, *base* and *user defined*.

Base data types

A base data type is one that is explicitly supported by Executable UML. As of this writing, I do not have a complete list of official base types or their structure. I believe they will be: numeric, ordinal, symbolic (like string), enumerated, time, duration and boolean. The numeric, time and duration types can be further qualified with units, range and precision.

---

[2]A subject matter domain is a system (modeled or not) that can be configured for use by a user (such as another domain). Word processing, animation, database, program language, GUI toolkit, ultrasound image management, cardiac physiology and gas chromatography are all examples of subject matter domains. Most systems are built using a dozen or more domains all configured for use by one another.

User data types   All user data types are built up from one or more base data types. So you might create a user data type named distance as numeric with units = cm, range = 0..100 and precision = .001. The duration base data type also requires the specification of units, range and precision. So you might define a user data type like videoFrameTime as duration with units = milliseconds, range = 0..1000 and precision = 1. Finally, a data type like additivePrimaryColors could be: enumerated [red, blue and green].

Implementation independence   The most radical thing going on here is that no assumption is made about how these data types are implemented. The numeric type, for example could be implemented as string, float or integer in C++. That's why some of the data type names (symbolic, for example) may seem a little weird to programmers. That's the whole point!

Armed with these definitions, we are ready to look at some example domain descriptions.

Domain descriptions

What follows are several examples and practical tips where I've defined domains for various attributes.

Don't be wishy-washy   Here is a descriptive attribute with a tentative domain description.

Scanner.Power_level

This is the amount of power applied to the infrared scanner. The value is provided as a control input to the scan control hardware.

☹ Domain: Some type of number (to be determined).

A domain description like this might be deferred for many reasons. Maybe the hardware design isn't complete. Maybe there is controversy as to whether the control will be a whole integer or a real number. Maybe the author of the model is worrying about more important problems. Or maybe the author is too lazy to track down the correct information.

If you review a model containing a domain description like this, you should find out why it is incomplete. If the author responds, "it's a design detail," then you know that the author is too lazy to track down the correct information. Nothing in the software design or implementation process will resolve the issue. One benefit of building an executable model is that it brings to attention details that need to be nailed down. The analysis is not complete if the attribute domains are undefined.

In any event, I would rewrite the example domain description like this:

☺ Domain: An integer between 1 and 10 inclusive, where 10 is the maximum possible. Conversion of this value into milliwatts is performed by the hardware. (Sarah — let me know if this changes.)

Here I am inventing a domain policy out of thin air. This statement will no doubt freak out the hardware folks. Admittedly, that's a little underhanded, but you've got to do something to get people to read your documents in sufficient detail.

The intent of a decisive description is to get the hardware engineers to make a decision, or at least to let them know that you are making default assumptions that may have to be corrected. This kind of writing may even help you to establish the hardware requirements that you want to see.[3]

---

[3] In the long run you will get more respect from the hardware folks. They think that us software weenies can never make up our minds.

Measurements need units

The following domain description is incomplete:

> Reflecting Body.Distance
>
> The distance from the sensor to the reflecting body.
>
> ☹ Domain: A positive real number.

A measurement doesn't mean anything unless it is defined precisely. Also, units should be specified when describing measurements.

> The distance from the center of the sensor to the surface of the reflecting body.
>
> ☺ Domain: type:numeric, units:nm,
>   range:[0..Game_Spec.Max_distance], precision: .001

In the second example, units are specified and distance is defined precisely.

Quantities don't need units

With quantities, the units are reflected in the attribute name and the attribute definition, so the domain description need not specify units.

> ☺ Flot.Defect_quantity
>
> The number of defects detected in the latest scan of this Flot.
>
> Domain: type:Quantity

Here I've defined quantity as a user data type built on the numeric base type.

Precision   Specify the precision demanded by the application — not the precision supplied by the implementation.

Tank.Pressure

☺ Domain: type:numeric, range:[Tank Spec.Min_pressure..Tank Spec.Max_pressure], precision:.01, units:psi

It's perfectly okay to make reference to other attributes in a domain description. Just make sure that the statement is unambiguous and the referenced attributes really exist.

Don't specify the implementation   Don't tell the model compiler how to do its job.

Environment.Temperature

☹ Domain: A floating point value (implementation specific)

☺ Domain: type:numeric, units:kelvin, range:0 to Chamber_Spec.Max_temperature expressing kelvins.

Coordinates   Coordinates like x, y, z, q are common examples of descriptive attributes. Sometimes it is tempting to lump coordinates together.

☹ Grabber.Position

The location of the grabber.

Domain: Real numbers x and y expressing a distance in microns.

But this is bad practice because you can easily overlook important distinctions among the attributes that have been lumped together.

☺ Grabber.X_position

The position of the grabber on the X axis. This axis runs horizontally along the face of the machine. The grabber is moved along this axis to line up with one of the two loading robots.

Domain: type:numeric, range:
    [Axis_Spec.X_low_limit..Axis_Spec.X_high_limit], units:
    microns, precision:1 (An operator facing the machine has
    the negative extreme on his or her left. Zero is at the center
    of the front panel door.)

Grabber.Y_position

The position of the arm on the Y axis. This axis runs vertically from inside the inspection chamber to the top of the front panel. The grabber takes a sample from the load robot and brings it to the inspection chamber (and vice versa).

Domain: type:numeric, range:
    [Axis_Spec.Y_low_limit..Axis_Spec.Y_high_limit]
    expressing microns. (Zero is at the top of the front panel.)

Specify the coordinate system

All coordinates should be described with respect to a coordinate system. Here is an example from a user interface application.

☹ Cursor.X

Location on the X axis.

Domain: A real number in the range [-.5, .5].

Where is the X axis? Is the position relative to a specific window?

The screen? Is distance measured in pixels or millimeters?

☺ Domain: type:numeric, range [-.5, .5] expressing a location on the X
   axis in Normalized Device Coordinates. (See model
   appendix.)

When a description applies to multiple attributes, you can put the
information in a class description or in an introduction or appendix
to the model. Diagrams are useful for showing how coordinate systems relate to one another.

Internal constraints   Often a domain is restricted by the current value of some other
attribute.

☺ Child Window.Lower_right_x

   Domain: type:numeric, units:pixels, prec:1, range:
   [Display_Spec.Min..DisplaySpec.Max] A distance in
   pixels along the X axis from the left edge of the Parent
   Window. This value is a positive integer N such that
   Upper Left X < N < Parent Window.Lower Right X.

It's probably a good idea to say more about the attribute constraint
in the attribute description (just before the domain description).

Type attribute   This attribute usually refers to subclass names. Here is an example where the domain of a type attribute is the set of subclass names.

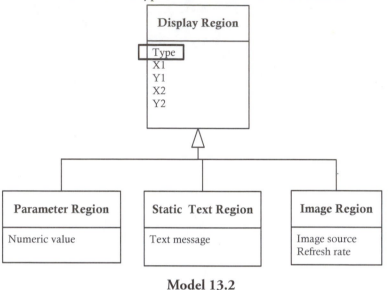

Model 13.2

Display Region.Type

This is the type of data that can appear in this Display Region. Only one type of data can be displayed in a single Display Region.

Domain: type:enumerated, values:(Parameter, Static Text, Image)

If you add a new subclass to the class model, then you have to update the Display Region.Type attribute domain description. Since you are updating the class model anyway, this is not such a big problem. Though, you have probably noticed that the addition of the type attribute adds no new information to the model. With a robust action language, you should not have to use type attributes.

Enumerated vs. numeric domains

With some set domains, it is not easy to determine whether you should enumerate the domain or specify it using a numeric range. Here's the enumeration approach.

> Flot.Thickness
>
> The nominal thickness of a Flot. A number of standard Flot sizes are defined within the industry.
>
> Domain: type:enumerated, values:(5mm, 10mm, 20mm, 25mm)

Contrast this with the range approach.

> Domain: type:numeric, units: mm,
>   range:[0..Flot_Fab_Spec.Max_size].

Either domain description could be correct. We need to know more about the application. The following note argues for the enumerated domain description:

APPLICATION NOTE

> Flot sizes are based on an industry standard that is updated infrequently. You would like the system to recognize only the standard sizes. The user should be presented with a list of standard thicknesses to choose from. We don't want the user to type in just any number and then have to reject it or round it because the number is nonstandard.

But this next note leads us to express the domain as a numeric range.

APPLICATION NOTE

> While it is true that the industry standard is updated only once a year, it is, nonetheless, updated. Also, what is to keep someone from fabricating a nonstandard flot for research purposes? True, you would still like to have the user choose from a list of standard flot sizes, but you would also like to provide an advanced option where a nonstandard size can be specified.

We have seemingly contradictory requirements. How do we model both restricted standard and unrestricted nonstandard flot thicknesses at the same time? Solution: Extend the class model with a specification class.

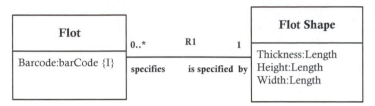

Model 13.3

Constraining a domain with a specification class

Here's how it works. First, you create instances for all the industry standard sizes in the Flot Shape class. The user interface restricts the user's selection to the current set of Flot Shape instances. If the user wants to define a nonstandard shape, a new instance must first be created in the Flot Shape class. The attribute domain of Flot Shape.Thickness becomes open ended.

We are restricting the domain of acceptable thicknesses explicitly using a set of instances in the Flot Shape class, rather than implicitly in the attribute domain description. So the domain of Flot Shape.Thickness is properly expressed using the numeric range option.

If the geometry of a Flot Shape were more complex (containing sophisticated internal features, for example), then you would need more than one specification class. In fact, you may uncover a whole subsystem's worth of specification classes.

Text names   Naming attributes are often described as being nothing more than text strings. This is a bad practice.

> Video Effect.Name
>
> The user can assign a string with arbitrary content to label a Video Effect.
>
> ☹ Domain: An ASCII string.

Here is a more complete description that defines the purpose and usage of names without specifying an implementation.

> Video Effect.Name
>
> A user assigns a descriptive name to a Video Effect so that he or she can recognize the effect in the future. Names are not, however, guaranteed to be unique.
>
> ☺ Domain: type:symbolic, length
>   [1..Video_System_Spec.Max_name_length]

The second domain description is better because it does not tell the model compiler how to do its job. The use of ASCII strings might be a requirement imposed by the database or a software architecture but not the application.

Summary

Be sure to describe the meaning and purpose and domain for every attribute on your class diagram. Every attribute. I know this seems like a tedious documentation task, but the technical quality of your models will improve dramatically.

Chapter 14

How to write relationship descriptions

Classes seem to get all the attention. This is unfortunate because relationships are equally important. Many of the critical policies in an application are formalized by the naming, multiplicity and conditionality of the associations. In fact, minor changes to a relationship can seriously alter the definition of the connected classes. Just as it does with classes and attributes, you will find that the careful definition of relationships almost always exposes errors in your logic (which, of course, is a good thing).

Why relationship descriptions are neglected

Here are some reasons why I think relationship descriptions are neglected:

1. Classes seem more tangible than relationships. What can you write about a relationship?

2. The class descriptions are generally written first. Once you write 15 or 20 class descriptions, you don't have much energy left over for the relationships.

3. The phrase "object-oriented" is taken much too seriously.

In this chapter I hope to address reasons 1 and 2. Good luck with 3.

What can you say about relationships?

As with any model description, you want to clear up confusion when you write about a relationship. To understand what to write, you need to understand where there is likely to be confusion. And what better place to find confusion than in someone else's model?

Take a look at any of the model examples in this book[1]. Or go look at a model built by one of your colleagues. Are there any cases where the model would make a different statement about its application if the name, multiplicity or conditionality of one side of one of its associations were to change? Are you confused about the exact meaning of the model because you can't tell what some of the associations really mean? If you didn't answer "yes" emphatically, let the model sit on the shelf for a few weeks and try again.

> **If you don't understand the relationships, you don't understand the model.**

Let's get confused   Consider a factory management system. In this system we track process stations (factory machines) that apply operations like cutting, drilling and surfacing to a variety of materials. The process stations are organized into Station Groups.

---

[1] Lots of model description examples are available in my book Executable UML: A Case Study. See the "Where to learn more" section.

Let's take a look at one of the associations in this application's class model.

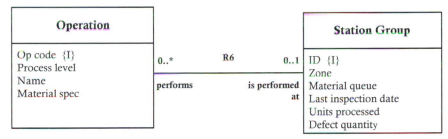

Model 14.1

Association R6 in Model 14.1 looks perfectly reasonable at first glance. But do we really know what R6 means? It says that a Station Group PERFORMS Operations. Does that mean at the present time? Can a Station Group perform multiple Operations at the same point in time? Or does R6 refer to configuration — a Station Group is configured to perform one of several Operations. Just because a Station Group has the capability of performing an Operation doesn't mean that the Operation is necessarily being executed at the moment. Or maybe the term PERFORMS means that a Station Group consists of machines that have the physical capability of performing a specific Operation. Are there any other possible interpretations of R6?

Okay, so we don't know the meaning of R6 — what about the multiplicity and conditionality? Model 14.1 says that an Operation is performed by zero or one Station Group. Why only one? Why can't multiple Station Groups perform the same Operation? If it is a consequence of the definition of Station Group — "a collection of Stations with the same capabilities" — then we should find out by looking at the Station Group class description. But the class description of Station Group wouldn't necessarily explain the circumstances when an Operation exists that is not performed by any Station Group. R6 also says that a Station Group might not perform any Operation. Why is that? Is it because a Station Group might exist that is not yet configured? Or is it because some Station Groups are not designed to perform machining Operations? If we knew the precise meaning of PERFORMS, we might be able to figure it out, but we don't.

What every association description must contain

Consequently, every association description should address the following:

- Number, name, multiplicity and conditionality

- Meaning

- Why it's 1 or * on each side

- Why it's conditional (0) or unconditional (1) on each side

What a generalization description must contain

Even though generalization relationships always have the same implicit name "is a", there is still a need to explain the meaning and purpose of the generalization. The following should be described:

- The basis for abstraction

- The policy which guarantees that the superclass is completely partitioned (alternatively, the policy that guarantees that an instance of the superclass is always an instance of exactly one of its subclasses — the mutual exclusion principle)

- The policy that guarantees that a subclass is really a special case of the superclass

Each of the association items is present in the following example association description:

Relationship descriptions

R6 — Operation IS PERFORMED AT Station Group (0..1:0..*)
Station Group PERFORMS Operation

A Station Group can be set up to perform any number of Operations. Since all the Stations in a Station Group are always configured identically, Operations are defined for Station Groups — not individual Stations. The process of making a Station Group capable of performing any given Operation can require many preparation activities. It depends on the machinery and the machining process. Bits, dies or other fittings may have to be installed, programs and parameters may have to be downloaded, and operating conditions may have to be met.

A Station Group may be capable of performing multiple Operations. A wide variety of cutting Operations, for example, may be executed at the same machining station. (This is especially true at the new MeltBoy 9000 laser reducing station.)

During retooling, a Station Group is taken out of service and is therefore incapable of performing any Operations.

To simplify material transport, an Operation may be set up at only one Station Group. This does not affect throughput since there is no limit to the number of Stations within a Station Group.

An Operation can be defined by a manufacturing engineer without necessarily setting it up at a Station Group. This can happen when an Operation isn't needed for the current Run or when the corresponding Stations have not yet been installed.

Let's examine each component.

The heading

The heading displays the number and name of the association so that you can match it to the multiplicity expression on the class diagram. The name is stated from each direction so that you can prove to yourself and to others that the association makes sense from both points of view. As I write up the association, I usually find myself changing the name as I consider how it looks from each point of view. I am generally more capricious when I jot the name down on the model graphic than when I name it in the description. Sometimes this renaming process will make me realize that what I thought was a single association actually breaks down into two separate associations.

The multiplicity and conditionality are stated just to be complete. We want to ensure that the descriptions contain a complete statement of the class model. If you throw the graphic part of the model away, you should be able to reconstruct the whole thing using only the descriptions.

The meaning

An association name alone can almost always be interpreted in more than one way. Your goal is not just to explain the meaning to other people, but to make sure that you really understand it yourself. Sometimes it helps to ask yourself when an instance of the relationship would be created or deleted. It often helps to draw a picture. Whereas instances of classes are often visualized as icons, instances of relationships can be represented several ways. Throughout the figures in this book, in fact, I have used the following methods to illustrate relationships: connecting lines, enclosed sets, relative proximity of class icons and similar shading.

Multiplicity and conditionality

The multiplicity and conditionality nail down specific application policies. These policies often have subtle yet far reaching implications. Since these policies may not be evident to the model reviewer, you need to write down your reasoning. State the policy and use examples to justify the multiplicity and conditionality statements on each side of the association. In the example relationship description, there is a subtle policy that could be easily questioned: "To simplify material transport, an Operation may be set up at only one Station

Group". This statement explains why the association is 1:1..* and not 1..*:1..*.

It takes a lot of analysis effort to figure out where to put the 0's on the class diagram. They capture critical application policies. Imagine how you are going to feel weeks or months later when a colleague comes along and changes them without appreciating the implications. When you go to straighten him or her out about why the PERFORMS association is conditional on the Operation side, you find that you can't remember exactly why. All you remember was that there was lots of discussion and deliberation leading up to the decision to make it conditional. So you just stand there looking silly, confirming your colleague's suspicions that your model needs to be rethought.

So right now, while you remember the reasoning, write it down!

Don't write the relationship descriptions last!

One key to writing good, useful relationship descriptions is to interleave them with the class descriptions. If you put all the relationship descriptions in a separate document, you will probably end up doing them last. Here is a generic outline of how I organize my model descriptions so that the relationships don't get the short end of the stick.

Class A

Class description

Attribute descriptions

Attribute A

Attribute B

Relationship descriptions (if any)

Relationship A

Relationship B

Class B (new page)

...and so forth

For easy reference, each class starts on a new page. In the relationships section I choose any of the relationships connecting to the described class when this class seems to be the main participant. If a relationship is already written up as part of another class description, then I just skip it. If all the connected relationships are covered elsewhere, then this section is omitted. I put a relationship index up front so that reviewers know which class to look under to find a given relationship.

When you write up the class description, you usually start thinking about some of the relationship rules. Since the relationship section is right there at the bottom of the page, you can easily skip down, fill in the details, and then jump back up to the class description. When you finish the class description, the relationship descriptions at the bottom are pretty easy to finish up because you've already filled in the meaty parts. It makes the description process much more natural than the alternative. I mean — think about it. Doesn't it seem a little odd to describe all the classes in one pass and then to describe all the relationships?

Summary

Well, that's it. Remember that precise relationships express critical rules. A seemingly innocent choice of a 0 vs. 1 on one end of an association can have serious implications that won't be obvious to most reviewers — including yourself. If you write descriptions that expose your thinking, the technical quality of your models and, thus, your software will improve dramatically. Get to work.

Model patterns

3

Chapter 15

Is zero-one-many specific enough?

Standard UML allows multiplicity expressions that can specify any number, 1, 5..7, whatever you like. Executable UML limits you to only three multiplicity expressions:

- 0..1
- 1
- 0..*
- 1..*

that's it!

This might seem strange, since numeric limitations appear frequently in requirements and in the real-world in general. And I know from experience that they come up in real-time, embedded systems all the time. If you know, for example, that your system will have two DSP's (digital signal processors) on every board, why not make the multiplicity expression more precise by sticking a 2 in it, as shown below?

Model 15.1

What's wrong with specific numbers?

First, let's review the reasons why you don't want specific numbers on most associations.

1. The logic that handles seven instances shouldn't be any different from the logic that handles eight instances. The model compiler doesn't care about this kind of distinction.

2. The logic that handles zero instances is often different from the

logic that handles one or more instances, so distinguishing 1, 0..1, 1..* and 0..* is of interest to the model compiler.

3. A data structure that might reference multiple instances will probably be designed differently than a data structure guaranteed to reference exactly one instance. Again, the model compiler cares.

4. A requirement with a number in it is likely to change (today we absolutely will have two DSP's on each board — next month it could be three). If you have to accommodate this change by editing your model, then you have to recompile the model, reintegrate it, retest it, etc. You should be embarrassed if you create a model that must be recompiled just because a number changes.

5. By their very nature, associations are dynamic, so they should be characterized qualitatively, not quantitatively.

6. It's consistent with the relational model of data.[1]

Reason 4 is enough to keep me from quantifying the DSP relationship example.

Quick comment: In fact, there is a good reason for using specific numbers on associations in Executable UML, but we don't embed the numbers in the class model itself. We'll come back to the DSP example and see why at the end of this chapter.

---

[1] For those familiar with the popular Saturday night TV show, say this with a Scottish accent, "If it's not relational,... *it's crap!*" In other words, when it comes to modeling complex information, anything that can't be reconciled with the relational model is worthless. Now that doesn't sound anywhere near as funny.

A case where zero-one-many isn't enough

But consider this example:

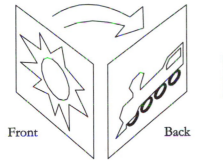

Front   Back

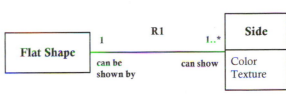

Model 15.2

Here we have a Flat Shape in a graphic animation system that can have a different bitmapped image painted on each side. We could model it as shown here, but a few realities nag at us.

- A Flat Shape has two sides and planar geometry isn't likely to change. So much for reasons 4 and 5.

- If we were to code this in C, let's say, the structure would probably incorporate this numeric fact. For example,

```
struct flatshape
{
        struct side front;
        struct side back;
}
struct side
{
        int color;
        int texture;
}
```

There goes reason 3 (reasons 1 and 2 generally follow 3 right out the window).

So the argument for modeling the two-ness of a planar shape is compelling. And it's easy enough to specify the number in UML. But, hey, you can do anything you want in standard UML. We need something consistent with our execution and translation goals. So what do we do?

An attempt at modeling two-ness

We could try using two one-to-one associations to more precisely enforce two-sidedness:

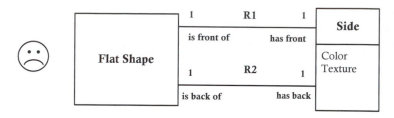

Model 15.3

This class diagram says that a Flat Shape has both a front and a back Side. But it also says that a Side is both the front and back side of a Flat Shape. No good. A Side is either the front or back of a Flat Shape.

Can we fix it by making the associations conditional?

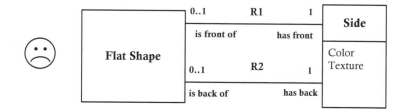

Model 15.4

Now the model says that a Side might exist that doesn't belong to any Flat Shape. Still no good.

We could try solving the problem with attributes instead of relationships. Since a Flat Shape always has two sides, why not just give it front and back side attributes?

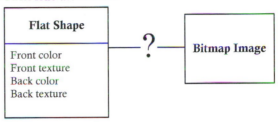

Model 15.5

This model ensures that every Flat Shape has exactly two sides, so it seems to accurately model the application. But we need the Side class to model relationships between a specific side and the Bitmap Image class.

This leads us back to Model 15.4.

The trick is to abstract the positional roles as classes

When you keep staring at the same handful of classes and relationships without arriving at a solution, it sometimes means that you have the wrong classes. Consider breaking the Side class down into Front and Back Sides. This may seem silly, because a Front Side behaves exactly the same way as a Back Side. But there is a relative difference when they are attached to a Flat Shape. This relative difference can be captured by modeling the Front/Back roles played by a Side using generalization.

Now we can make statements about Sides in general by building associations to the Side class. We can make rules about Front Sides that may be different from rules about Back Sides. It is not clear that we need this flexibility, but it won't hurt either. As you can see below, it does solve our relationship problem:

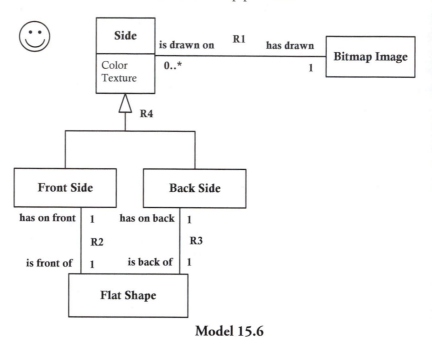

Model 15.6

This model says that a Flat Shape has exactly one Front Side and exactly one Back Side. It also says that a Front Side is always on exactly one Flat Shape and that a Back Side is always on exactly one Flat Shape. Success!

Okay, but what about the DSP example?

So we know that we have to drop the illegal "2" symbol in Model 15.1. That leaves us with this:

Model 15.7

R1 is just one-to-many since there is no point in specializing roles like we did in Model 15.6. There is no top-down, left-right, incoming-outgoing rule to model. We have two DSP's because that's how the hardware people have always said they were going to do things. I don't know about you, but I find no comforting stability in that statement.

Nonetheless, I know that a Signal Board is unlikely to have more than two DSP's on this project. Okay, maybe three. Probably not four. And five is right out. I know that if I were writing the code by hand, I would take the following facts into account:

Compile time assumptions

- There are less than four instances of DSP at any one point in time, and probably exactly two.

- An instance of Signal Board will be associated with exactly two or maybe exactly three DSP boards, period.

- The total number of Signal Boards in our system is probably less than four (I just made that up, but let's assume it's true).

- The total number of DSP's will consequently be 2 x 4 = 8 or maybe 2 x 3 = 6.

- Very important: Links along R1 are static during run-time. We initialize them all during boot-up, and that's that.

Well, if this information would be useful to write efficient code shouldn't it be useful to the model compiler? Sure! So we want a way to specify those bulleted items to our model compiler when we compile. But we absolutely do not want to embed that information into our class model. Why? Because all those bulleted items are volatile assumptions. Model 15.7 represents an eternal reality. Once we start mucking it up, we'll continually thrash the model on every little implementation change.

Coloring to the rescue

So we use a thing called coloring. Imagine that you lay a clear acetate sheet on top of our pristine Model 15.7. Now you get out a colorful highlighter and start marking up the acetate with notation that represents our compile-time assumptions. We designate the DSP class, for example, as having less than 8 instances total. We mark R1 as a static association, and so forth.

Now we can submit both the model and the coloring sheet to the model compiler. In practice, the model is in a database repository and the coloring data is submitted as one or more cross-referenced files or tables. The model compiler takes the coloring data into account so that it can generate efficient code.

What's really cool about this whole process is that, not *if* but *when* your compile time assumptions change, you can leave the model alone and just change the coloring. If your model compiles fine using Model Compiler A, but is too inefficient when it runs through a different compiler, Model Compiler B, you may be able to tweak the coloring so that Model Compiler B generates better code — assuming of course that Model Compiler B is designed to utilize the relevant coloring.

Conclusions

If you find yourself in a situation where you want to model the twoness or three-ness of an association, first consider how strongly the numeric constraint is enforced in the real-world. If the constraint is important because someone put it in boldface in the requirements document, then it is subject to change and not worth modeling. But if it is a fundamental law of geometry, math, physics, or some other relevant field, then it is probably worth embedding in the structure of your system. If that is the case, then consider the different roles played by the two or three things relative to one another. Use generalization to capture these roles.

Specific numbers do become useful when you color your models for efficient compilation. These numbers are never mixed directly into the class model, however.

Chapter 16 — Reflexive patterns

A reflexive association is an association drawn on a single class like this:

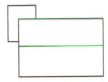

This type of association abstracts connections among instances of the same class. The basic characteristics of this type of association were introduced on page 121.

Reflexive associations and graphs

Reflexive associations are necessary when you encounter a bunch of things — all of the same type — that systematically associate with one another. Consider some examples: a network of hypertext links (Link CAUSES NAVIGATION TO Link), a linear sequence of destinations to be visited by a robot (Destination IS VISITED AFTER Destination), and a hierarchy of relative coordinate systems (Coordinate System DEFINES SPACE RELATIVE TO Coordinate System).

These examples correctly suggest that links among objects of the same class can always be drawn as some type of graph.

Network of instances

Abstracted network pattern

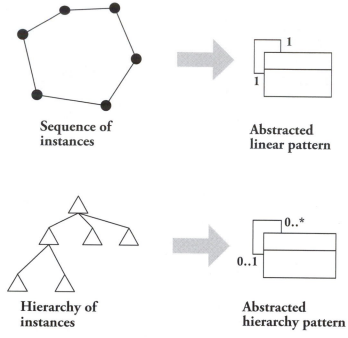

Sequence of instances

Abstracted linear pattern

Hierarchy of instances

Abstracted hierarchy pattern

Figure 16.1

When you model a class that references itself, you are modeling a graph. Fortunately, graphs are well studied things. A discrete math book[1] will provide you with a list of common graph types (networks, trees, lists, etc.) and graph properties (cyclic, acyclic, connected, directed, multiedged, etc.). The accuracy, precision and completeness of your self-referencing association depends on how thoroughly you have addressed the relevant properties of the type of graph that you are modeling.

---

[1] I've got a dusty old version of *Discrete Mathematics with Computer Science Applications*, Skvarcius, Benjamin/Cummings Publishing, 1986, ISBN: 0805370447. It covers the topic well. Good luck finding it!

Let's say, for example, that you have just drawn a model of communication channels opened between processes on a computer:

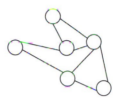

A familiarity with common graph properties will prompt questions like: Does this model allow processes with no communication channels (unconnected)? Processes that communicate with themselves (cycles)? One-way versus two-way communication (directed)? As you answer each of these questions you must make appropriate refinements to the model.

Modeling graph constraints

You probably won't get (or haven't gotten) very far in an application before you find yourself trying to model associations conforming to one of the graphs in Figure 16.1. I can tell you from painful experience that graphs are not always easy to formalize in a class model. This is especially true when the application permits instances in the graph to be created and deleted during runtime by a human user. The more dynamic the associations among instances, the more precise the constraints that must be formalized. Of course, you can always wimp out and leave all the constraints to be enforced in the state and procedure models, though you will probably find this even more difficult. As always, choose the best tool for the job. All things being equal, try to minimize the control threads you will have to test by capturing as many rules as possible in the class model.

Reflexive models can be trivial

Here's the good news. The typical reflexive association can be modeled with a straightforward one-class, one-association solution. This type of solution permits potentially illegal or nonsensical associations, but that's okay if instances are either (1) manually instantiated prior to runtime by an engineer (as is often the case with specification classes) or (2) managed internally — so the user has no opportunity to enter incorrect data. **IMPORTANT**: Before you use one of the elaborate reflexive patterns in the upcoming chapters, reread this paragraph and make sure that you build the appropriate set of constraints and rule checking for your domain's requirements!

Reflexive models can get ugly

When a graph — even an apparently simple graph — needs extensive constraints, you may spend weeks deriving a sophisticated arrangement of classes and relationships that does the job.

But don't worry

In the next few chapters, we will look at several ugly self-referencing scenarios that I've modeled myself into (and out of). The resulting models formalize reflexive patterns that I've seen resurface in several disparate applications. Even if your requirements call for something different, the examples should be interesting to study.

Before moving on, I want to address a source of confusion that often muddies the waters of reflexive association modeling. Oddly enough, experience designing self-referencing code structures can hinder the modeling of reflexive application policies as much as it helps. To build good models, you must recognize the difference between reflexive policies inspired by implementation needs and those that are truly essential to the application.

Self-referencing in analysis and programming

The reflexive concept — the idea that a thing can reference another thing of the same type — is encountered both in analysis and programming. Your goals, however, are different in each activity. I will point out the differences so that the programming goals (which are perfectly reasonable when you are programming) don't become intertwined with your analysis goals.

Isn't self-referencing an implementation concept?

It might be argued that lists, trees and other types of graphs are implementation ideas that belong in program code and not in the class model of an application. That depends.

Take a factory application, for example, where bar coded Trays are transported single file on a Conveyor Belt.

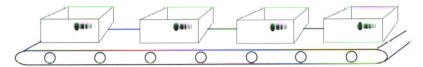

Figure 16.2

The fact that Trays are sequenced is an application fact. It is not a computer software fact. Consequently, we must formalize the sequencing of Trays in a class model — just as we would formalize any other application fact:

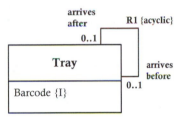

Model 16.1

Quick comment: The {acyclic} constraint on R1 means that a Tray must arrive before/after an instance of Tray other than itself. (A Tray can't arrive before itself!)

You will use some kind of self-referencing code structure to implement the application fact formalized by Model 16.1. One possibility is a doubly-linked list:

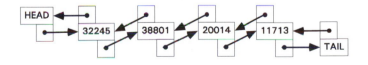

Figure 16.3

The class model states that Trays relate to one another in a linear fashion. Period. No determination is made that a linked list will be used and, if it is, whether it will be singly or doubly linked. The choice of single or double linkage is based on factors like the time it takes to traverse a list, the storage requirements of the list and the complexity of managing the list. Maybe an array will be used instead (or in combination). The analyst does not care. The programmer is required, however, to employ a mechanism that somehow implements the fact that Trays follow one another on a conveyor belt.

Implementation mechanisms disguised as application policy

Sometimes the distinction between application and implementation structures is subtle. Consider the following example taken from a semiconductor wafer test program. Here is a picture of a Wafer that will have each of its dies probed and tested.

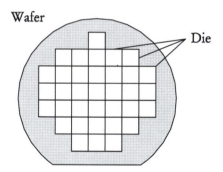

Figure 16.4

A numeric test code is returned for each die. Further action will be taken based on the value of this test code, as shown in the table below. This table data structure was extracted from program code written for the wafer test application:

Test result action table

Test Code	Ink	Retest	Skip
0	Y	N	N
1	Y	N	N
2	N	Y	N
3	N	N	Y
.	.	.	.
.	.	.	.
.	.	.	.

Sample data has been entered for a range of test codes. The actions are:

- Ink: paint an ink spot on the presumably defective die.

- Retest: test the die again.

- Skip: do nothing, move on to the next die.

Given the task of re-engineering this application, a novice analyst might construct the following model:

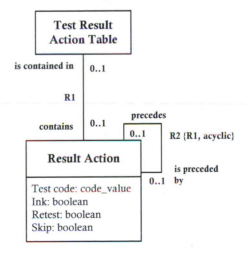

Model 16.2

319

which uses a reflexive association to capture the test result action table structure. Rather than analyze the problem, our novice has simply modeled the existing implementation.

The following model is better:

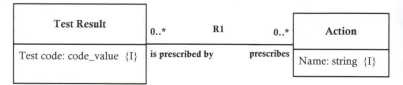

Model 16.3

because it doesn't attempt to model the programmer's data structure choice. It captures the requirement that actions be prescribed for different test results as minimally as possible. As a consequence, some faults in the programmer's design decision are avoided.

1. Mutually exclusive actions can be avoided. The "skip" action, for example, is handled by not making any links in R1 for a given Test Result.

2. New actions, "scratch" instead of "ink" for example, can be added without changing the class model.

Before modeling a reflexive association, make sure that you are modeling essential application policy and not an artificially imposed structure.

Simple and complex graphs

The following chapters are organized in order of ascending graph complexity and, hence, an increased need for constraints. A network graph (Chapter 17) has relatively few constraints to enforce and so it is easily modeled. List and tree graphs (Chapter 18) and (Chapter 19), on the other hand, present some intriguing modeling challenges.

Network patterns

A many-to-many reflexive association models things that connect with one another in a networked fashion. This chapter explores two such things, adjacent territories on a map and networked computer processors. As we will see, a single model pattern does not work for all types of networks. The model must be carefully sculpted to precisely match the details of the application.

Adjacent territories

The board game of Risk[1] splits a continent up into a number of territories.

Adjacent territories in the Risk board game

Figure 17.1

In this game, armies in one territory are allowed to attack the armies in any adjacent territory. Two territories are adjacent if they share a

---

[1] Risk® is a registered trademark of Parker Brothers.

common border. Every territory on the board is adjacent to at least one other territory. Island territories are connected to bordering territories with dashed lines. Madagascar, for example, is considered to be adjacent to East Africa and South Africa.

No islands, acyclic

The rules are:

* A territory is adjacent to any number of other territories.

* A territory cannot be adjacent to itself (no cycles — acyclic).

* Each territory is adjacent to at least one other territory.

This leads us to the following model:

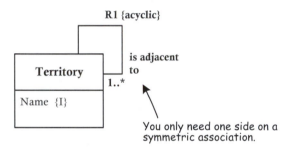

Model 17.1

Symmetry in reflexive associations

Model 17.1 says that an instance of Territory borders one or more other instances of Territory. R1 is acyclic because it makes no sense to say that a Territory is adjacent to itself. Since the roles on this association would be identical (is adjacent to 1..*/is adjacent to 1..*), this is a *symmetric* reflexive association. A reflexive association is symmetric if both directions on the association are absolutely identical. Only one side of a symmetric association has a verb phrase and multiplicity expression. By comparison, Model 17.3 features an asymmetric reflexive association.

The following table shows how Model 17.1 accommodates our map in Figure 17.1:

Borders

Territory A	Territory B
Brazil	Venezuela
Brazil	Peru
Brazil	Argentina
Peru	Venezuela
Peru	Argentina

Table 17.1

Each of the five borders on our map is represented as a row in the table above. Note that Brazil-Peru is identical to Peru-Brazil. It's the same border. If for some reason you need to abstract Border as a class, you need only attach it as an association class on R1. Were this a real-world map, attributes such as Length and Security might reside in a Border association class. I doubt these would be relevant in the game of Risk, however!

Making an association acyclic

The IS ADJACENT TO association is unconditional, so every Territory must border at least one other Territory. To prevent a Territory from bordering itself, the appropriate OCL is written and then referred to by the {acyclic} constraint.

Now let's move on to a less constrained network pattern.

Communicating processes

Consider computer processes that open and close communication channels with one another. When a channel is opened, it provides for the two-way exchange of messages between the connected processes. Here is a possible configuration.

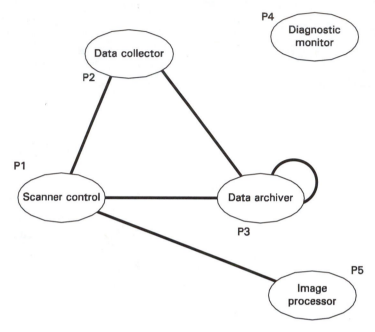

Figure 17.2

Cycles, islands, and single connections

Before jumping to the class diagram, let's make sure we have the rules straight:

- A channel is two-way (nondirectional).

- A process can open a channel with any other process.

- A process can even open a channel to itself (cycles ok — why not?).

- A process might have no channels open.

The following model captures our list of rules:

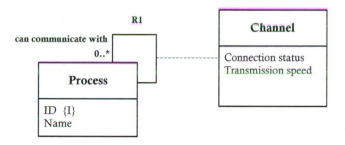

Model 17.2

A Process establishes communication with another Process or with itself by creating a link along R1 and hence, an instance of Channel. Since R1 is conditional, a Process like P4 in Figure 17.2 is accommodated.

In mathematical terms, we have just modeled an undirected, cyclic graph. Once again, the association is both reflexive and symmetric.

**Cycles, islands, and
multiple connections**

What if we want to open two Channels between a pair of Processes?

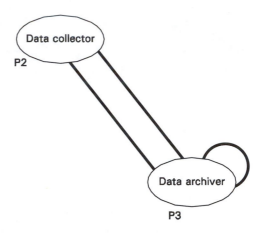

Figure 17.3

We need to incorporate the following rule into our model:

- Multiple Channels may share the same source and destination points.

But Model 17.2 doesn't accommodate multiple connections between the same source and destination. Why?

This limitation is apparent if you try to fill out a table of Channel instances for Figure 17.2 like the following:

Channels

A PID	B PID
P1	P2
P1	P3
P1	P5
P3	P3
P2	P3

Table 17.2

Since this is an association class, there is exactly one instance of Channel for every link along R1 in Model 17.2. This means that between any two Processes, P1 and P2 let's say, there can be at most one Channel. And since the association is symmetric, P1-P2 is the same thing as P2-P1, so you can't cheat and try to make two Channels between P2 and P1 or any other pair of Processes. Since R1 is not constrained to be acyclic, like our map example, you can also accommodate the P3-P3 Channel in Figure 17.2. But once again, there can only be a single P3-P3 Channel.

Directional and multiple

We need to clarify our rule. Why do we want to allow multiple Channels? Is it to make our Channels directional? Or do we just want multiple nondirectional Channels? Each answer demands a different solution. Let's take a look at the directional solution first.

Making the graph directional

Here is a directional configuration:

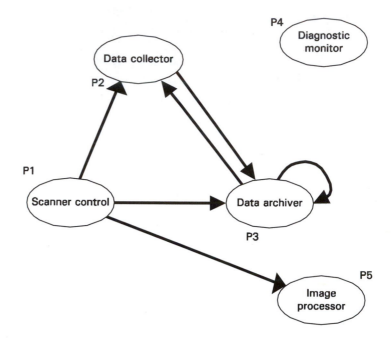

Figure 17.4

And here are the new rules:

- A Channel permits the passage of data in one direction only.

- There may be no more than one Channel in any given direction between the same two Processes.

Here is a model that formalizes these rules.

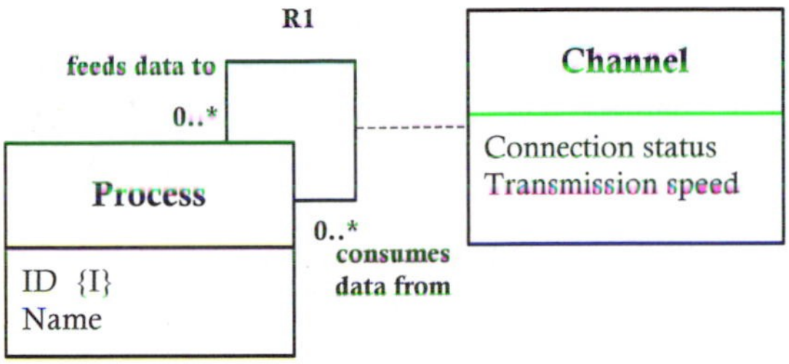

Model 17.3

The association name is reworded to make it directional — FEEDS DATA TO / CONSUMES DATA FROM. So now we have an asymmetric reflexive association. Even though the multiplicity happens to be the same on each side, the verb phrases are now complementary.

You can see how the Channel table subtly changes.

Channels

From PID	To PID
P1	P2
P2	P3
P3	P2
P1	P5
P3	P3

Table 17.3

Since there is a semantic difference between From and To, we can consider P2->P3 to mean something different than P3->P2.

But what about P3->P3?

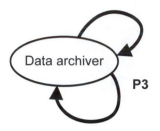

Figure 17.5

The above situation is not allowed by Model 17.3 because we can have only one instance of Channel on P3->P3. And Figure 17.5 is nonsensical anyway, because you can't distinguish one arrow from the other. And that's probably okay, because if a Process is sending data to itself, an extra Channel isn't necessary for two-way communication. If there is some need for multiple loops on a single Process, directional or otherwise, we need to further explore the idea of multiple Channels.

Multiple nondirected Channels

Let's say we want to allow multiple two-way Channels between Processes like this:

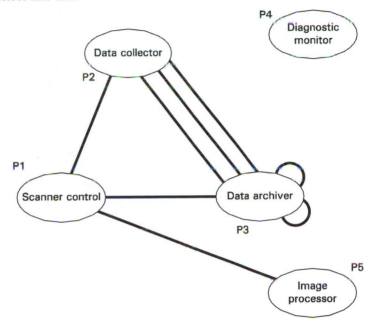

Figure 17.6

The new rules are:

- Any number of Channels may be opened up from one Process to another (or to the same process).

- Channels are not directed.

Here is the new model:

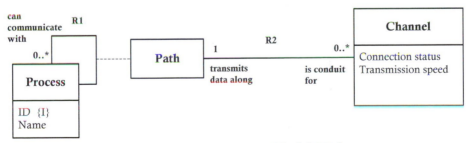

Model 17.4

We must now distinguish the concept of a Path from that of a Channel. Data is permitted to flow along specified Paths. A Channel is a line of communication down a specific Path. As you can see from the following table, we have addressed our requirement of allowing multiple nondirected Channels from one Process to another or to the same Process.

Channels in Paths

Channel ID	A PID	B PID
C1	P1	P2
C2	P2	P3
C3	P2	P3
C4	P2	P3
C5	P1	P3
C6	P1	P5
C7	P3	P3
C8	P3	P3

Table 17.4

Channel 7 on the P3-P3 Path is distinct from Channel 8 on the same Path. There can be as many loops as we like on a single Process, now that Channels are one level removed through the R2 association.

Multiple directed Channels

To model one-way Channels, we just change R1 back to its asymmetric FEEDS DATA TO / CONSUMES DATA FROM form:

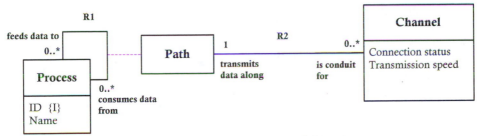

Model 17.5

Data flows in the same direction for all Channels in a Path. But two Paths can be constructed between any two Processors, one in each direction.

Bidirectional Channels

Model 17.5 supports multiple directional Channels. But maybe all we want are bidirectional Channels. Can we constrain our model somehow?

Specifically, we want to capture these rules:

- A Channel is one-way.

- There can be no more than one Channel for each direction of communication between two Processes (or the same Process).

Up to this point, we have handled added constraints and features with slight modifications to a basic model. But clever attribute naming and precise multiplicity expressions get you only so far. We need to think about the problem in a new way.

For example, we could think about Channels as coming in two flavors.

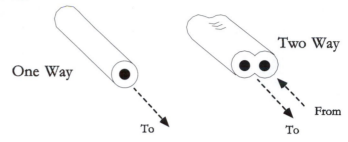

One Way

Two Way

To

From

To

Figure 17.7

Let's model this new concept.

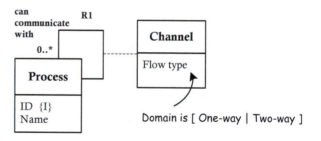

Model 17.6

This model says that between any two Processes (or the same Process) there may be one Channel. The Channel provides either one-way or two-way communication.

Let's see how the following Channel instances:

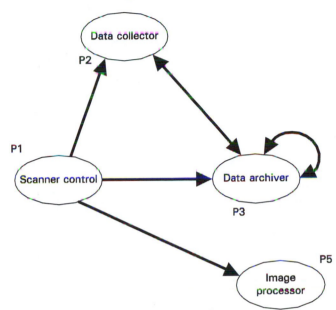

Figure 17.8

appear in a table:

Channels

A PID	B PID	Flow type
P1	P2	One-way
P2	P3	Two-way
P1	P3	One-way
P1	P5	One-way
P3	P3	Two-way

Table 17.5

While this model accommodates the stated rules, it doesn't model the data flow inside a Channel. When we thought about a Channel as being a one-way flow of communication, that wasn't a problem.

Both the data flow and the Channel were pretty much the same thing. But this is not the case with a two-way Channel.

What if you wanted to attach a message to a particular data flow during runtime? And notice that I dropped the Connection_status and Transmission_speed attributes in Model 17.6? That's because in a two-way Channel we need two pairs of values, but in a one-way Channel we need only one pair of values.

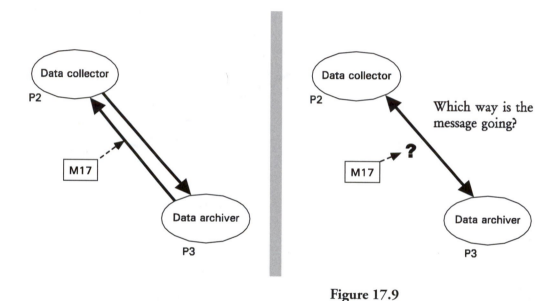

Figure 17.9

Let's see if we can extend our model to handle this situation.

Separating Channel from Data Flow

We need a class that represents communication in a single direction. We will call this class a Data Flow. The connection between two Processes (or the same Process) will still be referred to as a Channel. We want to say that a Channel consists of one or two Data Flows.

This leads us to the following model:

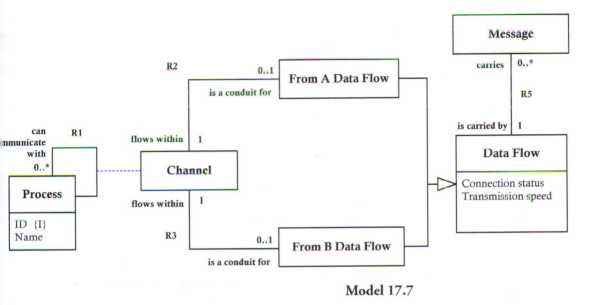

Model 17.7

Specialization by role   You might be uncomfortable seeing From A Data Flow and From B Data Flow as separate classes. After all, each type of Data Flow behaves the same way. I am supposed to be modeling the real-world, not introducing artifacts just to make the model work.

But I am modeling the real-world. The Data Flow subclasses are differentiated by the roles that they play. Positive and negative wires function similarly, but we distinguish them with different words, symbols and colors. I once attached jumper cables backwards to a friend's old BMW car battery (the cable colors or symbols were opposite the US standard). Oops. I think my friend would concur that the role distinctions are critical.

Model 17.7 says that a Channel contains a From A Data Flow, a From B Data Flow, both types, or neither. The Executable UML style generalization relationship gives us the mutual exclusion we need. I picked the names From A/From B for the Data Flow subclasses. You might prefer A Out/B Out, From A/To A, or even Positive/Negative.

Now we are able to associate Messages with Data Flows. And we can even specify which way a Message is going.

Summary

In this chapter we modeled cases where many things connect to many things; nondirectionally, unidirectionally and bidirectionally. The following techniques are helpful to remember:

- Draw tables and fill in instances to verify that you aren't breaking the model formalism (table rules) and to visualize how the abstract model handles tangible instances.

- Draw pictures and think up alternative paradigms (like the two-way channel concept) to transform a difficult modeling problem into a trivial modeling problem. You may not be able to change the application requirements, but you might find a different way to think about the application so that it is easier to model. Informal, nonmodel drawings (like Figure 17.7) are indispensable to this rethinking process.

Important advice about using patterns

There is more to modeling a network than just selecting a self-referential many-to-many association from your repertoire of model patterns. Pattern selection usually amounts to a good start. To develop an adequate model, you need to carefully inventory the application rules and verify that each rule in your list is captured by the model. Your initial pattern will cause you to ask more detailed questions about the application. The answers to these questions will almost always necessitate adjustments to the initial model. At best, you may need to change an attribute name or two. At worst, you may uncover application policies that mandate a serious modeling effort. In either case, this additional effort will add valuable insight into the application.

Chapter 18

Linear patterns

In this chapter we will look at different ways to model linear patterns such as:

- items in a queue

- a list of commands in a script

- a physical sequence of sensors, actuators or the like

- control points in a spline

- a data filter pipeline

All these applications look like they can be handled with a model like this:

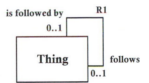

Model 18.1

which is definitely a good place to start. Upon closer examination, you may find that the application requirements require a more sophisticated model. We will model two or three linear patterns as precisely as possible. I plan to demonstrate two things:

1. How thoroughly you can capture rules and exceptions in an class model.

2. It can take many classes and associations to precisely model a simple list!

Example 1: Mission editor in a flight simulator

To start off, I will use an application problem taken from flight simulators on personal computers.[1] The more sophisticated flight simulators give you the capability to preprogram the movement of air and ground units. As you fly your plane around in the flight simulator, you can observe activity in the air and on the ground. Looking at the ground, you might see a bunch of tanks moving in one direction where they will encounter several enemy tanks coming from another direction. Looking ahead, you see a squadron of enemy planes going northeast and then turning south to support the enemy tanks.

To program all this activity, you call up a mission planning editor. Here you can plan routes for various types and quantities of battle units. These routes are laid out on a battlefield that might look like this:

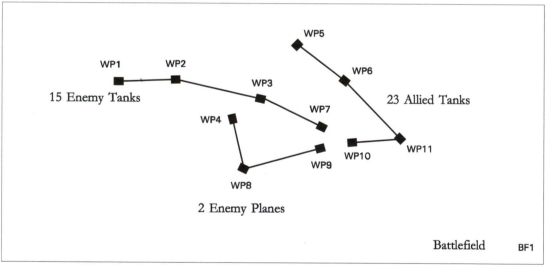

Figure 18.1

In this battlefield, separate converging routes have been planned for a group of 15 enemy tanks, 2 enemy planes and 23 allied tanks.

---

[1] Well, that's one of the reasons this book took so long to write.

A square represents a Waypoint where a new heading is specified. The legs drawn between Waypoints illustrate the movement of the associated battle units. When the game is initiated, the battle units will move along these legs.

Connecting the Waypoints

Let's model the waypoints and the battlefield first:

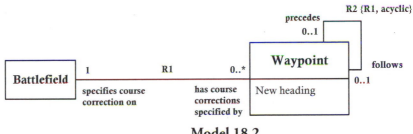

Model 18.2

This model says:

- Zero, one or many Waypoints may be specified on a Battlefield (R1).

- A Waypoint may or may not follow another Waypoint (R2).

- A Waypoint cannot follow itself (R2 {acyclic}).

- One Waypoint can follow another Waypoint only if they are both on the same Battlefield (R2 {R1}).

All these rules agree with our sketch in Figure 18.1. The FOLLOWS association is conditional to allow for the first Waypoint (which does not follow a Waypoint). But this conditionality also makes it possible to specify a completely independent Waypoint. Is that okay? Sure. A tank at a single Waypoint would stay put; a plane at a single Waypoint would maintain a hold pattern.

Adding Battle Units to follow the Waypoints

Now let's add the battle units. We need to know which Waypoints are to be visited by enemy tanks and which are to be visited by allied planes.

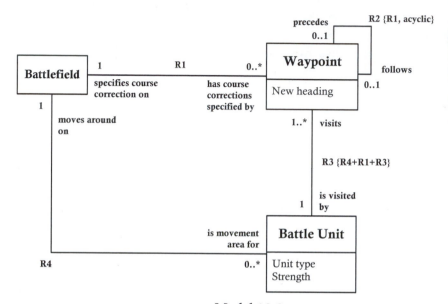

Model 18.3

This model ensures that:

- Every Waypoint is assigned to only one visiting Battle Unit (R3).

- A Battle Unit moves around on exactly one Battlefield (R4).

- A Battle Unit is on the same Battlefield as the Waypoint it visits ({R4+R1+R3} constrains the specified loop).

- A Battle Unit must visit at least one Waypoint (R3).

Unfortunately, no constraint ensures that a Battle Unit visits a contiguous sequence of Waypoints (a route).

Model 18.3 would allow the specification of a Battle Unit that jumps between unconnected Waypoints like this:

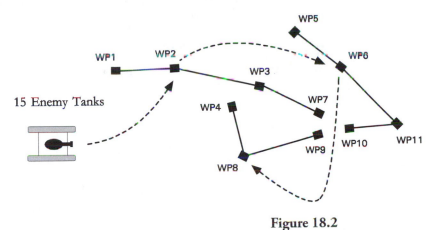

Figure 18.2

And that's definitely not what we want.

One way to constrain units to follow a route is to replace the VISITS 1:1..* association with a STARTS AT 1:0..1 association:

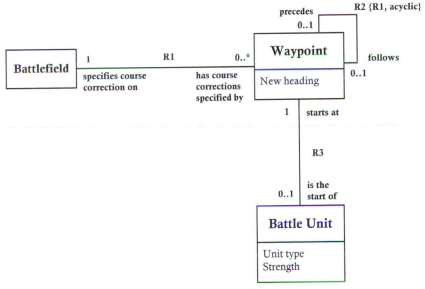

Model 18.4

By referencing only the point where the Battle Unit starts, association R2 can be accessed to find all the other Waypoints on the route. There is less to specify and, consequently, less potential for mis-specification.

If we assume that a Battle Unit cannot be specified until its starting Waypoint is created, we can dispense with association R4 from Model 18.3.

Unfortunately, Model 18.4 allows a Battle Unit to start somewhere in the middle of a route, like so:

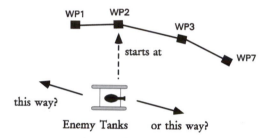

Figure 18.3

This is not good. A Battle Unit always starts at one end of a route and follows it all the way to the other end. We need to know the order in which all the Waypoints will be visited within a route.

Adding the Route class

We are getting into trouble because we have overlooked a critical class, Route. It should serve as a clue that a class is missing when a word central to the problem statement doesn't make its way into the model.

A Route is a connected sequence of Waypoints like this:

Figure 18.4

We want a Battle Unit to always move within a Route, so it makes sense to relate the Battle Unit class to the Route class instead of to the individual Waypoints. The Route class has other uses. We might want the ability, for example, to move and resize a Route, rather than moving all the Waypoints individually. Maybe we would even like to keep a library of Routes that can be loaded up like templates when planning a Battlefield mission. Actually, the best reason for modeling a Route may simply be that it exists.

The Route class is added to our class diagram below:

```
                    ┌──────────────────┐
                    │   Battlefield    │
                    └──────────────────┘
                         │
              1          │  specifies
                         │  movement of
                         │  ground units on
              R3         │
                         │
              0..*       │  has units that
                         │  move along
```

Model 18.5

A Battle Unit is assigned to an entire Route, but there is a problem with the definition of Route.

Those unsightly gaps between Waypoints

We would like to define Route as a completely connected set of one or more Waypoints. But since the FOLLOWS (R2) association is conditional, an unconnected Route like this could be specified:

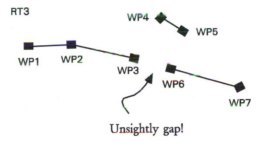

Figure 18.5

which we don't want.

Closed Routes — another dead end

We could try making the FOLLOWS (R2) association unconditional,

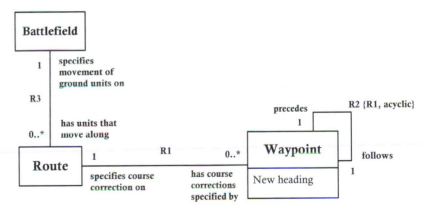

Model 18.6

but then all our Routes would have to be closed, like this:

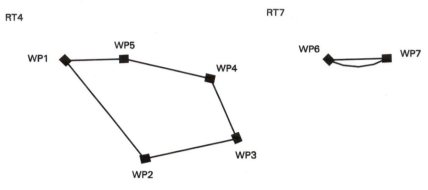

Figure 18.6

since every Waypoint would have to follow another Waypoint. Furthermore, the unconditionality of R2 would require that every Route contain at least two Waypoints: a starting Waypoint with a now mandatory following Waypoint, which cannot be the same Waypoint.

This is another example where twiddling the knobs and dials on the model takes us only so far. We need to stop model hacking and take another look at the problem.

Taking another look   Why is such a simple structure so difficult to model? Because the associations among Waypoints in Route are not so simple. Here are some observations.

Observations about Waypoints in a Route

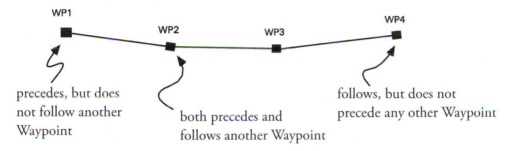

Figure 18.7

The way one Waypoint relates to another depends on whether a Waypoint is the start, middle or end of a Route. Specialization should make it possible to differentiate these roles.

Specializing by position

Here is a proposed specialization with the observed associations sketched informally.

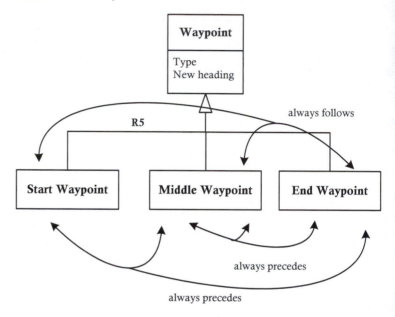

Model 18.7

We want to model the fact that a Start Waypoint must precede either a Middle Waypoint or an End Waypoint. A Middle Waypoint must precede either another Middle Waypoint or an End Waypoint, and so on. It is difficult to formalize the associations due to all this "either" stuff. We need more certainty. We need to be using the word "always".

Specialization by referencing role

Note that both Start and Middle Waypoints always PRECEDE and that both Middle and End Waypoints always FOLLOW. So maybe this is a better specialization.

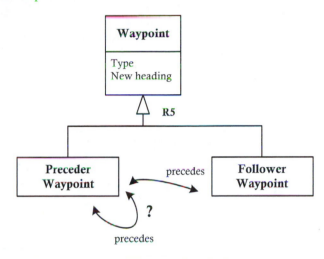

Model 18.8

Specialization both ways

A Start Waypoint is always a Preceder. Good. An End Waypoint is always a follower. Good. A Middle Waypoint is both. Bad. But it is always both. Good!

Check this out.

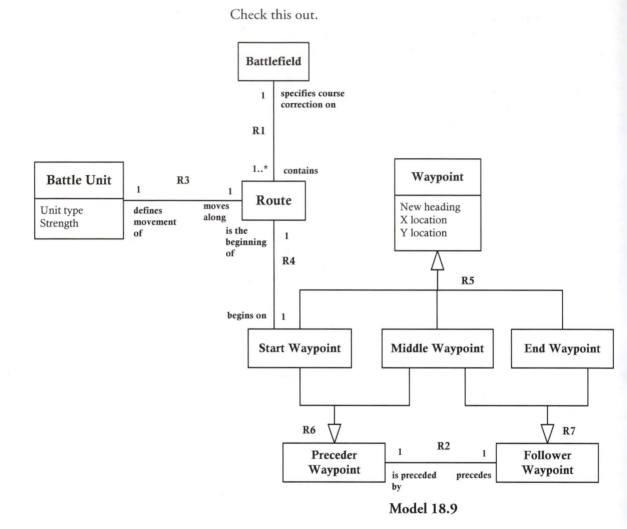

Model 18.9

Model 18.9 says that every Waypoint is a Start, Middle or End Waypoint. Furthermore, each Start and Middle Waypoint PRECEDES a non-Start Waypoint. Non-Start Waypoint is synonymous with Follower Waypoint. Conversely, every Middle and End Waypoint IS PRECEDED BY a Non-End Waypoint (Preceder Waypoint). Notice that each Middle Waypoint serves both as a Preceder and as a Follower Waypoint.

Model 18.9 also addresses the problem of Route direction discussed earlier. A Route begins at a Start Waypoint. All the other Waypoints are related to a Route through relationships R6, R7 and R2.

It may be interesting to note that the self-referencing linear pattern in our application is now captured with a collection of nonreflexive associations.

Does this interweaving of relationships look suspicious? It might seem that generalization overlapping like this breaks the relational table formalism. So let's test it by trying to stuff this Route:

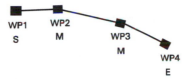

Figure 18.8

into these tables:

Waypoint

WP1
WP2
WP3
WP4

Start Waypoint	Middle Waypoint	End Waypoint
WP1	WP2	WP4
	WP3	

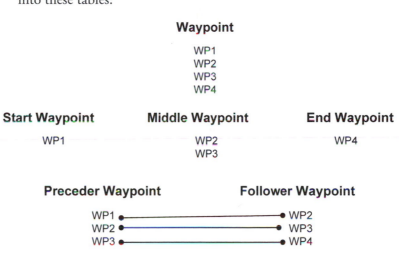

Figure 18.9

Figure 18.9 demonstrates that Model 18.9 specifies a legitimate set of relational tables that can be populated by an example Route. Two questions remain:

1. Is it possible to enter illegal/malformed Routes into the tables?

2. Can we handle all the legal boundary conditions?

Let's address these questions in order.

Precluding malformed Routes

It would be nice if the following malformed routes were impossible to specify in our class model.

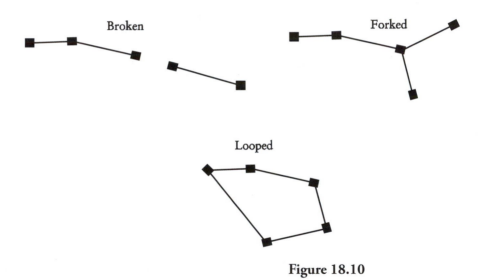

Figure 18.10

Forks are impossible because there are no one-to-many associations in our model. Broken routes can't be specified because the PRECEDES association is unconditional. But what about the loop? Loops are

not possible, again, because the PRECEDES (R2) association is unconditional. In fact, this

WP1   WP2
S   E

is the smallest legal Route. When a Waypoint is appended after
WP2, WP2 changes into a Middle Waypoint, so the new Waypoint
can be instantiated as an End Waypoint.

**The boundary
condition — minimal
Route**

This brings us to our second question, boundary conditions. It is
impossible to have a Route with zero Waypoints since R4 is unconditional. But it should be possible to specify a single Waypoint
Route:

WP1
S

Unfortunately, this case is illegal in Model 18.9. This minimal case
will come in handy when we draw the first Waypoint of a Route!
But how can we change the model to allow a single Waypoint in a
Route? We can't make the PRECEDES (R2) association conditional
because that would permit broken Routes and a few other bad
things.

**The solution — adding
a special case for the
Start Waypoint**

A single Waypoint might be classified as a Start Waypoint since it
represents the beginning of a Route. But a single Waypoint is not a
Preceder Waypoint (yet).

We could create a special kind of Start Waypoint through specialization, as shown.

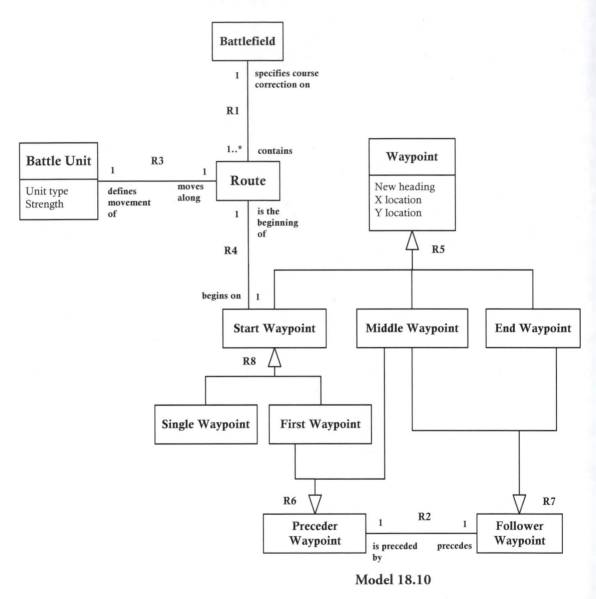

Model 18.10

Now we have two kinds of Start Waypoints — one that precedes and one that doesn't. Lesson: Putting a 0 in a multiplicity expression is only one way to express a conditional fact. In fact, throughout this exercise we have handled a problem replete with exceptions without the need for a single 0!

Mission editor summary

So what are the important things to remember?

- You can model a sequence of points relationally.

- Even with a simple linear pattern, there can be a lot of rules to capture.

- If you capture these rules in a class model, it may take a lot of classes and associations to get it right.

- A simple 1:1 or 0..1:0..1 reflexive association may not suffice for every linear pattern.

- Overlapping generalizations can really come in handy.

Which linear pattern model should you use?

Model 18.10 is a more comprehensive statement of the mission editor application rules than any of its predecessors. But do we really want to use it? Good question. Models 18.9, 18.5 and 18.4 capture progressively less of the application, but they are simpler.

The less rules in the class model — the more complex the state model

Any of these models can be made to work, but the number of application rules remains constant. So the less sophisticated the class model is, the more rules you must enforce in the state and procedure models. Procedures are more difficult to debug and prove reliable than class model structures. Since the mission editor is an interactive game, a full set of edit operations must be supported. Consequently, the choice of Model 18.4 would leave quite a few actions and exceptions to be specified. So I would probably go whole hog and use Model 18.9 or 18.10 (especially since I don't have to build them from scratch — I can just pull them out of my pattern library).

But let's say we were building a flight simulator that did not provide mission editing capabilities. Instead, the developers would supply a library of selectable missions. In that case, I would probably go with Model 18.4. Why? Because I would leave it up to the developers to make sure that they entered correct application data into the Battle Unit and Waypoint classes. Since the state and procedure models wouldn't enforce the entry of correct Routes, they wouldn't become complex.

Expose detailed policies as soon as possible

Visibility of application policy is another criteria. Model 18.10 exposes all the ugliness of the mission editor, so we see the full complexity of the application up front. This early exposure may inspire the analysts and the application experts to simplify or reinvent the application so it becomes less complex.

Example 2: Polyline draw tool in an illustration program

Maybe you think the mission editor model could have been simpler if we had taken a different approach. Would the final model have been more straightforward if we tried to model a list of segments instead of a list of points? Let's find out!

In the mission editor exercise, we found that a linear structure looks nonthreatening at a distance, but gets ugly when you grab it by the ears. This is because, relationship-wise, a linear pattern exhibits subtle complexity that you just don't appreciate until you get up close.

But sometimes a model is inordinately complex because you aren't thinking about it the right way. By recasting a problem's conceptual model you might end up with a less complex and more intuitive class model.

We modeled a sequence of Waypoints as connected vertices:

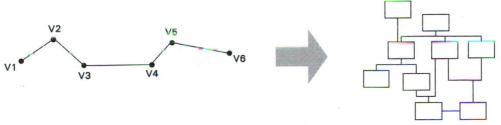

Figure 18.11

Would we get a less complex class model if we modeled a series of segments instead?:

Figure 18.12

For the mission planning editor application, the answer is no. This is because a single Waypoint was allowed, and a single Waypoint can't be modeled as a segment.

But a segment approach might work for the following problem. Consider a tool in an illustration program that can draw a polyline like this:

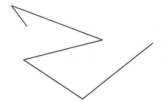

The smallest polyline possible consists of a single segment:

If someone starts to draw a line and doesn't finish

Second point is not created

then the initial point is deleted and nothing is drawn.

Let's start with this model:

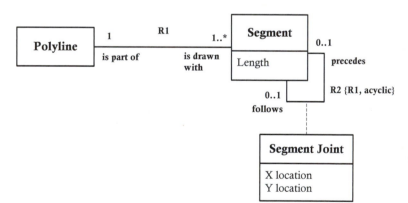

Model 18.11

This model says that:

• A Segment has length (Segment.Length).

- One Segment can be connected to another Segment within the same Polyline (R2 {R1}).

- The joint between two Segments is formed at an x,y location (Segment Joint.X,Y location).

- A Polyline must contain at least one Segment (R1).

- A Segment may not be joined to itself (R2 {acyclic}).

But as you can see, making the x,y location attributes of the Segment Joint class leaves us without the start and end locations of a Polyline, as shown.

The position of Segment S2 is specified, but...

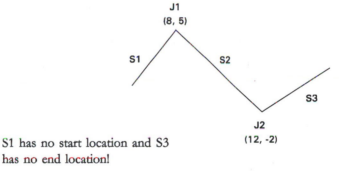

S1 has no start location and S3 has no end location!

Figure 18.13

Worse yet, if you have only one Segment, then there can be no Segment Joint and, consequently, no x,y locations at all!

We can fix this problem by attributing a start and end coordinate position to Segment instead.

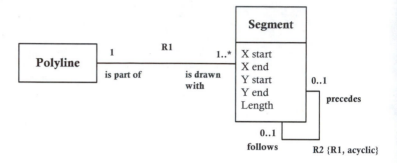

Model 18.12

Now we have a sequence of Segments with start and end points that is pretty good. Ideally, however, we would like to guarantee that the end x,y coordinate of one Segment coincides with the start x,y coordinate of the next Segment.

As it stands, Model 18.12 would allow specification of this set of supposedly connected Segments:

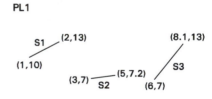

Figure 18.14

Fortunately, we can make the X,Y locations identifiers force the Segments to touch each other:

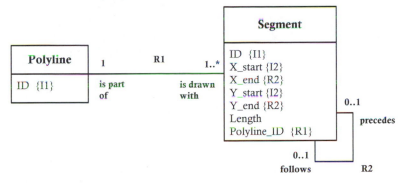

Model 18.13

We can now use the X,Y Start of the next segment as the X,Y End of the current Segment. The drawback to this approach is that the following case becomes illegal:

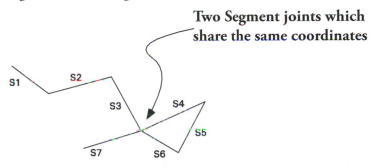

Figure 18.15

because you would end up with duplicate identifier values.

We just have to face it, there is no way to connect the end points of a Segment without modeling them as independent classes.

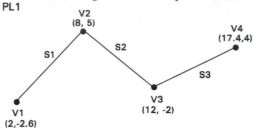

Figure 18.16

This leads us back to casting the problem as connected Vertices instead of connected Segments, as we did with the mission editor solution (Model 18.9, with a few of the names changed).

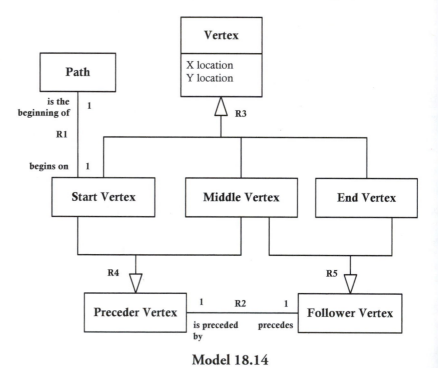

Model 18.14

We didn't use Model 18.10 because it permitted the existence of a lone Waypoint. A minimum of two Vertices is required in the Polyline application.

Conclusion   The original plan of modeling a Polyline as an association between Segments didn't get us too far. A better model was produced by modeling a Polyline as an association between Vertices. Consequently, the same pattern that worked in the mission editor application also works here.

Summary

As you can see, linear patterns are more constrained than network patterns. It is important to study the rules of your application and ensure that they are precisely captured and exposed in your model.

Chapter 19

Tree patterns

So how exactly do you model a tree or hierarchical pattern with Executable UML? This chapter explores an application that requires the analysis of a tree pattern. We are going to start off with a simple (one class, one association) class model. Then, step by step, we will identify limitations and devise improvements until we end up with a sophisticated class model that does a better job of capturing our application requirements. Even if you aren't especially interested in hierarchical structures, this modeling process will address more pragmatic modeling issues such as:

- the degree to which application rules can be expressed in a class model

- the degree to which application rules should be expressed in a class model

just as we did in the previous chapter.

Sound good? Great. Let's get to work! As always, we start off with a few words about our example application.

APPLICATION NOTE

The purpose of this application is to track a variety of automobile parts (engines, pistons, doors, door handles, etc.) stored in a warehouse. The warehouse is owned and supplied by the AutoWare car company. The warehouse must service orders placed by mechanics and auto parts stores.

When there is a shortage of parts of a certain type, it may be necessary to obtain those parts by pulling them out of some other assembly. A door, for example, might be taken apart so that an order for a window crank can be filled.

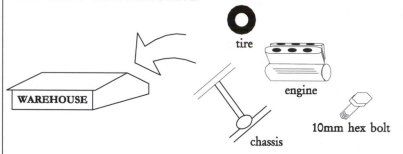

Not all the parts in the warehouse are manufactured by AutoWare. Some parts (usually things like bolts, gaskets, etc.) are bought from outside sources. These are stocked and shipped just like AutoWare parts. The only difference is that outside supplied parts are never disassembled.

For inventory and material control reasons, it is necessary to maintain a complete database of parts and part assemblies. It is not enough to know that an engine is in stock. It may be necessary to generate a complete list of all components in the engine, down to the piston rings and bolts.

A simple tree

A simple tree of parts

Here is an easy way to model the contents of the AutoWare warehouse:

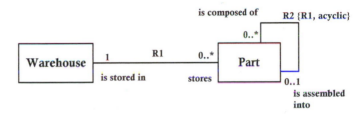

Model 19.1

Association R2 is a 0..1:0..* reflexive association that organizes Parts into an assembly hierarchy.

This model says:

- A Part is always in a Warehouse (R1).

- A Part may be assembled from other Parts (R2).

    A bolt would be an example of a Part with no subparts.

- All of the Parts in an assembly are in the same Warehouse (R2 {R1}).

- A Part cannot be assembled into itself (R2 {acyclic}).

- A Part may be assembled into one other Part (R2).

    This assumes that R2 really means "is a direct subassembly of," in which case the rule that "a Part can be built directly into no more than one other Part" is plausible. (This just highlights the importance of writing good relationship descriptions — See Chapter 14.)

    What about the conditional case? A door is an example of a Part that is not assembled into any other Part (assuming that it is intended to be shipped as a distinct unit). A spare bolt is also an example of a Part that is not built into anything.

- A Warehouse contains a bunch of Parts (R1).

  But it could be empty.

There is one application rule that Model 19.1 does not address. This becomes apparent when we consider specific instances of the Warehouse and Part classes.

Problem: Part storage is sloppy

Let's say that Part B is assembled into Part A. Obviously, if Part A is in Warehouse 3, then Part B must also be in Warehouse 3. But our simple model would let you say that Parts A and B are in different Warehouses! Or, put another way, Model 19.1 requires that you specify the Warehouse where each Part is located.

This is what our Parts tree looks like with Model 19.1:

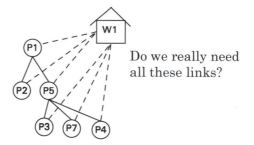

Do we really need all these links?

Figure 19.1

Figure 19.1 contains lots of superfluous links (dashed lines). We would prefer a model that (1) lets us specify the Warehouse containing a complete assembly and (2) forces us to infer that the constituent Parts are in the same location (a better reflection of reality).

A tree with a root

A glance at Figure 19.1 suggests that we should relate Warehouse W1 to Part P1. To model this situation, we need to distinguish a complete assembly (the top of the tree) from an installed Part (the rest of the tree). Here is the idea.

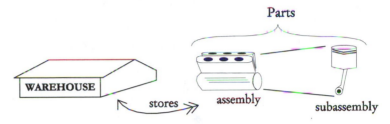

Figure 19.2

Then we can say that a complete Assembly is stored in a Warehouse and simply assume that the Parts built into the Assembly are at the same place.

Only Assemblies are stored

Here is the improved model.

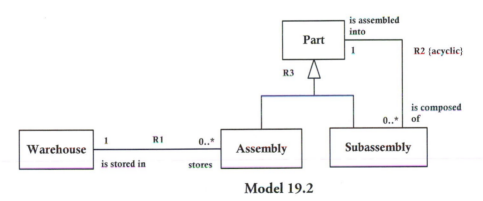

Model 19.2

To figure out where a Subassembly is stored, using Model 19.2 you must first find the encompassing Assembly using R2. This procedure eliminates the need to specify a link for every Part instance. Model 19.2 also precludes the possibility of specifying the physically impossible situation where an instance of Subassembly is stored in a Warehouse other than the one that stores the encompassing Assembly.

Here are the specific rules enforced in Model 19.2:

- A Part is either an Assembly or a Subassembly (R3).

- A Subassembly is *always* built into a Part that is either an Assembly or another Subassembly (R2).

- An Assembly, which is a Part, may or may not be built up from Subassemblies (this rule is given by the relationships R3➔R2).

- A Warehouse stores zero, one or many Assemblies.

- A Part still cannot be a Subassembly of itself. Up until now, the acyclic constraint has only been applied to reflexive associations. R2 isn't technically reflexive since it spans two classes. On the other hand, a Part is a Part. In fact, the OCL for this acyclic constraint will be written differently since a generalization association is involved. But it's the same idea.

There are two reasons why Association R2 is conditional on the many side: (1) A Part may be the lowest level Subassembly in an Assembly. (2) An Assembly may consist of only one Part and, thus, require no Subassemblies — a spare hubcap, for example.

Model 19.2 and Figure 19.2 are an elaboration of Model 19.1 and Figure 19.1. The specialization of Part made it possible to single out Assembly for Warehouse storage and Subassemblies for building a Part hierarchy. By abstracting the Assembly class and pulling it out of the version of R2 in Model 19.1, we are assured that an Assembly is always at the top of any Part hierarchy.

If we populate Model 19.2 with the instances from Figure 19.1, our Parts tree now looks like this:

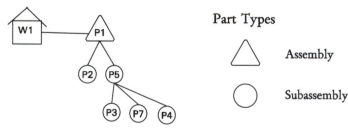

Figure 19.3

Model 19.2 is a definite improvement on Model 19.1, but it doesn't treat Parts that come from outside suppliers any different than proprietary Parts. Does that matter? According to the application note, non-AutoWare Parts are handled differently in at least two ways: (1) we have no visibility into the internal structure of a supplied part, and (2) supplied parts are supplied by a vendor.

A tree with leaves

Vendor supplied parts

First let's take a look at a typical vendor supplied Part. A rubber seal, for example:

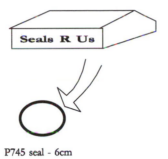

P745 seal - 6cm

Figure 19.4

For these kinds of Parts, we need to know the supplier/vendor information. Furthermore, we don't ever care about the components of a vendor supplied Part, even if it happens to be a complex assembly, because we would never disassemble and repackage it. Consequently, a supplied Part is never assembled from Subassemblies. The generalization of Model 19.2 does not handle this case. How do we fix it?

We could extend our specialization as shown:

Model 19.3

but how does the IS COMPOSED OF Parts association (R2) fit in? Remember that we want to prevent a Supplied Part (or any type of Part for that matter) from being built into another Supplied Part.

To solve this problem I found it helpful to stare at some real examples instead of those tedious rectangles and connectors. So I drew several sketches. Here's one.

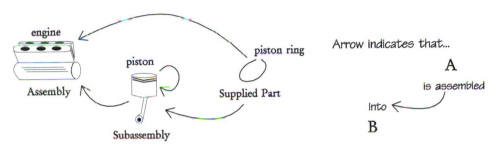

Figure 19.5

Stealing and adapting the linear pattern

Figure 19.5 shows that there is a reflexive association on Subassembly only. This looks a lot like the reflexive association sketched on Model 18.8. It's so similar, in fact, that I stole the whole linear pattern and adapted it to our hierarchical structure, like this:

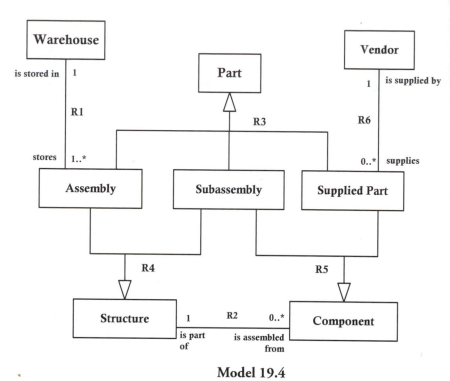

Model 19.4

You can see that the specialization of Structure and Component in Model 19.4 is analogous to the specialization of Preceder and Follower in Model 18.9. Also notice that, while the FOLLOWS association in the linear pattern is 1:1, the IS ASSEMBLED FROM association in Model 19.4 is 1:0..*. It makes sense that the only difference between a linear pattern and a tree pattern would be a change in the multiplicity of R2 from one to many. But is there some reason why our AutoWare application is conditional on R2 while the corresponding association in Model 18.9 is unconditional?

A review of parts vocabulary

Whether R2 should be conditional depends on our class definitions. Let's review them:

Assembly: A kit or fully built unit that is stored awaiting a shipping order. An engine would be an example of an Assembly if it was packaged as a kit or as a complete unit for sale. An engine built into a car, on the other hand, would be classified as a Subassembly.

Subassembly: A unit that is currently built into either an Assembly or a Subassembly. A piston Subassembly might be built into an engine Assembly, for example. If someone orders a piston individually and none is available as an Assembly, we might scavenge one from an engine, reclassify it as an Assembly and then ship it.

Supplied Part: A Part that a vendor has supplied. It has no internal structure as far as we are concerned.

Okay, now let's review some of the more interesting rules established in Model 19.4.

- Part is an Assembly, Subassembly or a Supplied Part.

- Assemblies and Subassemblies are Structures.

- Subassemblies and Supplied Parts are Components.

- A Component is always assembled into a Structure.

- A Structure is built up from zero, one or many Components (again, we allow for the case when we have a one-piece Assembly with no lower-level Components).

Let's populate our model with some example instances.

Part Types

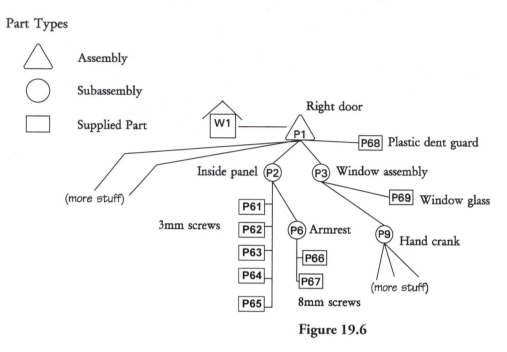

Figure 19.6

Figure 19.6 illustrates how we differentiate the root, leaves and intermediate nodes of our Parts tree. Our model accommodates the "Right door" example just fine.

Boundary cases We have at least two boundary cases to consider. First, can we handle an Assembly like "hubcap" that consists of only one Part?

Yes. Since R2 is conditional, we can define an Assembly that contains no lower level Parts.

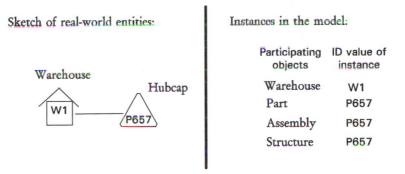

Figure 19.7

Second, can we handle a Supplied Part that is not assembled into anything? AutoWare might buy a bolt from Bolt Barn that we simply resell as a spare part. Do we classify the bolt as an Assembly or a Component? We can make it an Assembly with no Components. Since R2 is conditional, that is no problem. Unfortunately, Model 19.4 wouldn't prevent me from saying that a Supplied Part, an engine let's say, was broken down into Components. But that violates the application requirement that says we don't ever break down Supplied Components. The easiest solution might be to convince the application experts that this is a stupid requirement, but for the purposes of this exercise, let's say that we are stuck with the requirement. In that case, it would be nice to make Model 19.4 a little more bulletproof. Before doing that, can we just classify the bolt as a Component? We would have to change R2 to make it conditional on both sides, since Model 19.4 says that every Component must be built into a Structure.

The danger of diluting class meanings

Wait a minute — a Component that is *not* built into a Structure? And a Structure that is not made up of Components? Aren't we corrupting the whole idea of Structure and Component?

If we loosen up our semantic foundations, we are opening ourselves up to strange situations. We could end up with a Subassembly that isn't stored in a Warehouse.

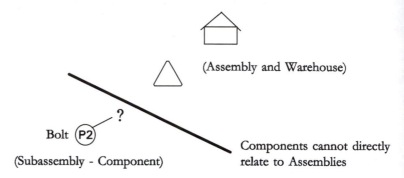

(Assembly and Warehouse)

Bolt (P2)

(Subassembly - Component)

Components cannot directly relate to Assemblies

Figure 19.8

Better semantics

We can increase the semantic integrity of our model by making R2 unconditional on both sides. To accommodate spare and supplied Parts, we need to change the way we specialize the leaves of our Parts tree. Here is one approach.

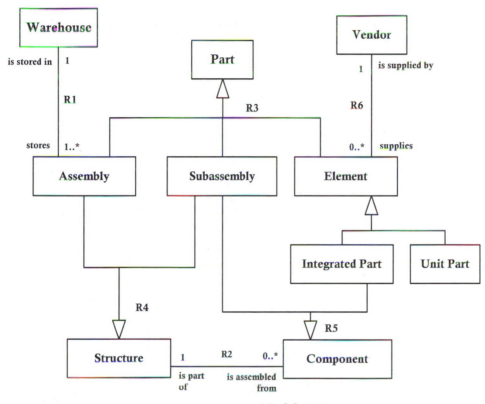

Model 19.5

The Supplied Part class from Model 19.4 has been replaced by the Element class in Model 19.5. An Element is a Part that cannot be broken down (by AutoWare) into subcomponents. This makes the specialization on R3 more homogenous. Each subclass represents a level of assembly. Just because a part is at the bottom level of assembly doesn't necessarily mean that it is vendor supplied. AutoWare might stamp a special type of brace or hinge out of sheet metal, which can't be broken down.

When is and when isn't a Part in an Assembly?

To ensure that all elements clearly fall into one or the other of its subclasses, I chose the names Integrated and Unit Part. Unit Part takes the place of what I've been referring to as a spare part. In other words, an Element is either a Part that is integrated into the bottom level of an Assembly or it is a totally separate unit that cannot be further broken down.

What does a Warehouse really store?

There is one problem, however. We managed to leave Unit Parts completely out of the Warehouse! A Unit Part is an Element that is not a Component. We say that a Warehouse stores Assemblies, but a Unit Part is not integrated into an Assembly. We would like to draw another association between Warehouse and Unit Part, but having two such associations leads to a loop requiring some ungainly constraints. No, what we really need to do is redefine what exactly it is that a Warehouse stores.

Let's focus on the kinds of things that the Warehouse can ship and draw another sketch.

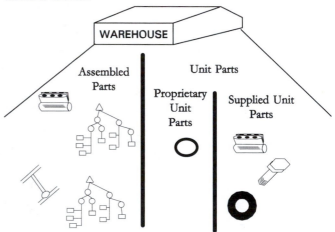

Figure 19.9

The nice thing about this sketch is that it both identifies all items that a Warehouse contains and it designates those classes that must have a direct relationship to the Warehouse class.

Now let's take the perspective of a Vendor.

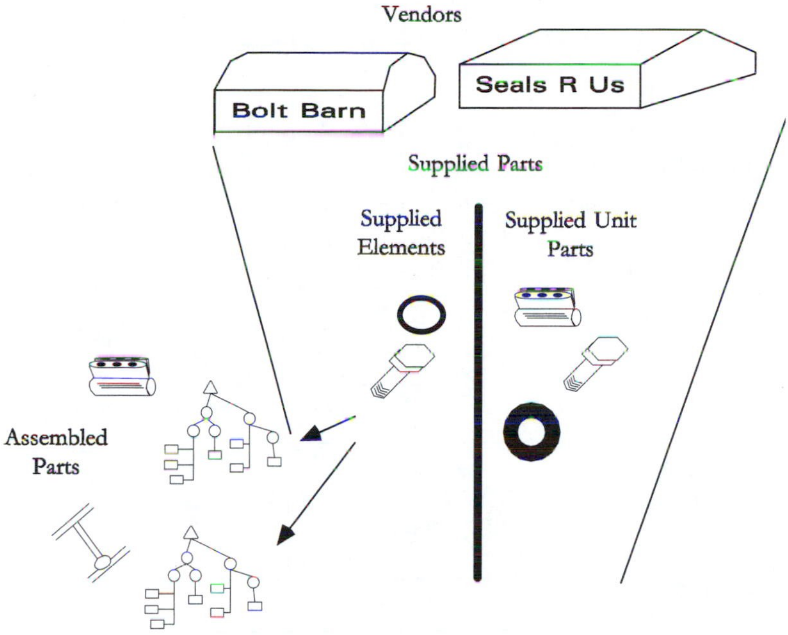

Figure 19.10

With the sketch in Figure 19.10, we establish that every vendor supplied Part is either an Element integrated into an AutoWare Assembly or a separately sold unit.

The finished product   Putting it all together we end up with this model.

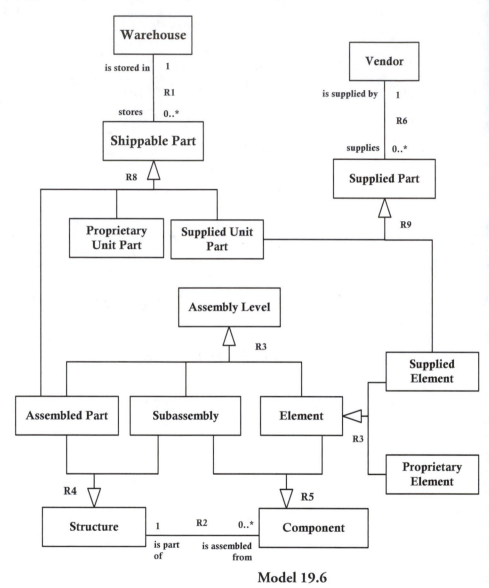

Model 19.6

So what?   After looking at Model 19.6, your first thought might be, "Why are there so many classes?" or maybe, "Geez — there are a lot of subclasses!" Hold that thought for a moment while we consider some of the application rules integrated into our latest model.

- An Element is either supplied or proprietary.

- A Shippable Part is either fully assembled or it is a Proprietary or Supplied Unit Part.

- A minimal Assembled Part consists of at least two Assembly levels: the top of the parts tree (Assembled Part) and the bottom (Element).

The nice thing about Model 19.6 is that it captures so many application rules — not in algorithms, not in procedures, but directly in the class structure. The state and procedure models built on Model 19.6 will have to handle fewer exceptions than those that would be built on our earlier class model versions.

How much modeling is too much?

So what's the best choice, Model 19.1 or Model 19.6? Working with nothing more than the application description at the beginning of this chapter, there is no way to tell. I can say with certainty that Model 19.6 captures the application rules more thoroughly and precisely than Model 19.1. I can also say that the state and procedure models built on Model 19.6 will be much less complex than those built on Model 19.1. Beyond that, you must consider your current degree of modeling skill and the needs of the project to make a good decision. Here are some things to consider:

- How important is it to verify that the informal application description is accurate? The author of Model 19.6 has a much better understanding of the application than someone who stops at Model 19.1.

- Have you solved a similar problem before? Is there an existing class model pattern that you can borrow and adapt? If so, it won't take long to knock out Model 19.6, so you might as well do it.

- To what degree has the rest of the application (neighboring subsystems) been modeled? Maybe you should build Model 19.1, model the neighboring subsystems, and then come back to Model 19.1 and extend it later. With the context of the rest of the application established, you may realize that Model 19.1 isn't so important in early versions or releases of the system that you are building. Then again, you may find that the subject matter covered by Model 19.1 is more central than you thought, leading you to build Model 19.6.

- If you lack Executable UML modeling skill, it may take a considerable amount of time to produce Model 19.6. Are you more concerned about finishing the class modeling, even at the risk of missing some important issues, or are you more concerned about developing modeling skill? At the point of diminishing returns you have to move on.

- How much time do you have? That's easy — not enough! In my experience, a decision to skimp on the class model so that you can quickly get to the state and procedure models is usually a bad decision when it comes to saving time.

Make a decision, move on and learn from it

Having considered these factors, don't feel bad if you still aren't sure which approach is best. My advice is this: just make a decision — right or wrong — and forge ahead. What's the worst that can happen? If you build Model 19.1 and it turns out to be a mistake, you will find out somewhere in the middle of the state and procedure models. If the state models seem excessively complex because they handle too many application-related special cases and weird exceptions, then go back and fix the class model! On the other hand, if you build Model 19.6 and it turns out that the state and procedure models are too awkward because they perform a lot of overhead functions (managing unnecessary class and relationship instances) that have little to do with the application policies, then go back and simplify the class model. Ultimately, that's the only way to learn how thorough you should be when you build class models.

Summary

In this chapter we modeled a tree pattern in an auto parts inventory application. We started out with a quick and dirty solution. This model was successively improved as we integrated more of the application requirements and exposed our model's limitations. We could see similarities between our tree model and the linear graph model we produced in Chapter 18. We finally arrived at a strong and extendable model that captured all the stated requirements.

Where to learn more

As of this writing, Executable UML is a relatively new thing. The underlying technology (definitions, time interpretation rules, semantics, action language) that now makes UML executable and, hence, translatable began evolving in 1984. In fact, the UML notation itself is the only new kid in town. Many of us have been executing object-oriented models and translating them into embedded code since the first model compilers were developed back in 1991 — and even before that to 1984 when you consider the projects where we translated the models by hand.

Since the debut of UML 1.0 in 1997, more and more companies have begun promoting the use of Executable UML models and the generation of code from UML models. You can verify this for yourself by attending one of the conferences listed under "Conferences" on page 393.

Until early or mid-2002, unfortunately, there will be no comprehensive text available that explains the complete Executable UML profile. (Welcome to the leading edge!)[1] Existing resources focus on specific topics. To help you make sense of which resources might be relevant to your interests, I will identify the key topics and then classify the resources accordingly.

Key topics

UML notation There are about a million resources showing you how to draw the UML symbols. I'm sure you'll have no trouble finding them.

---

[1] When I started learning C and Unix in 1979, all I could find was one thin book with a big blue C on it and a binder full of man pages. And with no C debugger in existence, the only diagnostic error I could get was "a.out - core dumped". But I don't regret getting the head start on everyone. By the time there are tons of Executable UML resources available you'll no doubt be on to the next big leap in technology!

Executable semantics
The definitions and timing rules that make UML executable were originally defined in the Shlaer-Mellor method. Many of these resources still use the old Shlaer-Mellor notation. They are all being updated with the UML notation. You can wait for these updates or, if you like to stay ahead of the game, just pick up the Shlaer-Mellor books, mentally superimpose the UML notation, and focus on the important part — the executable semantics.

Model entry/editing tools
Many tools allow you to draw UML symbols. There are only a few tools as of this writing that support Executable UML. Such tools interpret the executable content of your drawings. They check your syntax and provide a simulation environment where you can run and debug your models. Your model specifications are stored in a repository where they can be extracted by a model compiler.

Model compilers
A model compiler converts an executable specification into running code. Good model compilers allow you to supply deployment and performance coloring so that the compiler can generate efficient code and allocate it to separate implementation units (processors, tasks, etc.). Really good model compilers open the translation process so your development team can change the compilation rules as best fits your project.

Books and Papers

Executable UML: The Models are the Code
This is the book you want. This book (to be published mid-2002) provides a complete description of the Executable UML language. Steve Mellor, Marc Balcer, Addison-Wesley, 2002, ISBN 0201748045.

Executable UML: A Case Study
A complete set of fully documented models that you can run on your computer. This book includes class, state and procedure models. The featured case study is an elevator control application. This book ships with a trial version of the BridgePoint model devel-

opment environment and a sample model compiler. Leon Starr, Model Integration, LLC., 2001, ISBN 0970804407.

Shlaer-Mellor texts

While you're waiting for Steve Mellor's book to be published, here are some books which describe the executable semantics that form the foundation of Executable UML. They use Shlaer-Mellor notation, but many of the concepts are still relevant.

Object Lifecycles — Modeling the World in States

This book and its supplement (OOA 96 Report, below) define the executable semantics used in the elevator model. Emphasis is on state models, event delivery and time rules. Sally Shlaer, Steve Mellor, Prentice Hall, 1992, ISBN 0136299407.

Object-Oriented Systems Analysis — Modeling the World in Data

This book provides the set theory foundations for thinking about class models in an executable way. Sally Shlaer, Steve Mellor, Prentice Hall, 1988, ISBN 013629023X.

OOA 96 Report

This is a white paper you can download for free from www.projtech.com. It adds supplemental chapters to the two Shlaer-Mellor books listed above.

Courses and Consulting

Executable UML for Real-Time, Embedded Systems

Absolutely the best course on the topic! Leon's company, Model Integration, offers a 1-2 day introductory version as well as a full week intensive course.

Model Integration, LLC.

www.modelint.com

We offer expert training and consulting in the application of Executable UML to real-time and embedded systems development.

Contact us! **info@modelint.com**

Companies

These companies sell Executable UML development environments and model compilers.

Project Technology, Inc.

www.projtech.com

Lots of information on their website — papers, conferences, training, etc.

Kennedy-Carter, Ltd.

www.kc.com

Also lots of information — papers, conferences, training, etc.

Kabira Technologies, Inc.

www.kabira.com

Focused on e-commerce technology, Java, Corba, that sort of thing.

Pathfinder Solutions   *www.pathfindersol.com*

Tools, consulting, training

Rox Software   *www.roxsoftware.com*

They sell an excellent embedded systems model compiler that generates tight C for 8 and 16 bit CPUs without the overhead of a commercial operating system!

Conferences

Executable UML Conference   www.projtech.com — Small, but focused on the Executable UML technology. Getting bigger every year!

Embedded Systems Conference   www.esconline.com — If you are in the industry, you already know about this one. Most of the companies I listed have booths at this show.

Bibliography

Executable UML

Executable UML: The Models Are the Code	Steve Mellor and Marc Balcer, Addison-Wesley, 2002, ISBN 0201748045
Executable UML: A Case Study	Leon Starr, Model Integration, LLC., 2001, ISBN 0970804407

UML

OMG Unified Modeling Language Specification	Object Management Group, Version 1.4 draft, 2001, www.omg.org
The Unified Modeling Language User Guide	Grady Booch, James Rumbaugh and Ivar Jacobson, Addison-Wesley, 1999, ISBN 0201571684
The Unified Modeling Language Reference Manual	Grady Booch, James Rumbaugh and Ivar Jacobson, Addison-Wesley, 1999, ISBN 020130998X
Instant UML	Pierre-Alain Muller, Wrox Press, 1997, ISBN 1861000871
UML Distilled	Martin Fowler, Addison-Wesley, 1997, ISBN 0201325632
The Object Constraint Language	Jos Warmer and Anneke Kleppe, Addison-Wesley, 1999, ISBN 0201379406

Shlaer-Mellor Method

The OOA96 Report   Sally Shlaer and Neil Lang, Project Technology, 1996, www.projtech.com

Object Lifecycles   Sally Shlaer and Steve Mellor, Prentice Hall, 1992, ISBN 0136299407

Object-Oriented Systems Analysis   Sally Shlaer and Steve Mellor, Prentice Hall, 1988, ISBN 013629023X

How to Build Shlaer-Mellor Object Models   Leon Starr, Prentice Hall, 1996, ISBN 0132076632

Relational Theory and Software Engineering

An Introduction to Database Systems   C.J. Date, Addison-Wesley, 7th edition, 2000, ISBN 0201385902

Foundation for Future Database Systems: The Third Manifesto   C.J. Date, Addison-Wesley, 2nd edition, 2000, ISBN 0201709287

Software Engineering Economics   Barry Boehm, Prentice Hall, 1981, ISBN 0138221227

Discrete Mathematics with Computer Science Applications   Skvarcius, Benjamin/Cummings Publishing, 1986, ISBN 0805370447

Movies

The Terminator (1984)

Index

A

abstract class 37–38, 40
abstraction vii–viii, 110
abstraction vs. instances 109
Acceleration Profile class 39
access optimization 167
Account class 38
accounting application 38
acquired data 258
action execution 21
action language 173, 288
Active Route class 267
Activity Specification class 266
acyclic constraint 176–177
    example 322, 360–361, 369, 371–372
    explanation 317
additivePrimaryColors 282
adjacent territories 321–323
Aerodynamic Profile class 42
after
    reflexive meaning 123
aggregation 161–163
air traffic control application 180–190
Air Traffic Controller class 188–189
Aircraft class 41, 180, 182–184, 187
Aircraft Specification 42
Aircraft Specification class 40–42
aircraft vs. helicopter 182
Airplane class 39
Airport class 61, 70
Album class 34
Alignment class 47
amusement theme park 236
analysis 17, 24, 143, 147, 161, 191, 193, 219, 232, 257, 299
    essential tasks 233, 235

analysis decisions 162
analysis paralysis 10
analysis process
    diagram 241
analysis tasks 84
analysis time allocation 235
analyst 39, 84, 143, 154, 162, 167, 178–179, 189, 263, 268
    coloring 20
Animatable Entity class 39
animation 247, 267
animation application 196, 236–238
animation service domain 39
application 25, 285
    accounting application 38
    air traffic control 180–190
    animation 196, 236–238
    artificial intelligence 38
    audio library 33–34
    communicating processes 315, 323–338
    data pipeline 258–262
    defect inspection 226–227
    draw tool 358–365
    DSP 303–304, 309
    elevator 278
    elevator control 14, 38
    factory management 294–296
    flight simulator 39–42, 340–358
    flot inspection 126–130, 271
    graphic animation 305–308
    illustration program 358–365
    inventory 33–34
    laser scanner 277
    material transport 38, 131–136
    mission planning editor 340–359
    Monopoly game 51–53
    motor speed 71–72
    motor transport 39
    movie player 88

F

factory machining application
    application
        factory machining 136–140
factory management application 294–296
Feature class 47
feedback 252, 283
feedback on model 233
file 147
File Cabinet class 166–168
Filter class 259–260
filter function 261
Finishing Operation class 136–140
Finishing Requirement class 136–140
Fired Auto Seek Torpedo class 216
Fired Torpedo class 279
Fixed Wing Aircraft class 187
Fixed Wing class 182–184
flaky specifications 24
Flat Shape 49
Flat Shape class 49–50, 305–308
Flight class 46–47
flight simulator application 39–42, 340–358
Floor class 38–39
flot 271
    definition 126
Flot class 126–130, 271, 284, 289–290
Flot Handler class 271
Flot Illumination class 127–130
flot inspection application 126–130, 271
    application
        flot inspection 289–290
Flot Shape class 290
flowchart 8
Folder class 166–168
Follower Waypoint class 351–356, 376
frame rate 248
frameworks 19
frequency band 259
frequency filter 261

Front Side class 50, 307–308
functional specification 6
fundamental law 311
Fuselage Type 42
Fuselage Type class 42
future extensions 255
fuzziness 13
fuzzy specification 3, 12

G

gap
    application and implementation 24–25
general rules 191
generalization
    bad 226
    hacking 219
    overlapping 357
    sets and subsets 182
    when to use 196
generalization relationship 104–106, 179–228
    corresponding instances 183–184
    description key components 296
    disjoint,complete 186
    eliminate n/a values 74
    example 49–50, 76, 79, 94, 194, 288, 308,
        337, 371, 374, 376
    FAQ 199
    for mutual exclusion 337
    multidirectional 202–212, 227
        set partitions 209
    multidirectional partition scheme 213
    multilevel 212–214, 225, 228
    multilevel partition scheme 213
    mutual exclusion 104, 190, 197–198
    nonoverlapping subsets 105
    notation 186
    overlapping sets 106, 214–219, 228
    pattern summary 201

M

S

saving time 252, 386
Scan class 45
Scanner class 197–198, 282
Scanning System class 267
scenario 13, 110
schedule pressure 44, 234
schematic 10
scheme 40
Screen class 39
script 339
Script class 165, 174–177, 266
search algorithm
    optimizing 23
Search Program class 206, 216
Segment class 360–364
Segment Joint class 360–361
segments vs. points 358–359
selecting instances 172
selective generalization 214–219
self-referencing and implementation 316–318
semantics vii, 10
Semaphore class 38
semiconductor wafer 267
sequence 123, 339, 345, 357
sequence and numbering 124
service domain 24, 32, 196, 267
    animation 39
    archival 45
    configuration 39
    definition 39
    example 196
    examples 39
    reuse 39
Session class 267
set of attributes 35
set of instances 34
set theory 97
sets within sets 106
Shaft class 38–39

Shape class 92, 94
Shape Template class 92–95
Sheared Brace class 226
Sheet class 93–94
Shippable Part class 385
Shlaer, Sally xi
Shlaer-Mellor method ix
Side class 50, 305–308
Signal Board class 303
simulated class 39–40
simultaneous events 13
single attribute class 51–53
single loop 174–177
    example 194
single player rule 52
singleton class 53–54
sketch 111
sloppy approach vii
sloppy thinking 162
smooth interpolation 236
snapshot 112
    association class 125
    instances and links 97
Socket class 119
soft class 38–51, 268–269
    description 266
    drawing 265
software architecture 19, 21, 268, 291
software blueprint 10
software weenies 283
source code 19
Space class 51–52
special effects application 39, 113–114
specialization
    example 349–350, 372
    See also generalization.
    when to use 196
specific exceptions 191
specification 3–4, 7–9, 17, 23–24, 117
    correctness 14
    destruction by elaboration 22

U

ultrasound diagnostic application 145–155, 192–198
UML 13, 110, 162
    * and 0..* 146
    association class 129
    generalization constraints 105
    limitation 147
    multiplicity expressions 303, 305
    official specification 243
    profile vii
    relationship types 181
unambiguous interpretation 239
unconditional expression 99, 112–113
unconstrained loop 170, 173
unidentifiable instances 84–85
uniform code structure 21
uniformity of data 32
unique instances 36
Unit Part class 381–382
units 281–287
Update Frame class 237
use cases vii
useless documentation 257
user data type 282
user interface 251, 290
user interface application 286–287
uses 143

V

vacation
    returning to model 236
vacuum 264
validation 232
value
    not applicable 73–74
value assignment 70–71
variable 189

verb phrase 156–161
    on symmetric association 322
verb phrases vs. role names 156–161
version control application 268–269
Version Number 269
Vertex class 364
VHDL 104
Video Effect class 291
video effects application 39, 247–251
videoFrameTime 282
visualizing associations 97
vocabulary
    of domain 239

W

wafer 264
Wafer class 48, 265, 267
Wafer in Process class 48
wafer inspection application 264–265
wafer test application 318–320
walkthrough 253
Warehouse class 369–384
Waypoint class 100, 341–359
whiteboard 110, 233
Widget class 42
Widget Specification class 42
Widget Surface class 136–140
wimpy qualifier 270
Window class 287
Wing Type class 42
wire guided torpedo 221
Wire Guided Torpedo class 74, 216
wishy-washy descriptions 270–272, 282

Z

zipCode 281

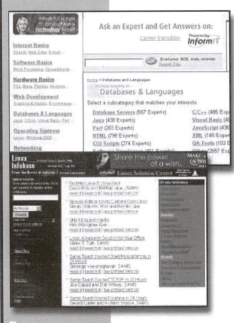
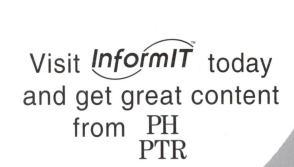

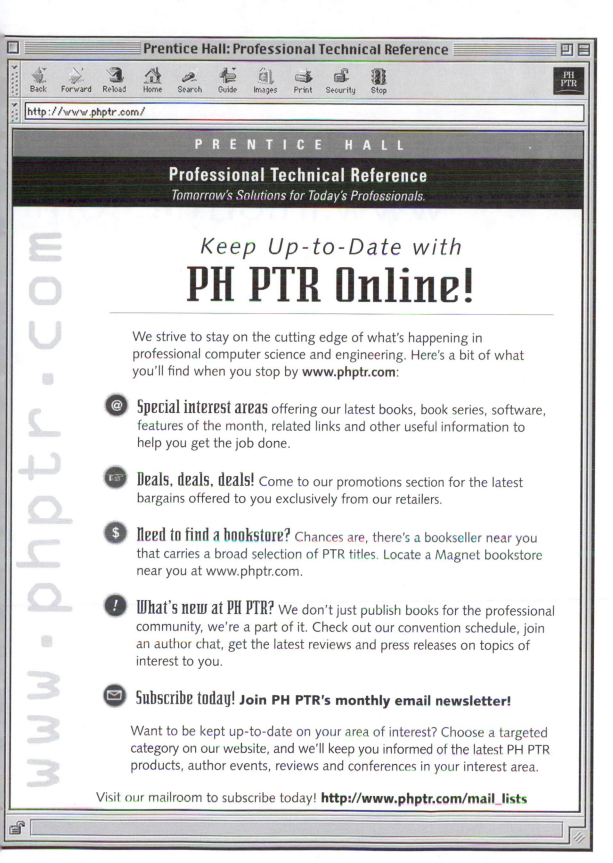

Prentice Hall: Professional Technical Reference

http://www.phptr.com/

PRENTICE HALL

Professional Technical Reference
Tomorrow's Solutions for Today's Professionals.

Keep Up-to-Date with
PH PTR Online!

We strive to stay on the cutting edge of what's happening in professional computer science and engineering. Here's a bit of what you'll find when you stop by **www.phptr.com**:

@ Special interest areas offering our latest books, book series, software, features of the month, related links and other useful information to help you get the job done.

Deals, deals, deals! Come to our promotions section for the latest bargains offered to you exclusively from our retailers.

$ Need to find a bookstore? Chances are, there's a bookseller near you that carries a broad selection of PTR titles. Locate a Magnet bookstore near you at www.phptr.com.

! What's new at PH PTR? We don't just publish books for the professional community, we're a part of it. Check out our convention schedule, join an author chat, get the latest reviews and press releases on topics of interest to you.

✉ Subscribe today! Join PH PTR's monthly email newsletter!

Want to be kept up-to-date on your area of interest? Choose a targeted category on our website, and we'll keep you informed of the latest PH PTR products, author events, reviews and conferences in your interest area.

Visit our mailroom to subscribe today! **http://www.phptr.com/mail_lists**

www.phptr.com

Executable UML

Training, Consulting and Resources